Survey of Applied Soviet Research in School Mathematics Education

The University of Chicago

Soviet Studies in Mathematics Education

Volume 3

The Development of Spatial Thinking in Schoolchildren

Soviet Studies in Mathematics Education

Volume 3
The Development of Spatial Thinking in Schoolchildren

I.S. Yakimanskaya

Volume Editors,
English Language Edition

Patricia S. Wilson and Edward J. Davis
The University of Georgia

Translator

Robert H. Silverman

National Council of Teachers of Mathematics
Reston, Virginia
1991

Survey of Applied Soviet Research in School Mathematics Education

Izaak Wirszup, Principal Investigator
Department of Mathematics
The University of Chicago

Series Editorial Committee

Jeremy Kilpatrick, Chairman
The University of Georgia

Izaak Wirszup
The University of Chicago

Alphonse Buccino
The University of Georgia

Robert Streit
The University of Chicago

Financial support for the *Survey of Applied Soviet Research in School Mathematics Education* has been provided by the National Science Foundation.

Originally published in 1980 by Pedagogika, Moscow, as *Razvitie prostranstvennogo myshleniya shkol'nikov.*

English Translation © 1991 by the University of Chicago
All rights reserved

Set in Adobe Postscript Times Roman with Helvetica display.

Printed in the United States of America

Second printing 1995

Library of Congress Cataloging-in-Publication Data

Ǐakimanskaǐa, I. S.
    [Razvitie prostranstvennogo myshleniǎ shkol 'nikov. English]
    The development of spatial thinking in schoolchildren / I.S. Yakimanskaya ; volume editors English language edition, Patricia S. Wilson and Edward J. Davis ; translator, Robert H. Silverman.
        p.   cm. — (Soviet studies in mathematics education ; v. 3)
    Translation of: Razvitie prostranstvennogo myshleniǎ shkol 'nikov.
    On verso t.p.: Survey of Applied Soviet Research in School Mathematics Education.
    Includes bibliographical references.
    ISBN 0-87353-298-8. — ISBN 0-87353-289-9 (set)
    1. Space perception in children—Soviet Union. 2. Cognition in children—Soviet Union. 3. Visualization. I. Wilson, Patricia S. II. Davis, Edward J. III. Title. IV. Series.
BF723.S63I3413   1991
155.42'42142—dc20   91-17060
                                                          CIP

Contents

Series Preface

The series *Soviet Studies in Mathematics Education* is a collection of translations of books from the extensive Soviet literature on research in the psychology of mathematics instruction. It also includes works on teaching methods directly influenced by this research. The series is a product of the Survey of Applied Soviet Research in School Mathematics Education at the University of Chicago and is funded by the National Science Foundation. The final editing and preparation of manuscripts was a cooperative undertaking by the Survey and the Department of Mathematics Education at the University of Georgia, with the valuable collaboration of a team of leading scholars from around the country. The *Soviet Studies* series comprises outstanding works selected for their value to the American mathematics educator and translated for the first time into English.

In view of Soviet social and political doctrines, several branches of psychology that are highly developed in the U.S. have scarcely been investigated in the USSR. On the other hand, because of the USSR's emphasis on education and its function in the state, Soviet research in educational psychology and teaching methods has received considerable moral and financial support. Consequently, this Soviet research has attracted many creative and talented scholars who have made remarkable contributions.

Even prior to World War II the Soviets had made great strides in educational psychology. The creation in 1943 of the Academy of Pedagogical Sciences helped to intensify research efforts and programs in this field. Since then the Academy has become the Soviet Union's chief educational research and development center. One of the main aims of the Academy is to conduct research and train research scholars in general and specialized education, educational psychology, and the methods of teaching various school subjects. Members of the Academy (51 in 1987, with another 85 associate members) are chosen from the ranks of distinguished Soviet scholars, scientists, and educators.

The Academy of Pedagogical Sciences comprises 15 research institutes, most of them in Moscow and Leningrad. Many of the studies reported in this series were conducted at the Academy's Institute of General and Polytechnical Education and Institute of Psychology. In 1987 the research institutes had available some 15 laboratory schools in which experiments were conducted. Developments in foreign countries are closely followed by the Bureau for the Study of Foreign Educational Experience and Information.

The Academy has its own publishing house, which produces hundreds of books each year as well as a number of periodicals, including *Proceedings of the Academy of Pedagogical Sciences of the USSR* (Izvestiya Akademii Pedagogicheskikh Nauk SSSR), the monthly *Soviet Pedagogy* (Sovetskaya pedagogika), the bimonthly *Topics in Psychology* (Voprosy psikhologii), the journal *Special Education* (Defektologiya), and the remarkable enrichment monthly for secondary school mathematics and science students (Grades 6-10) *Quantum* (Kvant).

Soviet psychologists have concerned themselves with the dynamics of mental activity and the principles of the learning process. They have investigated such areas as the development of mental operations; the nature and development of thought; the formation of mathematical concepts and the related questions of generalization, abstraction, and concretization; the mental operations of analysis and synthesis; the development of spatial perception; the relation between memory and thought; the development of logical reasoning; the nature of mathematical skills; and the structure and special features of mathematical abilities. Over the years, they have created a vast and impressive body of research.

This research has had a notable impact on the recent Soviet literature on methods of teaching mathematics. Experiments have shown the student's mathematical potential to be greater than previously assumed. Consequently, Soviet psychologists have advocated various changes in the content and methods of mathematics instruction. They participated in designing the revolutionary Soviet mathematics curriculum of the late 1960s and have been actively involved in more recent school reforms. Studies conducted with the assistance of the Survey of Applied Soviet Research in School Mathematics Education and the University of Chicago School Mathematics Project show that Soviet and American elementary school mathematics textbooks differ strikingly, with the Soviet books featuring many more types of word problems, treating a more even distribution of problem types, a much higher percentage of problems whose solution requires more than one operation, more varied sequences of problems, earlier introduction of multidigit addition and subtraction, and an emphasis on methods of mental calculation for single-digit operations. Furthermore, Soviet elementary school mathematics texts contain a continuous treatment of intuitive geometry, which by mandate comprises at least 20% of the mathematics curriculum in grades 1-5. The Soviet textbooks have clearly been constructed to reflect careful analyses of learning tasks and students' responses to them.

The USSR's apparent successes in the mathematics classroom, especially in the lower grades, have spurred American interest in Soviet research in educational psychology. One of the first opportunities to examine that research came with the appearance of the 14-volume series *Soviet Studies in the Psychology of Learning and Teaching Mathematics*. A joint publication of the Survey of Recent East European Mathematical Literature at the University of Chicago and the School Mathematics Study Group at Stanford University, that series had a broad and beneficial impact on mathematics education research in the United States and elsewhere and led directly to a great number of influential research projects.

At the time the earlier *Soviet Studies* series was published, American educational research was beginning to turn from its strong quantitative-experimentalist orientation toward the qualitative-interpretivist view so prominent today. The *Soviet Studies* helped bring to the attention of American researchers a tradition in which case studies and intensive work with small groups of children were the norm rather than the exception. Of particular interest to Americans was the *teaching experiment*, in which children were studied in the process of learning mathematical concepts, usually in ordinary classroom settings over a substantial period of time, and the teaching was continually modified in the light of the children's responses to it.

American researchers were interested not only in the approaches Soviet researchers used in their research but also in the topics they studied. One volume in the series concerned the structure of mathematical abilities. It brought the seminal work of V. A. Krutetskii to the attention of English-speaking mathematics educators. Subsequent publication of Krutetskii's landmark book *The Psychology of Mathematical Abilities in Schoolchildren* by the University of Chicago Press stimulated a variety of investigations into children's memory for the problems they have solved and how they perceive problems as being related. A subsequent book by Krutetskii is included in the present series.

Another volume in the earlier series dealt with studies in the perception of three-dimensional space. In the United States this ability had long been considered relatively static and little influenced by school instruction. The Soviet research demonstrated clearly that spatial abilities could be developed; again, that work is represented in the present series.

The earlier series was drawn primarily from journal articles published prior to the mid-1960s. The present series picks up where that one left off and consists entirely of translated books, for the most part monographs, all of which underwent thorough review by experts before they were originally published. Each manuscript was recommended by a scholarly committee or editorial council of either a university, a research institute of the Academy of Pedagogical Sciences, or the Ministry of Education.

The aim of the present series is to acquaint mathematics educators and teachers with directions, ideas, and accomplishments in the psychology of mathematical instruction in the Soviet Union. This series should assist in opening up avenues of investigation to those who are interested in broadening the foundations of their profession, for it is generally recognized that experiment and research are indispensable for improving the content and methods of school mathematics.

We hope that the volumes in this series will be used not only for research by individuals but also for study, discussion, and critical analysis in teacher-training programs and in institutes for in-service teachers at various levels.

It goes without saying that a publication project of this magnitude requires the commitment and cooperation of a network of institutions and individuals. In acknowledging their contributions, we would like first of all to express our deep appreciation to the National Science Foundation. Without the Foundation's generous long-term support of the Survey of Applied Soviet Research in School Mathematics Education, these books might never have become accessible to the American education and research communities.

The Survey at the University of Chicago is very pleased that the *Soviet Studies in Mathematics Education* are being published by the National Council of Teachers of Mathematics. It has always been a major goal of the Survey to disseminate its translations to a wide audience at minimal cost. We believe that the NCTM's recognized leadership, publishing expertise, and steadfast support and encouragement have assured us of reaching that goal. We are particularly indebted to the NCTM Educational Materials Committee and the Board of Directors. Special thanks are due Ms. Cynthia Rosso, NCTM Publications Business Manager, whose expertise, counsel, and energetic efforts were critical to the publication of this series.

The Editorial Committee would like to acknowlege the special assistance provided by Steven Young and George Fowler, who made a meticulous review of the translations; Jack Kirkman of the University of Georgia, who supervised the preparation of the edited manuscripts for publication; and Birute Tamulynas, who worked tirelessly on the manuscripts at the University of Chicago. We gratefully acknowledge the dedicated efforts of the volume editors and translators whose names appear on the title pages, as well as the valued contributions of the many language editors, typists, proofreaders, and production specialists who helped bring this extraordinary research to the English-speaking public.

Jeremy Kilpatrick
Izaak Wirszup
Alphonse Buccino
Robert Streit

Introduction to the English Language Edition

Patricia S. Wilson and Edward J. Davis

In this volume, I. S. Yakimanskaya discusses the complex nature of spatial thinking and how to observe and improve it. The first chapter presents the results of a considerable effort to explain the nature of spatial thinking according to Soviet psychological literature and philosophy. The second chapter details a theoretical structure of spatial thinking based on the foundation laid in the first chapter.

Although the literature base is predominately Soviet research, many of the foundational ideas can be seen in research outside of the Soviet Union. Common propositions include:

1. Spatial thinking is developed through activities.

2. The individual must create his or her own image before it can be used in spatial thinking. (However, the activity of spatial thinking is manipulating spatial images rather than creating them.)

3. Representations and representational systems are a necessary but complex component of spatial thinking.

4. To study spatial thinking, there is a need for qualitative research.

5. Many individual differences exist .

6. Spatial thinking is dynamic and requires a continual recoding of images. Images are manipulated, resulting in new images which are manipulated, and the cyclic process continues.

The claim is made that educators can and should pay attention to developing spatial thinking skills. This development is not occurring in Soviet (or American) schools to the extent necessary. Yakimanskaya uses numerous examples from industry that illustrate the necessity of developing spatial thinking in all students. Although a strong utilitarian argument is presented, the familiar argument that improved spatial thinking improves the ability to operate with abstract ideas is also developed.

Yakimanskaya claims that students can be taught spatial thinking at a much earlier age than is presently attempted. The second part of the volume is an elaborate report of a number of investigations of the performance of children in Grades 4 through 8 in support of this claim. Children were given tasks involving two-dimensional representations of three-dimensional phenomena from different reference points such as "top view" and "side view."

The investigations are described as "experimental studies." The reports include both quantitative and qualitative data. The details of these investigations are not fully reported in some instances; the questions and tasks for children did not always follow a prescribed sequence or form but were often adapted as the interview progressed. Many conclusions and findings are given with limited supporting statistics. Several conclusions are based on expert opinion and interpretation. Although replication of some experiments would be difficult, it was possible to get a reasonably firm idea of what children were asked to do and how well they performed.

The reported successes of young children in geometric contexts requiring different perspectives are surprising. We were pleased to observe considerable success in a third-grade classroom in our area when we tried out some activities similar to those reported. After viewing and drawing various objects such as chairs, desks, fellow students, bicycles, and toy cars, from top, side, front, and bottom viewpoints, third graders could successfully show how the objects would look from various reference points.

One goal of the Soviet studies is to establish levels of spatial thinking. Yakimanskaya was sensitive to individual differences and separated students into three performance groups that were based on students' abilities to mentally manipulate spatial objects. She also considered the constructs of persistence of ideas and receptivity to teaching. Her diagnosis of students is compatible with Kaplunovich's developmental levels based on the structure of spatial thinking. Although the Soviet levels of spatial thinking are quite different from van Hiele's levels of geometric understanding or Piaget's developmental stages, the purposes for the classifications were similar. The levels were designed to describe student thinking and to inform teaching. In contrast to Piaget's theories, Yakimanskaya claimed "developmental differences depend . . . we believe, basically on the teaching technique." She argues that reliance on concrete visual aids is not a result of development but a product of current teaching techniques relying on concrete materials. A preferred teaching technique would encourage students to create mental images and to operate on their mental images.

Development of Spatial Thinking in School Children offers a detailed careful analysis of spatial thinking and interesting reports of investigations into the development of spatial thinking. Yakimanskaya makes a point that the nature of any object is more than the sum of the constituent parts; the observer must study how the parts interact. This is analogous to analyzing spatial thinking. This volume has given a close, technical look at the constituent parts of spatial thinking, but spatial thinking is much more than its constituent parts. Although the question of how the parts interact is not resolved, the experiments offer insights and suggest areas for further study.

Preface to the Soviet Edition

One of the central problems of educational psychology is the study of the laws governing the student's intellectual development during the learning process. An important component of this development is spatial thinking, by means of which the individual orients himself in space (both physically and mentally), acquires knowledge, and learns different forms of activity.

This book is devoted to a study of the structure of spatial thinking and the identification and evaluation of optimal techniques of stimulating it in schoolchildren. The importance of spatial thinking emerges from the fact that its development, both in the school as well as in higher educational institutions, is obviously inadequate, as is apparent from the numerous and stubborn difficulties which many students experience when they attempt to create and use spatial images. The study of the psychological nature of spatial thinking, along with the "motivating forces" and regular stages of its development, therefore, are not only of theoretical importance, but also of great practical value.

Interest in the needs and concerns of the general education school and constant efforts at applying the results of experimental investigations in actual teaching have led us to develop a diagnostic method which may be employed to identify and evaluate the level of development of spatial thinking in children. This method has been tested by an experiment involving many teachers, experts in teaching methods, and instructors at higher educational institutions in Moscow and other cities. We would like to express our deep appreciation and gratitude for their considerable assistance and selfless work.

The use of the diagnostic method for research purposes is of great importance in the analysis of compensatory mechanisms of spatial thinking and the identification of its individual and developmental characteristics. Many of the theoretical ideas treated in this book are oriented toward the development of a psychologically-based system of requirements for the development of spatial thinking in the educational process and the identification of the general and specific laws governing this development.

The present book considers more than just the educational aspects of spatial thinking. Proceeding from definite theoretical assumptions, we attempt to discuss more general methodological issues in the relationship between biological and social influences in the structure of thought, and consider the relation between the structure of spatial thinking and its function in everyday activities. A detailed analysis is made of the epistemological function of spatial thinking, and we show how the basic principles of determinism are manifested in the activity of spatial thinking. Special emphasis will be placed on the analysis of basic strategies in the modern approach to the study of thought.

Proceeding from the theoretical ideas of S.L. Rubinshtein, the present book approaches the study of spatial thinking as a dynamic unity of subjective and objective experience, which stand in an intimate relationship and enrich each other during the course of activity. It is demonstrated experimentally that the forms and levels of spatial thinking are determined, on the one hand, by the objective content of the subject matter (e.g., the degree to which it is visual, conventional, and generalized), and on the other, by the individual's cognitive activity in the course of solving problems which require the creation and manipulation of spatial images. The level of this activity depends upon the individual's mastery of the tools of activity, i.e., methods of representation.

Our analysis of spatial thinking (the structure, level of development, and conditions under which it is created) is based on many years of theoretical and experimental research and systematic observation of the learning process in schools, technical vocational institutes, and higher educational institutions. Since, in its most highly developed forms, spatial thinking is engendered basically on a graphical base, its distinctive features are be studied within the framework of the general characteristics of representational thinking.

This book reflects the results of systematic research begun by the author more than twenty-five years ago under the guidance of Rubin-shtein, and subsequently continued at the Research Institute of General and Pedagogical Psychology of the USSR Academy of Pedagogical Sciences. Our study of the distinctive features of spatial thinking has followed the work of Menchinskaya on the laws governing the learning process and the influence of spatial thinking on the mental development of children.

1

General Description of Spatial Thinking

The Importance of Spatial Thinking in Educational and Professional Activity

It is difficult to cite even a single area of human activity where the ability to orient oneself in space (visible or imagined) fails to play an important role. Our orientation in time and space is a necessary condition of social reality, a medium for the reflection of the world around us, and a precondition for successful cognition and active manipulation of reality.

The free manipulation of spatial images is a fundamental ability combining various types of educational and professional activity. It is one of the most important professional skills. It is therefore no accident that professional training in its various forms (general educational schools, technical vocational institutes, higher educational institutions, on-the-job training, etc.) has the basic task not only to foster professional habits and skills in students, but also to develop their spatial thinking. The latter is a major element of practical preparation for many occupations (engineering, architecture, construction, topography, drafting, machine operation, courier service, etc.).

Graphic modeling is now widely used in science and technology, where it makes it possible to establish more clearly certain theoretical relations and predict their occurrence in a variety of situations. Graphic modeling is also closely involved in the mathematicization and formalization of numerous disciplines, the combination of different disciplines into a system, the identification of structural relations, and so forth. Two major uses of graphic modeling may be noted.

The first is the creation of a visual system in which the form of selected signs or some other means of display recalls the objects being represented. In many cases, however, such a system is difficult to achieve because of the variety of and differences between the content of particular objects. The second method is to reflect the properties of objects by means of letters, numerals, and other conventional signs which in no way resemble the objects represented. This representation makes it possible to identify important relationships and features that are concealed from direct observation and cannot be deduced from an analysis of the individual objects taken in isolation.

In many branches of industry (e.g., instrument construction and electrical and radio engineering) we observe a growing tendency toward schematization and formalization of representations, and replacement of visual representation by conventional signs for the purpose of conferring on them a more universal meaning. It is hoped that this meaning would thereby make it possible to represent a large number of full-scale mechanical objects that differ with respect to a variety of properties and functions. In planning technological documentation, it has been suggested that descriptions of standard manufacturing operations could be replaced by conventional signs. The notation could be standardized and made uniform, creating a conventional notation for terms (e.g., weld seams, threaded joints) used in functional diagrams. This would make it possible to create a unified system of graphic representations for all types of scientific and technological documentation. Analogous trends can be observed in many branches of science, including biology, chemistry, physics, and mathematics, all of which make use of generalized and formalized tools for conveying information about objects by a systematic approach to the study of these objects.

All this inevitably affects the content and methods employed in the acquisition of elementary knowledge. Instruction in many subjects in the modern school regularly makes use of not just visual representations of particular objects, but also conventional images in the form of spatial diagrams, graphs, schemes, and so forth, which reproduce the general laws governing the structural, functional, and space-time properties of the objects and thus help students develop theoretical generalizations.

In learning, increasing importance is assigned to analysis of objects and events with a view to identifying by means of graphic diagrams properties and attributes of these objects that are not directly observable or deducible from an individual concrete object. Among the forms of knowledge which must be acquired are: 1) factual information about distinct objects and 2) descriptions of methods for obtaining concrete data. For example, mathematics students learn algebraic methods of solving problems of varied objective content and methods for transforming geometric objects as they simultaneously learn about the concrete attributes and properties of these objects.

In drafting, we may also observe a tendency to combine the subjective content of images with the extensive use of semiotic models, which conventionally supplant the object of the representation, losing all visual analogy with it. More universal methods of representation have been introduced, making it possible not so much to depict visually, as to denote (focus) structural features of objects hidden from direct observation, thereby simplifying the methods used to represent them. Thus, we may draw the general conclusion that comprehension of modern scientific knowledge and successful work in many theoretical and practical areas are inextricably linked to the use of spatial images.

Serious research is now under way designed to improve the content of education and teaching methods, in order to bring them as close as possible to the modern level of scientific knowledge and research methodology. Thus, principles are being developed in educational psychology for selecting subject matter in light of the advances of science and technology and creating optimal methods of imparting these principles. This work aimed at both verbal and visual material. Much less care is taken in the case of visual material, since in the learning process visual material is often given the role of a secondary prop. This is clearly the reason why, to date, no scientific classification of the types of visual aids used in teaching various subjects has been developed, and also why so little attention has been devoted to the complicated and multiple functions of visual aids in the course of students' intellectual development.

The importance of graphic material to learning has grown as never before, together with its range of application. The functions of graphic material have substantially changed, and new types of visual aids have been introduced in keeping with basic trends in science and technology (its integration, the development of new methods of research and control). Many commonly used visual aids are not merely auxiliary, illustrative tools designed to facilitate learning, but rather constitute an independent source of new knowledge. Alongside various formulations, verbal explanations, and definitions, processes and events are widely represented by graphic models in the form of three-dimensional models (diagrams, graphs) and mathematical expressions (formulas, equations, symbolic notation), which make it possible to describe processes and events more precisely and economically. Thus, the verbal form of the transmission of knowledge has become universal. In addition, a separate "linguistic" component of conventional symbols, signs, and three-dimensional representations has arisen.

Many modern scientific concepts are highly abstract. For example, in physics students study the properties and events in both a macrocosm and microcosm. The study of the microcosm presupposes visual representations that cannot be created by analogy with representations of objects in the macrocosm. The content of such representations still lacks adequate visual images. Here we are dealing with a theoretically different system of representation based on theoretical abstractions requiring orientation not just in physical space, but also in an abstract mathematical space. Such systems of representation cause great difficulty for students. To help them acquire these concepts, the visual material used here includes graphic models reflecting objects of the real world that cannot be perceived by means of our senses, but only by abstract mathematical relations. The models of the structure of the atom and nuclear reactions are examples.

As noted by a number of specialists (P.R. Atutov, 1967; V.G. Boltyanskii, 1970; A.D. Botvinnikov, 1966; and others), conventional graphic models constitute a visual aid which differs theoretically from images of the concrete object. The use of three-dimensional graphic models in many school subjects has become an independent form of classroom activity.

Changes in the content of the knowledge students must acquire, reflecting the contemporary level of development of many sciences, must affect teaching methods as well. Today the technique of learning whereby a system of concepts is formed through the gradual generalization of isolated facts has lost ground. In the most widely used technique, basic laws underlying the subject matter (grammatical, mathematical, physical, chemical, etc.) are first demonstrated, and then concrete material is analyzed in their light.

A learning technique whereby students first learn about natural connections and relations identified through a theoretical analysis, and only then investigate their manifestations in specific situations of a given subject area (language, mathematics, etc.), has been proposed and experimentally developed. The psychological foundation of this technique of learning was primarily developed by V.V. Davydov [1968, 1972], and his interpretation of semantic abstraction was creatively developed by his colleagues, including L.I. Aydarova [1978], A.K. Markova [1974], G.G. Mikulina [1968], L.M. Fridman [1977], and others. As a result, the principles governing the construction of subject matter and the design of exercises was substantially altered. In this method of teaching, generalizations are based not on a correlation of isolated cases, but rather on the identification of the roots of general theoretical relations in the subject matter. These relations are then visually established by a unique spatial and functional model in the form of a conventional semiotic representation.

Representations created on the basis of such graphic models are psychologically distinct from those formed through the perception of visual images of individual objects. Images which arise through using graphic models are closer in content to concepts than to individual representations.

Graphic modeling is widely used in teaching technical subjects. Drawings, graphs, electrical and functional diagrams, and instructional charts are used to describe various mechanical objects and manufacturing processes. Drawings constitute the language of technology. As visual images, drawings model the varied properties and relations inherent in mechanical objects. Work with images of mechanical objects is usually based on diagrams representing three dimensions, a key aspect of engineering thought (P.M. Yakobson, 1934; E.A. Mileryan, 1968; T.V. Kudryavtsev, 1975; I.S. Yakimanskaya, 1968; V.V. Chebysheva, 1970; and others).

Using technical images not only means having a representation of a particular object (machine tool, equipment, mechanism) in static state in space, but also seeing it in motion and change, dynamically interacting with other mechanical objects. Any graphic model is a two-dimensional image through which we must visualize the spatial position of a full-scale mechanical object.

Graphic models used to teach technology reproduce the most general relations and connections inherent to the various objects and events. Graphic models make it possible to isolate technical elements, which can then be specially taught.

Scientific and technological progress has led to the creation of new models of mechanisms and machinery which differ in production purpose and structural implementation. Furthermore, their common operating principles have grown more important. Thus, an ongoing process of standardization has made individual assemblies and parts increasingly interchangeable. The manufacturing processes and conditions for the organization of the production process have tended to converge.

These trends have also affected the methods of teaching technology. The road leading to true technological generalization lies through detailed and comprehensive analysis of a single mechanical object. This analysis reproduces the most essential relations, along with a concomitant review of other similar mechanical objects, based on the unified operating principle of all these objects. This is possible despite substantive differences in their structural implementation (T.V. Kudryavtsev and

I.S. Yakimanskaya, 1962, 1964). Spatial diagrams are an important factor in this technique of learning technology.

As a type of representational thinking, spatial thinking plays an important role not only in understanding fundamental ideas in the sciences, but also in many areas of production.

A distinctive characteristic of the contemporary production process is intermediated control of automated mechanical objects and manufacturing processes. In a host of professions, labor operations are carried out not with full-scale production objects (machinery, mechanisms, devices), but rather with substitutes, e.g., various instrument panels, control panels, three-dimensional mock-ups, etc. Various simulation systems create images of ongoing manufacturing processes, which are used to teach the machine operator how to solve complicated control and guidance problems involving real objects. Various types of systems allow the user to receive and reprocess far more information about control objects than is possible via direct contact and operation. These systems often help detect structural and functional relations which underlie ongoing manufacturing processes, but are hidden from direct observation.

Simulation systems differ not only in terms of manufacturing content, but also in their requirements for spatial thinking. From this point of view, all present-day systems may be divided into two large groups: 1) units which reproduce the actual properties of objects, and 2) units which represent them by a specialized system of symbols and signs.

The first type provides a vivid graphic representation of the ongoing manufacturing process, and virtually replaces direct perception of this process. The second type involves more than just direct replacement of the production situation. To understand the manufacturing process by the second means, it is necessary to: 1) be well trained in the system of conventional symbols and signs used in the control panel; 2) mentally convert standard notation into images of the actual object (i.e., see actual machine parts and manufacturing processes in the conventional signs); and 3) create dynamic images of the constantly changing situation based on the perception of a three-dimensional diagram, the control panel.

Psychological studies by B.F. Lomov [1967], V.P. Zinchenko [1968], V.N. Pushkin [1965], M.V. Gamezo [1977], and others have demonstrated that under these conditions, the speed and reliability with which visual information about the controlled objects is received and reprocessed depends largely on the operator's ability to create satisfactory visual images, readily pass from one graphic system to another, and recode incoming information. When he sees a system of signals on a control panel, the operator mentally decodes the incoming information, creating an image of an actual manufacturing situation based on this information, and repeatedly modifies it in light of the signal code dynamics. There must be no discrepancy between the perception of the signals that continuously appear at the control panel and the corresponding images of actual production objects. All this activity often takes place solely on the level of representation, without direct visual contact with the real mechanisms and processes. Results of reading out the information at the control panel must be superimposed on the image of the actual object, creating two distinct but correlated visual fields of analysis. This process requires highly developed spatial thinking (I.S. Yakimanskaya, 1969).

Thus, work in various engineering and manufacturing activities is based on conventional visual aids, and presupposes not only suitable knowledge and abilities, but also the existence of dynamic spatial images. In preparing students for professional activity, dynamic spatial imagery must be taken into account. This is also vital because of the growing importance of developing special symbols that reflect various attributes of the controlled object within an integrated spatial structure, i.e., spatial coding. This type of graphic indication does not represent the properties of the object; rather, by means of a hypothetical picture it exclusively transmits relations and connections which express actual characteristics of the production object.

The use of various semiotic systems in students' educational and professional activity significantly influences the development of their thought processes. This applies both to fundamental scientific concepts, as well as technological information, job habits, and skills. Considerable emphasis is now placed on the development of the latter. The need for professional education has been expressly emphasized in resolutions for the further improvement of teaching and training of students in the general education schools and their preparation for work (*Pravda*, December 29, 1977), and in the professional and technical educational system (*Pravda*, September 11, 1977). Both resolutions were approved by the Central Committee and Council of Ministers.

Aptitude for creating and using spatial images can be gauged by the student's success in graphic, artistic, construction, and technical assignments, where this aptitude constitutes an independent element. Students become keenly interested in activities where this aptitude is most fully realized. For example, applying the spatial relations discovered in an object by creating images has been shown to encourage successful lessons in geometry (I.S. Yakimanskaya, 1959; V.A. Krutetskii, 1968), drafting (B.F. Lomov, 1959; N.P. Linkova, 1971; L.L. Gurova, 1976), art (O.I. Galkina, 1955; V.I. Kireenko, 1959; E.I. Ignatev, 1961; and others), and geography (F.N. Shemyakin, 1953; E.N. Kabanova-Meller, 1956; M.V. Gamezo, 1977; and others). A number of studies have uncovered a statistically reliable relation between highly developed spatial thinking in students and persistent inclinations towards corresponding occupations (P.A. Sorokun, 1966; I.S. Yakimanskaya, 1971; G.I. Mikshite, 1974). Successful mastery of such activities depends in many ways on the level of development of spatial thinking.

Thus, we have considered the importance of spatial thinking in various educational and professional activities. The following factors work in concert to help people constantly create and use images in the course of their activity: 1) an increase in the theoretical content of knowledge; 2) the use of modeling and structural analysis to study events in the objective world; and 3) the development of semiotic fluency.

The Epistemological Function of Spatial Thinking

The term "spatial thinking" is not generally accepted in psychology. Its use is often disputed by claiming that every thought is a generalized and mediated reflection of reality in its connections and relations, including spatial relations.

Although this assertion is undeniable, it requires some refinement. First, the assertion denotes the epistemological function of thinking. However, this function is also characteristic of other psychological processes. For example, memory and imagination yields a generalized and mediated reflection of reality by means of images and concepts. Therefore, the assertion does not identify the specific nature of this type of thinking. A more useful line of investigation is to analyze thought as a special form or qualitative form of reality, which also makes it possible to distinguish individual processes in terms of their psychological content.

Second, it is rare that a reflection of reality's spatial relations, connections, and their use becomes an independent goal of thinking. In addition, there are areas of human activity in which any effort to establish and modify spatial relations requires a specialized and often highly complicated operation. The psychological reality expressed by the term "spatial thinking" is so unique that it can appropriately be distinguished as a special form denoted by a special term.[1] The content and nature of spatial thinking and its functions are determined by the conditions under which it is created, manifested, and honed.

In our study of spatial thinking, we have employed the basic methodological principles developed in Soviet psychology, the principle of practicality, systematic structural analysis, and the ontogenetic principle. In following these principles, we have tried to identify the psychological content and structure of spatial thinking, as well as trace its basic formation and development in the ontogenetic process. Let us first characterize the content of spatial thinking.

Due to the Marxist-Leninist philosophical foundation of Soviet psychology, the category of practicality occupies a paramount position. The introduction of practicality into the field of psychology has radically altered the way the mind is studied. In particular, it has made it possible to discover the real roots of the development of thinking and investigate the mechanisms by which it develops. Related studies carried out by S.L. Rubinshtein, L.S. Vygotskii, A.N. Leontev, and others have helped direct us to the sources of various types of thinking and their functions in cognition and the transformation of reality.

Because it is a generalized and mediated reflection of reality, thinking is directed at the analysis of qualitatively distinct aspects of reality. The content of thinking is defined by man's direct and selective cognitive activity and the needs and motivation mandated by societal conditions.

Society's division of labor imposes its own imprint on the nature of the thought process. People work in different fields and deal with different objects. The properties and relations of these objects are studied, modified, and created. It is precisely each person's sphere of activity which defines the content of his thinking, specializing and directing it towards the analysis of individual aspects of reality which are most important for the creative performance of this activity. Emphasizing this fact, B.M. Teplov wrote, "...intelligence in man is everywhere the same, and the basic mechanisms of thinking are shared by all, but the forms of mental activity are different, since the problems confronting the mind of man differ from one case to the next" (1945: 55). It is precisely the difference between problems (cognitive, educational, professional) and the distinctive techniques and conditions for their resolution which define the various forms of thinking and their actual content and degree of development.

From the epistemological point of view, thinking makes it possible to recognize distinct facts and events in the real world, together with their most important relations and connections. In the physical world, objects exist in time as well as in space. "In the world, there is nothing but matter in motion, " wrote Lenin, "and moving matter can travel only in space and in time" (*Complete Collected Works*, 18:181). According to Engels, to be in space means to be situated one next to the other; to exist in time means to exist in the form of a sequence of one after the other. However, as Engels emphasized, "... both these forms of existence of immaterial matter mean nothing and are merely empty ideas or abstractions existing in our head" (Marx and Engels, *Works*, 20:550).

The intimate and continuous relation of the spatial and temporal characteristics of objects is most clearly revealed by recent advances in such fields as quantum mechanics, nuclear physics, and cosmology. According to modern scientific ideas (above all, Einstein's theory of relativity), spatial and temporal relations are so intimately intertwined that it is difficult to isolate their material processes as independent elements. The geometric shape of objects may vary as a function of their speed, mass concentration, and direction of travel. For example, if an elementary particle, a nucleon, travels slowly relative to another particle, it will be spherical in shape. But if this particle is considered relative to a third particle hurling toward it at an extremely high velocity, it will be flattened into the shape of a moving disk.

The intimate relation of space and time is manifested most clearly in the various forms of motion. The simplest form of motion, or displacement, is described by quantities such as speed and acceleration, which express relations between space and time. The length of any body and the duration (and rhythm) of the processes occurring in it are not absolute, but relative properties. The directional character of any motion in time and space makes it possible to describe the developments of physical processes and their causal relations. Since time and space cannot be separated, we may speak of four rather than three dimensions. Time may be introduced into a system of three dimensions as a fourth, defining the position of any figure in space. There can be no doubt of the intimate and permanent unity of the spatial and temporal characteristics of objects in the material world.

Modern notions of space and time influence children's spatial thinking to a marked degree. Based on the latest notions of the permanent unity of space and time, the identification and discrimination of spatial properties and relations can only be accomplished through theoretical abstraction as a part of cognitive activity. In accordance with its purposes and tasks, thinking is "specialized" into the identification of distinctive features and the application of specific relations.

As is well known, the most comprehensive spatial properties and relations are studied in mathematics. The first geometric concepts arose as a result of an abstraction from all the properties and relations (excluding relative position and magnitude) of the real world. For example, the concept of a geometric body first came about as an abstraction of a real object, retaining only the shape and size of the object, apart from all its other properties. The very concept of shape and size is thought of as precise and defined in mathematics, whereas in real objects shape and size are ill-defined and variable. In fact, the subject of any science is always an abstraction isolated from the specific relations and connections in which objects occur.

Since individuals can identify properties of reality from experience, it is appropriate to isolate spatial thinking as a special form of thinking and designate it by a special term. The epistemological function of "spatial thinking" is to help identify spatial properties and relations and use them in the course of solving problems related to orientation in real (physical) and theoretical (geometrical) space. Spatial thinking arose from the deep practical need for orientation in a terrain full of real-world objects. In the course of ontogenesis, spatial thinking was isolated as an independent form of mental activity.

In its most highly developed form, spatial thinking utilizes images whose content is the reproduction and modification of the spatial properties and relations of objects, including their shape and size and the relative position of their parts. We understand spatial relations to mean the relations between objects in space or between the spatial attributes of these objects. These relations reflect such concepts as direction (forward-backward, up-down, left-right), distance (near-far), relative comparison (nearer-farther), location (in the middle), the dimensions of objects in space (tall-short, long-short), and so forth.

Determining the spatial distribution or relative position of objects requires a system or frame of reference. The initial position of an observer is most often taken as the reference point. A change in frame of reference often entails a rearrangement of the entire system of spatial relations. For example, to describe the interior of a classroom, whether perceived or represented, we must not only reproduce the structure and attributes of the objects in the classroom, but also know how to arrange them properly in space. The description of a specific interior may vary substantially, depending upon the selected point of observation. The spatial distribution of objects remains virtually unchanged, but the mental reflection in the image changes for every change in the reference point.

The spatial image created in this way is dynamic, since the mental distribution of objects in space relative to a given observation plane or point may vary. The selection of this point may be determined by the individual or given by the conditions of a problem. Compare one person's idea of the relative position of objects in a room when he stands at the entrance to the room with the view from across the room, with his back to the window opposite the entrance. The arrangement of the objects remains the same, but their position relative to the observer changes, and this leads to the creation of different spatial images. The same may be observed in the creation of images on a graphic base.

A drawing reflects the position of the observer relative to the object. In terms of structure (shape and interrelation of parts), the object does not change, but depending upon which point of view is taken (e.g., a frontal view), the images of its projections in the plane, along with the models of these projections, change.

The initial observation point constitutes a fixed frame of reference common to man and animals. Guided by a "body image," the individual orients himself in space relative to the objects located in it. We identify spatial relations with respect to our own position (nearer-farther, to the right-to the left, in front-behind, above-below). Let us call this type of relation the "subject-object" (S-O) relation.

In many instances, objects in the real world interact without the involvement of any individual. In these cases, we must take into account the spatial relations between the objects themselves, and the observer's position plays no major role. This type of relation will be referred to as the "object-object" (0-0) relation.

These relations are relative in nature, since the individual who is temporarily excluded from an integral system of spatial relations is nevertheless always present in it. A person does not merely alter spatial position by changing viewpoints. As he interacts with objects, a person can change objects and exert a decisive influence on the spatial relations between the objects. Spatial properties and relations, therefore, are highly variable, unlike other objective relations. These relations may be denoted as a complex of dynamic interaction between objects and the individual:

$$O\text{-}S\text{-}O$$
$$|\ |$$
$$O{=}O$$

By observing interacting objects, the individual can reflect their spatial relations and connections. However, he does not simply contemplate these relations, but actually becomes a definite part of the system of relations, and transforms them. By reproducing an already novel system of relations, the individual designs his own behavior, adjusts this behavior, and controls it.

An important element of spatial relations, as emphasized by V.G. Ananev [1961], is that they constitute one form of reflection on the connection between objects. That is, the full variety of spatial properties is not exhibited in individual, isolated objects and frozen geometric shapes. They may be identified, studied, and applied only through the individual's positive transforming activity. Only during the course of this activity may spatial properties and relations be discovered.

This assumption remains meaningful both for practical and theoretical activity. Psychological studies have demonstrated that people actively identify and mentally construct spatial relations in objects of cognition according to the goals of activities. Our experiments in developing methods of analyzing geometric diagrams [1958, 1959] demonstrated that students see various numbers of regular polygons in the same drawing, depending on which methods of spatially transforming the elements of an image they have learned. In S.L. Rubinshtein's excellent expression, the act of "plucking" desired spatial relations and connections from an object manifests specifically human cognition: conscious, assertive, and transforming.

Examination of certain epistemological aspects of spatial thought can help us approach an understanding of its psychological nature and the laws governing its formation and development. Spatial thinking is a psychological construct created through both practical and theoretical activities. Its development is enhanced by creative forms of activity: building, drawing, scientific or technical work. As students learn these activities, they consciously acquire the ability to represent the results of their actions in space and represent them in paintings, drawings, constructions, and crafts. The ability to alter them mentally and create new versions in accordance with the particular image (schema) is an acquired ability. Other acquired abilities include planning the result of ones work along with the basic stages in which it is performed, and taking into account not only the temporal sequence of the stages, but also their spatial sequence.

Not only full-scale objects, but also their conventional semiotic substitutes in the form of various graphic models, i.e., paintings, drawings, diagrams, and outlines, may serve as objects of the space to be analyzed. This qualitatively diversifies the content and forms of spatial thinking, and complicates its functions in various forms of activity.

The transition from the representation of real space to a system of conventional graphic substitutes entails the development of appropriate techniques and methods designed for the creation of conventional images and their use. This transition does not take place automatically, but through teaching students to acquire a specialized conceptual apparatus, and use various frames of reference and methods of representation. The mechanisms underlying this transition have yet to receive adequate study.

The general development of spatial thinking may be traced, on the one hand, to a stable system of orientation relative to the body image, and, on the other hand, to the specific formations which arise under the influence of a specially organized instruction in various forms of activity (play, educational, professional) in the process of ontogenesis. It is important to study the common (vertical) lines of development, the

psychological mechanisms which make development possible, the intermediate, critical points of development, and the most sensitive periods.
Without such study, it is difficult to understand the psychological nature
of spatial thinking and determine optimal techniques for teaching it to
students.

We have considered the epistemological function of spatial thinking
and its objective content. Now let us attempt a more detailed description
of spatial thinking, taken as a psychological formation.

The Nature of Spatial Thinking as a Psychological Formation

Spatial thinking is a form of mental activity which makes it possible
to create spatial images and manipulate them in the course of solving
various practical and theoretical problems. In the course of ontogenesis,
spatial thinking passes through a number of natural stages in its development, initially intertwined with other forms of thinking. In its most highly
developed and independent form, spatial thinking appears in the form of
spatial images.

Arbitrary manipulation of images is seen particularly clearly at school
age, when rapid mental development takes place. At this point students
acquire appropriate techniques of intellectual activity, making it possible
to create and transform images, arbitrarily alter a system of reference,
and use different types of visual bases. Spatial thinking develops at this
age under the decisive influence of those school subjects which are
"responsible" for the formation of a given type of thinking and "involved" in its development. Without this it would be impossible to
effectively teach science. The study of the laws underlying spatial thinking, therefore, will be undertaken here using material from various
subjects, including geography, mathematics, painting, drawing, and
shop, along with a number of general engineering subjects studied at
special secondary educational institutes and higher educational institutions (special technologies, descriptive geometry, mechanical drawing).

The distinctive aspects of spatial thinking appear most clearly in the course of solving graphic problems in which spatial relations and their modification are based on conventional pictures (isometric drawings, diagrams). In our studies we have particularly emphasized the analysis of various types of conventional graphic representation, i.e., the visual base in which spatial thinking is formed.

In the process of activity, whether play, educational, professional, or sport, we identify spatial relationships in a perceived space and reflects them in representations or concepts. We are often compelled to predict new relations that we have not previously perceived, besides establishing prior relations and regulating our activity accordingly. Based on the sensory cognition of given spatial relations through a complicated system of mental events, we create new spatial images and express them in verbal or graphic form, (diagrams, drawings, paintings, outlines). This is achieved via the special activity of image expression, which makes it possible to perceive given spatial relations and mentally rework them, creating new spatial images.[2]

The activity of image expression constitutes the basic mechanism of spatial thinking, and consists in the use and transformation of images; it is often a lengthy and repetitious process. This process incorporates images that arise in various, and therefore spatial thinking involves a constant recoding of images, a transition from spatial images of real objects to conventional graphic representations of these images or from three-dimensional to two-dimensional representations.

The term "spatial thinking" denotes a rather complicated process including not only verbal and conceptual operations, but also a number of perceptual events necessary for the mental process of forming images. For example, we recognizes objects represented realistically or by means of different graphic techniques, and then create corresponding images and use them during problem-solving.

In order to discuss spatial thinking and its specific nature, we must define the concept of space. The term "space" has two meanings in science. It may be applied to an actual space or to an abstract, mathematical space. Modern mathematics identifies a number of different spaces, including topological projective space and metrical Lobachevskian space. The images of space formed in these systems are highly specific and are studied by mathematicians, logicians, and psychologists (R.Y. Shteinman, 1962; A. Grunebaum, 1969; J. Piaget, 1960, 1969; M. Janmer, 1964; R. Sperry, 1976; and others).

The school mathematics course treats two-and three-dimensional Euclidean space, employing various coordinate systems. Students study methods of transforming geometric figures defined as mappings of two-or three-dimensional space onto itself. These transformations include parallel translation, rotation, symmetry (central, axial, planar), dilation, parallel and orthogonal projection, and transformation of the graphs of functions. Students are taught basic concepts, e.g.: "a geometric figure is a set of points" and "a transformation is a relation between two figures whereby a given figure is transformed into a second figure." A figure is considered to be a definite spatial shape, including not only a body, surface, line, or point, but also any set of points.

The concepts of Euclidean geometry studied in school rest on the notion of realistic, physical space, and in this sense do not contradict our ordinary beliefs. As a result, this creates conditions for determining the common line of development of our understanding of space and investigating the psychological mechanisms underlying the transition from real to mathematical space.

In studying students' spatial thinking, we are assuming that, from both the practical and theoretical standpoints, it is derived basically from the material of Euclidean space and from a consideration of various inertial systems governed by the laws of classical physics, mechanics, and gravitation. In this way a variety of spatial images are created, including topographic, geometric, and projective images, images of mechanical parts, and handmade structures. Moreover, the school usually incorporates the foundations of scientific ideas about space, reflecting relations present in non-inertial systems that do not obey the classical laws of mechanics and the earth's gravitational attraction. In physics, advanced students learn about elementary nuclear physics, the theory of relativity, and the laws underlying both the microcosm and the macrocosm. Analogous trends may be observed in mathematics lessons designed to teach various geometric spaces and coordinate systems (i.e., rectangular, polar, spherical). Indeed, the student's acquisition of modern scientific notions and concepts of space is among the most important goals of intellectual development.

All these factors have led us to further develop topics related to the study of spatial thinking and the laws governing its formation and development. It is important to determine the direction in which spatial thinking should be developed and what form it should take. We must avoid merely analyzing how this development proceeds in the contemporary school, and not just because its development is still inadequate. If students are to be psychologically ready for educational and professional activity during the scientific and technological revolution, it is important to identify the main future lines of the development of spatial thinking.

Which qualities of spatial thinking are the most significant? We have already remarked that spatial thinking in various forms of professional activity is derived through extensive use of semiotic systems in which all necessary information is specified and reprocessed by means of certain codes. Semiotic systems expressed in the form of conventional graphic representations are also used in the school as a form of visual aid. Graphic modeling is applied not only as a method of scientific cognition, but also as a method for learning.

The real (psychological) content of spatial thinking is manifested as an activity directed at recoding spatial images of various degrees of abstraction, visualization, and generality. Solving many classroom problems requires various types of visual materials. The images obtained through their perception should be present in the student's mental activity not in sequence, but rather as part of a unified system that ensures logical transformation in the course of problem-solving. There should be no "discrepancy" between these images, for that would lead to rote learning and make it impossible to solve problems. The same phenomenon is observed in various professional activities.

Spatial images manipulated by thinking must be dynamic, flexible, and operational. These qualities follow from the condition under which they are created and manipulated. Flexibility and dynamism are necessary because the problem-solving process may require the routine transition from three-dimensional to two-dimensional images and vice versa. Moreover, it is also necessary to move from the perception of realistic objects to their graphic representations.

Starting with various static ("frozen") images or diagrams (e.g., functional or electrical), it is necessary to create dynamic images of real operating parts and processes in order to solve problems. The representation often contains the most general (structural or functional) properties of articles, which combine objects of various types and purposes.

When solving problems that require the use of spatial relations, it is necessary to abstract from any one frame of reference and shift to a second system specified by the conditions of the problem or selected independently. The operative units that make it possible to solve problems include a variety of spatial characteristics, including shape, size, spatial arrangement of elements, relations between the parts and the whole, and so forth. Successful rendering of the spatial properties of an object in the form of an image depends upon the function of the image in the structure of the problem. At various stages of the problem-solving process, images that differ in terms of content may emerge as operative images. These features of spatial images collectively define the basic paths for the development of spatial thinking in students at specified levels in the teaching process.

Numerous studies in educational psychology, as well as everyday experience in teaching, have demonstrated that spatial thinking develops unequally at school age even in students under identical teaching conditions. The developmental and individual differences in spatial thinking are manifested in complicated and ambiguous ways. We have attempted to identify the psychological factors that determine developmental and individual differences in this type of thinking and investigate the stability displayed by these individual differences. Thus, in summarizing the foregoing discussion, we may attempt to characterize spatial thinking by giving the following definition:

Spatial thinking is a specific type of mental activity which is manifested in solving problems that require an orientation in physical and mental space (both visible and imaginary). In its most highly developed forms, this is thinking in terms of images that establish spatial properties and relations. By operating with original images created within the framework of various graphic bases, thinking proceeds to modify these images, transforming and creating new images different from the original ones.

This type of thinking is principally characterized by the manipulation of spatial images in solving practical and theoretical problems. Spatial thinking is made possible by the activity of image expression, which is based on the perception of realistic objects or their graphic images. This process requires constant recoding of images created within the framework of various visual bases.

The image is the basic operative unit of spatial thinking. The spatial characteristics of an object are represented in the image. For example, shape, size, and the relative arrangement of constituent elements are spatial characteristics represented in the image. In this respect spatial thinking differs from other forms of representational thinking in which the identification of spatial characteristics does not constitute the central element.

Thus, spatial thinking is a complicated mental formation with its own line of development at all stages of ontogenesis. While it is rooted in practical activity (i.e., geographic orientation, measurement), it has gradually become an independent type of mental activity over the course of historical development.

Spatial thinking passes through a complicated developmental path in each individual. It is first intertwined with the child's object-manipulation activity, and only gradually isolated as an independent type of thinking performed by means of images, and converted into a variety of highly complicated professional activities. The basic lines of development of spatial thinking in ontogenesis and the conditions which underlie them have yet to receive adequate attention from psychologists.

We will limit our investigation to an analysis of the particular features of spatial thinking developed in elementary school during learning. In particular, we will deliberately neglect the various forms of practical and theoretical activity in which this type of thinking is manifested (i.e., measurement, construction, modeling, design, practical preparation of various objects, etc.). We will concentrate on features of spatial thinking that appear when the individual creates spatial images and manipulates them while solving various types of graphic problems. For this reason, we will devote a considerable portion of our study to the psychological features of various conventional graphic images and their role in representational activity.

This approach to research in spatial thinking is designed to meet the practical needs of elementary school teaching. As we have attempted to demonstrate, students' spatial thought processes are developed mainly within the framework of graphic and visual materials while solving classroom problems by recalling images from memory. Here we find a multitude of persistent difficulties that students have trouble overcoming. A study of the psychological nature of these difficulties may help us improve the content and teaching methods used in those subjects which develop spatial thinking.

Let us now attempt a more detailed analysis of individual aspects of spatial thinking. The three-dimensional image is the distinctive element and basic operational unit of spatial thinking.

Elements of the Spatial Image

The content of spatial thinking the manipulation of spatial images in visible or imaginary space based on various graphic images generated by the need to "recode" images created from visual stimuli.

The identification of spatial relations from an object of perception is often difficult because of its complex structure. Many features, such as the internal structure, are hidden from direct observation. For this reason the spatial relations inherent to an object can often be identified only indirectly, by comparison and correlation of different parts and elements of the structure. The common characteristics of any spatial image are derived from its reflection of the objective laws of space. However, this reflection is defined by the individual's active relation to the immediate space. The variety of conditions, modes, and methods of reflection define the differences in the content of a particular spatial image.

Spatial properties and relations are manifested through the perception of real objects as well as their substitutes. Furthermore, the graphic representation of a real object may diverge appreciably from the object itself, creating complications in the corresponding spatial images. Spatial properties and relations are inseparable from the concrete things and objects which bear them. This is most apparent in the case of geometric objects (solids, two-dimensional models, drawings, diagrams), which are idiosyncratic abstractions from real objects. It is no accident, therefore, that geometric objects (and various combinations of them) constitute the basic material with which spatial images are created and manipulated.

The objective configuration of any object is created by its contour, which makes it possible to distinguish one object from another and compare any two objects by applying socially developed sensory models. Indeed, spatial properties characterize not only the external view (configuration) of the object, but also its structure (construction). Spatial properties define the functional significance of the object (i.e., its purpose and range of application). Spatial properties occupy a dominant role in a number of other properties (e.g., color, weight, texture, etc.) which characterize an object. Based on these properties, the individual may recognize various objects, classify them, and make extensive use of geometric knowledge in practical and theoretical activity. Because they describe the contour of an object, spatial properties such as shape, magnitude, and breadth define, particularize, and individualize the object.

The position of one object relative to another is defined by its relative position in space. Determining this position means indicating its place in a collection of places occupied by other objects around it. Spatial relations describe not so much the object itself as its position within the context of other objects, and if a particular object is structurally complex, its structure may involve spatial relations between its parts and between the parts and the whole. Spatial relations often display a complicated structure, and their use is mediated by specialized knowledge and skills. The features of the spatial image are defined not only by its content and the conditions underlying its appearance. As we have already mentioned, an important aspect of spatial thinking is the recoding of images that appear within the framework of a visual base.

A visual base for learning may be a real (concrete) object, a theoretical model that reproduces its structure and the hidden processes within it, or a graphic image of an individual object or an entire collection of objects. Let us therefore consider the most commonly employed types of visual aids. There are three basic groups: (1) full-scale real models (i.e., real objects, molds, geometric bodies, mock-ups of various objects, engineering models) and perspective images (photographs, artistic reproductions); (2) conventional graphic images distinguished in form and content (i.e., drawings, graphic images as part of a system of perspective or isometric projection, cut-away views, cross-sections, sketches, various types of engineering and process flow diagrams); and (3) semiotic models (graphs, geographic maps, topographic maps, diagrams, chemical formulas and equations, mathematical symbols, and other interpretive semiotic systems).

All these types of visual aids are related in various ways to the represented object, and they fulfill different functions in uncovering the object's spatial properties and relations. They also extend the boundaries of our sensory experience, since it is impossible for us to directly perceive all these properties in relation to the object itself. They make it possible to model the properties of objects through theoretical transformation. Though they are descriptive in nature, they differ markedly in content; they also implement a number of different conditions which are necessary for creating suitable images.

Full-scale models and perspective images serve as simple substitutes for real objects, retaining full similarity. The descriptive nature of these models is clear from the fact that they may be used to create images of real objects or events which are fully accessible to direct observation.

These images are rich in detail, vivid, and "objectivized." They reflect the object in all its sensory content.

Full-scale models and perspective images serve as a visual basis for the student's acquisition of concrete images of objects they are studying. The student acquires scientific concepts based on these images. Full-scale models also stimulate thinking, since they help visually identify properties of the given object which have not been expressed in words. They impart an emotional tone to the learning process without which knowledge could not be understood or acquired to a sufficiently permanent extent. These visual aids usually convey the particular properties of individual objects in full completeness and multiplicity, and serve as illustrations for the learning process. However, their function is limited to conveying external, self-evident properties of the object (i.e., its external appearance, specific features, and its individual constituent parts), e.g., models express shape, size, the relation of parts to the whole, and so forth.

Unlike full-scale models, conventional graphic images help convey properties of the object that are more concealed from direct perception. Since they are free of the real features of the object, they express primarily the structure of the object, its geometric shape and proportions, and the spatial interrelation of its individual parts. Compare, for example, a model and a drawing of the same mechanical object. The model conveys solely the external, standard features of the object, whereas the drawing makes it possible to identify the geometric shape and features of the structure, along with the spatial relations of the object's elements.

Among conventional graphic images, we may cite three- and two-dimensional representations, which may be distinguished by their "remoteness" from the real represented object and by the level of visualization. For example, compare a geometric drawing of a pyramid and a drawing of a triangle. Among two-dimensional representations, we may cite functional, assembly, and construction diagrams. A functional diagram gives us an idea of the motion and interaction between the individual parts of an object, independent of their particular structural implementation. In an assembly diagram, the object is represented in the form of its constituent elements (parts and assemblies); this type of diagram may reveal the types of connections in the object. A process flowchart indicates a method of transforming an object (its shape or size) in the course of production.

Conventional graphic representations of an object are thus more abstract (more remote from the represented objects) than full-scale models. They make it possible to identify hidden spatial relations and connections, moving from the phenomenon to the essential nature. We should also note that the degree of schematization and abstractness may vary from one graphic representation to the next. In this respect we may distinguish functional, assembly, key, and structural diagrams.

Conventional representations may also be distinguished by the state (static or dynamic) of the object they describe. For example, a projective diagram represents the object in a definite, rigorously fixed position. Functional diagrams, process flowcharts, and assembly diagrams convey by means of conventional symbols not only the structural features of the object, but also its movement and the processes by which it is created, modified, and produced. This is important because any real object always moves, interacts, and changes in terms of shape, size, and spatial position as it is designed and produced.

Thus, full-scale models, along with their perspective visual representations, differ substantially from conventional graphic representations in content, method of representation, and the functions each fulfills in learning. The perception of the full-scale model resembles artistic perception, whose characteristic feature, as noted by N.N. Volkov [1947], lies in the identification of the most typical and expressive characteristics in the picture. The perception of conventional graphic representations is schematic and selective in nature, and somewhat one-sided, as a result of the distinctive features of learning—that is, the effort to identify and emphasize by means of graphic tools a single aspect of the object, temporarily isolated from all other aspects.

We should not neglect an additional feature that distinguishes conventional graphic representations from full-scale models and their perspective representations. Conventional graphic representations reproduce the object by means of certain graphic methods and a special system of notation.

We perceive simple illustrations directly. To create an image of an object through a painting or reproduction of a picture, we need only perceive it. Once we have seen the Kramskii's "Portrait of the Unknown Woman" in the museum, we can create a clear image of it and retain all its details in our memory for a long time. To perceive a conventional graphic representation, we must have special knowledge, for otherwise it is difficult to determine what object is being depicted. For example, without knowing anything of orthogonal projection, it is difficult to create an adequate spatial image of an object. For this purpose, we must have specialized tools for creating such a representation, and we must know how to mentally combine three given representations, transform a two-dimensional representation into a three-dimensional one, visually locate in space the image arising from the drawing, see exactly how the individual representations of the object are related to each other, and so forth.

The very creation of the image is mediated here by a corpus of knowledge and by specialized techniques that make it possible to create the image. The use of different projection systems depends upon basic knowledge of such sciences as descriptive geometry, topography, cartography, and machine production, and construction drawings. Without some knowledge of these sciences, it is impossible to create proper visual images. However, the descriptive content of these images is indirect.

Semiotic models differ substantially from the above visual aids. In essence, semiotic models totally lack any direct relation to the depicted object; however, this does not mean that semiotic models are not visualized. They lack any direct relation to the object in the sense that full-scale models and conventional graphic representations do.[3] Semiotic models reproduce not the material properties of the object or even its structural features, but rather emphasize abstract relations inherent to numerous objects, but not deducible from any one object. Semiotic models are highly specialized, fulfilling a more semantic than illustrative function. However, they are also visual in nature. By means of semiotic models, it is possible to reproduce different relations and connections. For example, structural relations displayed in chemical and mathematical formulas and causal relations studied in physics and biology in an accessible visual form reproduce relations and connections. The use of semiotic models as a special type of visual aid is particularly important whenever the object to be studied takes the form of highly formalized general relations and connections, such as the structural relations studied in linguistics.

The analysis of various types of graphic models demonstrates that highly particular knowledge about an object, as well as theoretical and abstract knowledge, may be reproduced visually. One of the basic functions of semiotic models is to reveal, by means of graphic techniques, material which cannot be discovered under ordinary conditions of perception.

Although these visual aids in education are all perceived and considered by means of our senses, the content they reproduce varies in basic respects. For this reason the resulting spatial images differ in degree of generality, abstractness, and dynamism. Particular features useful in the course of problem-solving are also determined here. Let us consider the notion of the generality of spatial images in greater detail.

Spatial images created within the framework of a graphic base may reproduce the spatial relations inherent to a single object (i.e., its shape, size, or position in the plane and relative to other objects). However, it may reproduce spatial properties inherent to a wide variety of objects, along with their various states (movement, rotation, etc.). In the former case, the spatial relations may readily be established empirically. They may be deduced from the particular object, reproduced by means of our senses, or represented in memory. In the latter case, they are constructed in the mind in the form of various spatial diagrams, since they are not given in any individual example. They may be extracted solely through the mental transformation of the object or by modeling their spatial properties and relations. These images reproduce and generalize not only attributes that may be visually detected in the actual object, but also "hidden" properties and relations that do not lie on the surface. For example, machine tools that differ when viewed from outside (with respect to overall size, shape, or material) may share a common functional basis. It may not be possible to detect a common element empirically by perceiving each particular tool, although the element may be discovered visually through the spatial model of a functional diagram.

Such a diagram may be realized in the image of a single machine or tool, although in that case it may seem to be absorbed in the structural features of this one tool. The image of this diagram seems to be "re-embodied" in a second image, which is more particular and less conventional. While it can exist as an independent image, whenever necessary it may be realized again.

Spatial images establish the geometric features of static objects that distinguish one object from another. For example, they establish shape, size, spatial relations between the parts and the whole, the breadth of the object, and its position in the plane or in space. But spatial images may also determine the dynamic process of transforming objects. The image that defines the method of transformation may also be generalized to various degrees. For example, it is possible to describe how the position of a particular object such as a doll may vary as it is rotated 180 degrees about its axis. It is also possible to describe a given image of motion relative to any object (i.e., a segment, angle, polygon, plane). In this sense, as emphasized by V.V. Davydov [1972], the reproduction of the method of transformation "is more realistic than the full-scale, sensory, particular thing." Here we may also establish the origin and method of obtaining various spatial combinations and relations. The spatial images that arise with different visual aids differ in content and level of generality.

An isolated image of a particular object, based on direct perception, is already generalized, since it reflects different variable impressions of its spatial position relative to the observer. An image created on the basis of a conventional graphic representation constitutes a diagrammatic image that reproduces in its content the most general spatial properties and relations inherent often to an entire class of analogous objects, rather than just one object. A diagrammatic image generates a whole series of other, more representative and particular images; e.g., a drawing of a screw makes it possible to create images of different individual screws that differ from each other in color, material, and method of use, though they share a common geometric shape, size, and spatial relation between the parts and the whole.

Thus, spatial thinking involves both spatial images of isolated objects as well as generalized schematic images. These images do not arise sequentially or independently of each other in the course of problem-solving, but rather routinely convert into each other, as if recoding each other. This defines the complicated and internally contradictory nature of this type of thinking.

Spatial images created on various graphic foundations are complex in their very nature. Spatial images describe what is unique and what is universal, what is particular and what is abstract, and what is empirical and what is theoretical. By means of these images, it is possible to establish spatial relations inherent to individual objects as well as to a whole class of objects that share a common design-engineering geometry.

In our study of the psychological nature of spatial images, the foundation of spatial thinking, we follow the majority of Soviet psychologists in understanding that the generalized nature of spatial images is derived from a unity of the sensory and the rational. "The sensory and the rational," writes P.V. Kopnin, "are not two levels of cognition, but rather two of its aspects, which penetrate cognition in all forms and at all stages of development. The unity of the sensory and the rational in the cognitive process denotes the indispensable participation of both aspects in our cognition, and is not simply the successive appearance of one after the other" [1969, pp. 177-178]. Furthermore, the generality, abstractness, and dynamism of the spatial image at any level are coordinated by theoretical knowledge, a conceptual framework, and specialized techniques of perception and representation.

With these remarks in mind, we can address a number of issues relating to the use of the visualization principle in the teaching process. The selection of visual material for educational purposes must reflect the psychological nature of the spatial image generated on the basis of the image itself. Suppose a student attempts to analyze a shop drawing in order to make some part shown on it. To achieve this goal, the student, glancing at the drawing carefully, following it step by step, and making sure not to forget any feature of the geometric shape of the part, must focus on the dimensions of the drawing and the standard notation used in it. But if this same student considers a geometric drawing necessary for proving a theorem, his attention will be focused on identifying the most abstract aspects of the drawing, rather than its specific features. Thus, it will be important to deduce that two sides of a triangle are perpendicular, independent of the position of the triangle in the plane. Whereas in the first case the drawing constitutes a special object of study, in the second case, it is simply a visual support the student uses to rouse his thought processes, and thus is a distinctive schematic image.

In the third case, the drawing may serve as a condition for the reproduction of various visual images of a particular object. Thus, if students are asked to depict some object in a drawing in three views and locate it in a set of objects (or visual representations of a set), a clear image of the particular objects can be generated and then compared to other objects given in a technical diagram. In all the cases we have considered, we find a recoding of images that differ in content and the level of generality of spatial properties and relations.

All these remarks indicate that using various types of visual aids for educational purposes, so that spatial images may be created and used, requires an analysis of the psychological content of the image. Unfortunately, the visual aids used in the classroom are classified solely in terms of their objective content, and are often used exclusively for purposes of illustration. Furthermore, the function of the spatial image in the development of the student's spatial thought processes has not received sufficient study.

The Structure of the Spatial Image and Its Function in the Solution of Graphic Problems

Earlier, we considered the conditions under which an image may appear and be manipulated. Among these conditions, we may cite the following: (1) the nature of the visual content in which the image first appears; and (2) the features of the graphic problem that define the requirements imposed on the image and its manipulation.

Depending upon the nature of the visual material (according to our classification of visual aids), images displaying different content and various degrees of generality and particularity may be created. Compare, for example, a picture of a doorbell, a perspective drawing of this bell, its assembly diagram, and a diagram of the path of the current in the circuit which makes possible its operation. It is possible to represent the same object, the doorbell, using different graphic techniques. Since this object is reproduced in each of the different representations in terms of different features and properties (structural, functional, etc.), the images differ in terms of internal nature, although they are closely interrelated.

In the course of solving problems, whether educational, industrial, or design-engineering, it is often necessary to use several graphic representations (i.e., isometrics, drawings, diagrams) rather than just one. As a result, we must not only create images corresponding to given representations, but also recode them. To solve such problems as determining the reason for a failure of the doorbell to ring, it is necessary, starting with different graphic representations, to see the object from a number of different points of view. The images created on the basis of these representations must be merged into a single, unified image. The isolated images derived from the perception of each representation may be distinguished by degree of clarity, generality, and schematization. They do not simply exist sequentially, but instead are modified and transformed in the problem-solving process. In the final or resultant image, therefore, we find reflected in the finished form the entire logic underlying the transformation of the initial images. The structure of these images depends upon the content of the visual material in which they initially appeared.

We have considered the case where the problem-solving process is based on the use of different graphic representations given as initial visual material. However, there is also a class of problems in which the raw data are given in a single representation, rather than several. In the problem-solving process, we must apply a different method for the graphic expression of a given result. This classic problem is extensively represented in drawing and in descriptive geometry, as well as in school mathematics. For example, in many drawing problems it is necessary to identify the shape of a geometric body and produce a perspective representation from an original drawing. The converse problem is often encountered. Let us present several examples of such problems.[4]

(1) Given a perspective drawing of models in three views, create a graphic representation from a set of figures.

(2) From a drawing of parts, construct their evolutes and, after cutting them out of cardboard, make a model.

(3) Guided by graphic representations, make a perspective drawing of a part.

In these problems, the initial condition is a single type of representation (drawing or picture), while solving the problem requires a second representation, switching from a two-dimensional to a three-dimensional representation, from a graphic to a diagrammatic representation, or vice versa.

Problems in which it is necessary to create a drawing, sketch, or graphic representation of an object from a verbal description are also common. In this type of problem, it is first necessary to mentally create an image of the object and locate it in space, and only then turn it into a proper graphic image. The converse problem is also feasible.

All the cases we have considered involve a recoding of spatial images which arise under various conditions. In some cases, the initial conditions for the creation and manipulation of the image specify several representations at the same time. In other cases, we have a single initial representation and must construct other images from it to create an entirely different graphic image. Finally, in yet other cases, images are recoded in words and graphic representations displaying varying degrees of abstractness.

In each case we are dealing a recoding of images, but the psychological nature of the recoding may differ from one case to the next. Let us not forget that an image of an object and a graphic image interact in a complex way. Various graphic images may be created for the same object, since it may be depicted in various ways. For example, its many spatial properties and relations may be emphasized in one image but not in another.

We should emphasize that in the examples considered here, we are concerned with various methods of recoding images of the same object. A certain object is specified while the method used for creating a graphic representation of it varies. However, a whole series of problems typically involves several different objects rather than just one, and the techniques used to create graphic representations of them vary. This complicates the process of creating suitable images and transforming them in the problem-solving process.

Thus, the structure of the spatial image depends greatly on the nature of the visual context in which the image first appears. Several different types of representations, rather than just one, may be used to solve graphic problems, and it may be necessary to switch from one to another, thus bringing about changes in the structure of the image. Each graphic image reflects the properties of the object established by its graphic representation.

However, the structure of the spatial image is defined not only by the nature of the visual context, but also by the function that the image fulfills in solving the graphic problem. Depending upon its function, the image establishes those attributes and properties of the depicted object which are necessary for realizing and successfully performing some activity, rather than all its properties and attributes. The selective nature of psychological reflection is a fundamental law manifested in the relation of the structure of an image to its function in activity. In its specific form, this law appears whenever spatial images are created. Let us consider this in more detail.

Marxist-Leninist philosophy and its theory of cognition presuppose that the origin of the image (its content or nature) may be understood only through analysis of the individual's practical and objective activity. This psychologically important assertion was successfully realized in a number of basic studies by L.S. Vygotskii, S.L. Rubinshtein, A.N. Leontev, B.G. Ananev, A.V. Zaporozhets, and their many students and collaborators. These studies established convincingly that in any real cognitive process, the structure of the image may change substantially, depending on how the individual formulates the problem, even though the object itself remains invariant. This underscores the positive and active nature of the image, understood as a reflection of reality.

By considering mental activity as objective and transformable, rather than sensory and contemplative, researchers approach the study of this form of activity from the standpoint of the unity of its reflective, orienting, and transformational function in the individual's cognition of the real world. The content of the images created by people and the mechanism by which they appear and function cannot be comprehended without taking into account the social nature of this activity. For the individual, any object assumes its own definite social purpose. The individual's means of handling this object and its functions are reinforced in the social and historical experience, communicated in the course of human interaction, used by individuals in their objective and transformational activities (play, educational, occupation), and learned and improved in the course of activity.

A.N. Leontev (1959, 1965, 1970) has offered a very useful interpretation of the essence of the image and its psychological nature. Under his interpretation, the image is likened not to the object per se, but rather to the object viewed through the effective relations and connections which link it to the individual. Many researchers (E.N. Sokolov, A.V. Zaporozhets, V.P. Zinchenko, L.A. Venger, L.M. Vekker, and others) have shown that the structure of the image depends not only on the physical properties of the actual object, but also on the signaling function that properties of the object perform for the individual. The structure also depends on the extent to which the individual has learned to engage in specialized perceptual actions that identify the most informative content in the object, and locate, recognize, and detect its individual properties and attributes. At any level of sensory organization, the origin of the structure of the mental image may be understood solely on the basis of a description of objective and practical activity (A.N. Leontev, 1975; E.V. Ilenkov, 1961; V.S. Tyukhtin, 1963; and others).

Because the individual formulates problems, in any real cognitive process the structure of the image may vary appreciably, although the object of cognition remains unchanged. In studying the mechanism of this event, S.L. Rubinshtein [1955, 1958] emphasized that the individual trying to solve a particular problem may consider the same object from various perspectives, and in various relations and connections. The observer seems to pick out different content from the object, reflecting the properties and attributes required for successful transformation of the object. In other words, the content of the image incorporates modal characteristics of the object that may be identified selectively, depending on the goals and aims of the activity, and serve as a reference point and source of practical or theoretical action. In view of this feature of human cognition, contemporary philosophical literature distinguishes between the concepts of the *object* [Russian *ob"ekt*] and *subject* [Russian *predmet*] of reflection (learning). The *subject* of reflection (learning) is the field of reality apprehended in the course of specially organized activity designed for the discovery or detection of desired relations and connections (V.A. Lektorskii, 1968; V.V. Davydov, 1972; and others). The subject of reflection (learning) does not encompass the entire object, but only some of its more important aspects or properties. The *object* of cognition, by contrast, can be the same while the subject of cognition varies because we considers only those properties and attributes of the object which are necessary to carry out a certain practical or theoretical activity, rather than all its properties and attributes. The subject of cognition is thus defined by each particular problem. The content of the image, therefore, depends on the type of activity organized for studying the object. The levels and goals of this organization may vary, depending on the goals set for cognition. Formation of the image can be understood as the special activity of observation (B.G. Ananev), perceptual activity (A.N. Leontev, V.P. Zinchenko, and others), or mental activity (S.L. Rubinshtein).

The image is mediated by activity. This creates the illusion that the image is independent from the object, but it is merely an illusion. The more complete the object's reflection in the image, the more meaningful is the image itself, and the broader its subjective content. The degree of completeness of the object's reflection in the image depends upon the organization of the individual's activity, as was demonstrated superbly by Descartes and Diderot in research that was subsequently extended along materialist lines by I.M. Sechenov.

In our analysis of the concept of the image in the "subject-object" system, we must particularly emphasize that the existence of the object is a necessary, but not sufficient condition for the creation of the image. Also essential is special organized activity to make this necessary condition sufficient for the creation of the image. In fact, a performance-based approach to the formation of the image makes it possible to comprehend the dynamics underlying its content and structure. The image establishes in the object precisely those properties and relations which are necessary for realizing a certain activity. The orienting, regulative, and predictive functions of the image are quite apparent from studies in educational and engineering psychology.

In emphasizing the selective information established in the image, a number of researchers (V.P. Zinchenko, B.F. Lomov, V.N. Pushkin, and others) have employed the concept of the *operative image*. This term expresses the fact that the image reflects only those characteristics of the effective object which the individual requires for the successful performance of some activity. The content of the operative image incorporates those properties of the object which enable effective cognition and regulation of the cognitive process. Among these properties, we may cite the structural and technological features of objects, various operational parameters, and dynamic states. The intellectual use of these relations constitutes the basic content of the machine operator's work under the conditions of various control systems. In carrying out this activity, it is important for the individual to utilize spatial properties and relations, since a variety of signal codes are distributed in the form of spatial diagrams.

Operative images arise in any type of activity. The creative content of any activity depends upon the flexibility, variability, and dynamism of these images. Images are always part of a mental process, and are organized according to the content of this process. In reflecting on same object, therefore, images may differ in terms of completeness, depending upon which mental problem is resolved by these images.

Idiosyncratic operative images also arise in educational activity. For example, in solving mathematics problems students in the younger grades may create images of objects involved in the conditions of the problem, especially when solving narrative problems. However, when confronted with specialized organized activities designed to deduce theoretical relations (mathematical, physical, linguistic, etc.), students create diagrammatic images which reproduce these relations in visual form. Furthermore, the content of the images differs in important respects between the two cases. In the first case, the image reflects all the particular features of the objects in the problem (i.e., their objective content), whereas in the second case it reflects only abstract theoretical relations (i.e., features dealing with magnitude, relation between speed and path traversed, shape and magnitude).

Thus, the image is "born" under the influence of two closely interconnected determinants: visual stimuli and the activity required by the conditions of the problem. This is important to bear in mind when applying the principle of visualization in the teaching process. Often the choice of visual graphic representation is dictated solely by the illustrative function it plays. However, it is also important to take into account the requirements imposed by the classroom problem and, therefore, select an adequate graphic representation. Psychological studies have shown that it is often more difficult to solve a problem because an inadequate representation of the problem has been given. V.I. Zykova (1965) found that certain sixth-grade students found it difficult to determine from the picture of a house what geometric shape its roof might have. Identification of the geometric shape was made more complicated here by the vivid colors of the house. Once the picture of the house was replaced by a geometric drawing, all the students solved the problem correctly. Thus, if a representation does not adequately correspond to a classroom problem, it begins to play a negative, rather than a positive role, despite the fact that it is intended to illustrate material for study (A.Z. Redko, 1955; E.N. Kabanova-Meller, 1958, 1972).

In studies by A.N. Leontev and M.N. Volokitina, it has been shown that children who rely on a graphic representation may often substitute a play problem for a classroom one. If the teacher represents the conditions of a mathematical problem in vivid graphic pictures so as to promote the goals of teaching (draw the attention of younger students), quite often this does not help the student solve the problem, but rather makes it more difficult. In such cases, the student starts by using the realistic content in place of quantitative relations. For example, the student imagines how the guns and tanks depicted in the picture were used in the battle, how the enemy was defeated, and so forth.

Our studies have also determined that giving students a graphic representation (geometric or projective drawing, sketch, diagram) still does not define, in and of itself, the nature of the image that arise on this basis. Students may extract different content from the same graphic representation, depending upon the specific subjective problem they wish to solve. The presentation of visual material does not automatically define the effectiveness with which this material may be applied for learning through problem-solving. For these reasons, it is important to take into account the actual function served by the graphic representation in solving the classroom problem, and not merely its content and nature.

The selection of graphic illustrations must be based on an analysis of the content of the classroom activity, just as it must reflect the actual problem the students are to solve. Particularly in the higher grades, it is necessary to give students some freedom of choice in using graphic representations in light of their function in learning specific subject matter and the flexibility with which they may be used. For example, when studying mathematics, and particularly when doing geometric proofs, it is necessary to use drawings as a visual prop. But, of course, this is not always necessary, nor do all students require it. Moreover, some students have no difficulty in representing the conditions of a problem from its symbolic description. Reliance on drawings often paralyzes the students, preventing mental application of the geometric properties given within the representation.

From our point of view, allowing students to independently select the form of representation they find most convenient for solving a problem can be an important diagnostic tool for identifying the level and nature of their representational thinking. Our studies have shown that students are accustomed to working with prepared representations. In experimental situations, they seem lost and helpless if asked to select on their own the type of representation (perspective drawing, diagrammatic drawing, symbolic notations) which, in their opinion, would help in solving the problem.

Psychologists consider students' ability to subordinate their own perception to a classroom problem an important index of mental development. The accessibility of any type of graphic representation to students of a particular age, as confirmed by a number of studies, depends on the actual organization followed in the learning process, and not on any features of the thought process. Studies by V.V. Davydov and his colleagues have shown that younger students consciously utilize and independently construct graphic models that reproduce theoretical relations and dependencies. Reliance on visual (narrative) pictures is by no means an idiosyncratic feature of the thought processes of younger students. If suitable learning conditions are created for this purpose, young students' representational thinking becomes theoretical, rather than visual and empirical.

Consequently, the structure of an image depends on its function in specially organized activity. The perception of visual aids is considered by many psychologists (A.V. Zaporozhets, P.Y. Galperin, N.N. Poddyakov, A.A. Venger, and others) a special orienting foundation of activity that determines individual success at implementing its performance element.

We have considered the complicated relations found in the process of creating the image from the standpoint of the initial graphic context and the content of the educational and vocational problem. Let us now analyze how this relation emerges when solving graphic problems aimed primarily at creating and using spatial images. The principle of selective image content here retains its full value, as is particularly apparent in the classification of the problems. Thus, in geometry we may identify computation, construction, and measurement problems. This underscores the selective nature of educational activity, based for the most part on using the geometric shape of mathematical objects and their size or spatial relations. Students who work with a system of problems involving varying content naturally create visual images that differ in structure.

In descriptive geometry, we usually say that there are measurement, positional, and mixed problems. While in the first case students primarily measure relations such as length, breadth, or magnitude, they employ spatial relations and connections to solve problems of the second type. V.S. Stoletnev's studies [1977] conducted under our supervision present a description of the types and content of spatial images used in descriptive geometry. This description made it possible to give a psychologically more detailed classification of positional problems by their degree of difficulty. Let us give several examples of problems where it is necessary to identify spatial relations and manipulate them mentally.

Problem 1 (establishing the spatial relations between geometric bodies by perceiving their shape). Determine which of the three bodies represented in the drawing touch each other. Which is closest to the observer? Farthest away? Farthest to the left? Farthest to the right?

Problem 2 (establishing the spatial relations between elements in space which have no shape). Indicate which of the points in the drawing belong to the line AB; which lies in front of it; behind it; above it; under it.

Problem 3 (establishing the spatial relations between line segments by determining their direction from a diagram). Using three given projections, create a graphic representation of a broken line in space, inscribing all its segments in a drawing of a cube to help visualize them.

These examples reflect the models for such problems. Various geometric bodies and concrete drawings which we will not present here may
be used as visual representations.[5]

We should emphasize that in descriptive geometry problems, the
image that initially arises in the given graphic context is only an initial
model possessing its own set of spatial and projective attributes. Which
attributes will be used depends on the conditions of the problem, since
the problem determines the mental transformations of the initial image
or model.

None of the transformations we have carried out, each requiring
representational activity, is specified directly by the initial representation.
The final image that establishes the solution is constructed in light of the
requirements imposed by the problem. Therefore, the structure of the
image (the set of elements, attributes, and properties it depicts) depends
upon the image's function within the context of the problem. The problem-solving process may reorient various attributes and properties. For
example, at the start of the problem-solving process the student may
concentrate on some attribute of the geometric shape or position of the
object. Properties connected with the relative position of the elements in
space may subsequently become more important and critical. In this type
of problem, the elements are understood to refer to abstract geometric
figures (i.e., points, lines, projective planes, surfaces, and lines of intersection).

Thus, problems in descriptive geometry often involve a dynamic
relation between spatial properties and attributes that are established
directly in the problem-solving process. Here we may also observe a type
of recoding, expressed not only in the transition from one graphic image
to another, but also in the transition from one set of spatial attributes to
another.

Drafting problems may be classified analogously; problems call for
determination of the geometric shape of an object (or group of objects)
depicted in a diagram, or computation of the actual and working dimensions of parts and their relations. Many problems require that students

understand the spatial relations between the elements of a cross-sectional or cut-away representation. Let us give examples of such problems.

Problem 1. Given the diagram of a part, determine: a) which geometric bodies' surfaces make up the shape of each part; b) the overall dimensions of each part.

Problem 2. Given cut-away diagrams, find visual representations, indicating the correspondence between the literal notation used in the cut-away view and the numerical notation in the diagram.

Problem 3. Given a group of geometric bodies in the form of a visual representation, along with one type of diagram, complete the diagram of the group of geometric bodies in light of their spatial position.

These examples demonstrate how the content of a problem often defines the selective perception of the graphic representation (precisely what is to be identified, underscored, modeled, etc.).

Also common are compound problems in which it is necessary to deal simultaneously with the shape, size, and spatial relations of the object when creating its spatial image. For example, suppose we are given the following description of a part: "The housing is in the form of a hollow rectangular parallelepiped (length 80 mm, width 50 mm, height 40 mm). The walls of the housing are universally of the same thickness, 10 mm. In the center of the upper base of the housing contains a hole measuring 30 mm in diameter, and in the center of the lower base there is a square hole with dimensions 20 x 20 mm. From this description, sketch the part, including the required number of views. Based on the sketch, draw the part.[6]

These examples of problems from various school courses demonstrate that the structure of a spatial image created using different types of graphic contexts depends upon the specific conditions and requirements imposed by the activity. It varies dynamically, depending on the content of the graphic problem, since we observe a constant transition: (1) from visual representations to conventional diagrammatic representations; (2) from three-dimensional to two-dimensional representations; (3) from one system of orientation to another, using various properties of the object (shape, size, spatial relations).

The structure of the spatial image must change because of its function in human activity (in the problem-solving process). The image which arises initially from a reading of the original representation can only perform the function of control, correction, and prediction of activity (i.e., a regulative function) when it is regularly transformed in the problem-solving process. Let us illustrate this by means of an example. In a number of manufacturing problems, it is necessary to represent the entire process of producing a mold and finished part based on comparative analysis of diagrams of each step, and then express the process in graphic form through sketches of the manufacturing steps. The first graphic image arises from reading the initial technical documentation (diagram of mold and part). Each subsequent image must take into account a preceding sketch of a manufacturing step that establishes changes in the shape, size, and spatial position of the mold. If the entire manufacturing logic of these changes is not taken into account, the engineer will be unable to correctly diagram the next sketch, because it will not be possible to predict all the necessary changes that must be made mentally in order to obtain a correct graphic image of the mold at the next stage of production. We must especially emphasize that sketches of manufacturing steps, since as unique graphic images, establish in their content particular features of the same object or part depicted by a diagram of the mold and the graphic representation of the finished part. However, these graphic images differ in structure, since they reproduce the features of the part at various points in its development.

In many graphic problems, the way images change and are transformed into one another is essentially the basic mechanism of the problem-solving process. This follows from the unique dialectical nature of the image. While the image cannot remain invariant relative to the visual context in which it is created, it must be adequate for this material. At the same time, the image cannot be something which remains fixed, static, and frozen, but must be dynamic, variable, and operative. Otherwise it could not fulfill its function in the problem-solving process, where it is necessary not merely to establish the existing, original situation, but also to transform it.

While the initial graphic material is specified in the conditions of the problem, usually as a stable invariant element, the function of the image varies constantly, and this makes it necessary to constantly reconstruct the image. The static and dynamic elements of the image are unified. Any discrepancies between the two give rise to difficulties in solving the graphic problem, a fact which has been demonstrated convincingly by teaching experience.

Thus, like any image, spatial images are dynamic in their very nature. Their structures are defined not only by the nature of the graphic material, but also by the degree of activity displayed by the individual. The direction and content of this activity are specified by the conditions of the graphic problem, and by previously developed methods or methods uncovered during the problem-solving process.

The initial graphic material is no more than an initial base for the creation of the image. The image itself is transformed repeatedly in the course of the problem-solving process. These transformations are closely related not only to retention of the image in memory, but also to the use of a conceptual apparatus that defines the methods which may be used to transform the image within the logic of the problem.

The solution of any graphic problem is based on the activity of *representation*, which takes on, as we have tried to show, a complex structure. The process of solving graphic problems is composed of a combination of: 1) initial images that arise in a special visual context through a selection of methods for transforming them (i.e., graphic modeling); and 2) images in the form of graphic diagrams of movements which reproduce the logic underlying the student's mental construction of the representation. These images should be interpreted on the basis of the extensive application of knowledge and concepts of types of representation and methods of constructing them. Both unity and interpretation help to establish correct strategies for solving graphic problems in which the visual and conceptual components merge into a unified whole.

The spatial image is a complex, multi-level structural formation. The image defines not only different modal characteristics of the object (i.e., shape, size, spatial relations), but also methods for their graphic (practical) transformation. The structure of the spatial image is highly dynamic. Any image, as we have shown above, reflects far from all the features inherent to the object, rather only those which are necessary for solving a particular problem and successfully performing some theoretical or practical activity. The image, therefore, is always operative, selective, and dynamic. This is particularly the case with the spatial image, which reflects the most varied and dynamic characteristics of the object (i.e., changes in its position in the plane, in space, and relative to other objects). Therefore, no description of the spatial image can be complete if it does not take into account the system of orientation in which the image appears and is manipulated.

The Use of Various Systems of Reference With Spatial Images

The use of various systems of orientation in space (visible or abstract) is a distinctive feature of spatial thinking. The body image is the most natural system of orientation, since it is related to all the individual's experience. This system is the basis for the individual's physical orientation relative to objects and events.

Spatial images serve as a basis for orientation in a locality. But they can never be entirely abstracted from the particular objects and spatial relations between them, which collectively make up the locality and distinguish it from all other localities. Nor can they be abstracted completely from the material reference point: the individual, the bearer of these images; nor from the system of reference specific to the individual's perception. Even if these representations arise from a conventional graphic representation of an actual locality (e.g., a topographic or geodesic map), rather than from perception of this locality, the individual nevertheless remains the conventional reference point. All the objects surrounding the individual (or their conventional substitutes) are distributed in space relative to an individual standing erect (in actual fact or in imagination). This orientation in real space has developed historically. It first arose as a practical necessity, so that people could adapt properly to local conditions. "Man could not become biologically adapted to the environment, " noted Lenin, "if his senses could not give him an *objectively correct* representation of it" (*Complete Collected Works*, v. 18: 185).

At a rather early age, the child begins to orient himself to the real space around him, and subsequently the imaginary space, based on the position of his own body. Studies by A.Y. Kolodna [1940], B.G. Ananev [1954], A.A. Lyublinskaya [1956], A.N. Sorokun [1965], and many others have demonstrated that the child's first spatial images arise once he is conscious of the arrangement of his own body, understanding the distinction between right and left hands or feet. All objects in space are perceived by children with respect to the vertical disposition of their own bodies (above-below, in front-in back, to the side, to the right-to the left, etc.). This natural position then serves as a reference point for the creation of a variety of corresponding spatial images.

Orientation with respect to the body is dominant not only in the practical understanding of space, but also in the transition from real (physical) to theoretical (geometrical) space. Children's pictures eloquently attest to this fact. As they begin to draw, children try mainly to reproduce in their pictures either themselves or other people. In drawing a self-portrait using conventional means, the child tries to create a compositional structure in the picture by spatially distributing all the constituent objects in the picture. Data obtained by N.P. Sakulina [1972] indicate that children proceed mainly from an understanding of the position of their own bodies when they attempt to reproduce spatial relations between objects in their representational activities. Sakulina showed that the child who has learned how to readily reproduce people in pictures will for a long time experience difficulty when trying to convey the forms and relations of the parts of animals.

Such difficulties, we believe, may be attributed to the fact that the spatial position of the parts of an animal's body differs from the arrangement of the human body. Though they share a common cruciform structure, the basic parts of the human and animal body are arranged differently in space. When depicting the human body, the basic reference point is the vertical axis, whereas when depicting the animal body, the reference point is the horizontal axis. The transition from one frame of reference to another creates understandable difficulties for children, difficulties which may be readily overcome by means of a specially organized teaching process. We must agree with Sakulina's conclusion that a child's acquisition of the ability to form spatial images requires more than just the development of sensory standards of shape and color. Also necessary is a scientifically-based system of standards, which makes it possible to identify spatial relations and use them when handling real objects and conventional graphic representations of real objects. Only on this basis is it possible to acquire a generalized understanding of the structure of different objects.

An orientation based on the body remains important in learning about geometrical (Euclidean) space. It is well known that Cartesian coordinate systems are theoretical abstractions, though in their very basis they retain the vertical-horizontal construction inherent to the human body. The rectangular coordinate system, which is a special case of affine coordinates, is especially reminiscent of the body's organization.

Indeed, the rectangular coordinate system is extensively utilized in various school subjects, e.g., physics, geography, and mechanical drawing. The three types of representations used in mechanical drawing are nothing other than distinctive projections of the object when viewed from three different points of view: from in front (a frontal view), from above (a horizontal view), and from the left (a profile view). The origin, or point of reference is usually the position of the observer at which the image plane is parallel to the frontal plane of the perceived object and lies above the level of its horizontal plane. In other words, the rectangular and parallel systems of projection widely used in mathematics, drafting, descriptive geometry, and other fields is based on the natural and physically important system of reference of the human body.

Orientation based on the body is also important in physical geography. It is well known that this subject has as one of its central topics the development of spatial images related to terrain orientation, as well as the understanding of geographic maps. The first geographic images are created from the use of the natural reference point, the human body, relative to which objects are either perceived or mentally arranged in space.

Students are introduced to the notion of terrain orientation by means of topographic plans, and are taught how to use the compass and identify the compass points. It is assumed that they must know how to determine the origin in their minds. The same occurs when students are taught how to read maps in the physical geography course. The following technique is recommended for determining the direction of stream flow from a map: "Imagine you are standing in the river and facing in the direction of the flow. In that case, to your right will be the right bank and to your left, the left bank."

Thus, learning to use geographic maps is closely related to the use of the body as a unique reference point. The transition from real terrain orientation to the conventional symbolization of this orientation contains nothing new in terms of psychology, since the transition itself is based on the use of the same frame of reference. This thought has been expressed distinctly by F.N. Shemyakin, who has written, "by the term 'topographic representations' we understand a mental plan of some terrain as a reflection in a person's mind of the spatial distribution of the local objects ('field points') in their relations to each other and to the individual there" [1959: 42-43]. A person seems to localize himself mentally at some locality by determining one's own standpoint. If he is not representing a real locality, but rather reading a topographic map, he must first orient it to his own position, and then try to "visualize" real objects from the conventional notations on the map. The mechanism of creating a spatial image of a real locality based on its perception or the use of conventional notations to represent it is, in this sense, one and the same thing. In both cases, the individual is guided by an empirically created frame of reference about himself. The only difference is that the image of some locality created from a map is mediated by knowledge of conventional notation. Experience in teaching geography, however, suggests that this notation can be learned without great difficulty.

The process of reading a map is based on the orientation of the objects at the site relative to the compass points (north-south-east-west), which is in turn related to orientation based on the human body. Consider the following example of reading a topographic map.

At the center is located a collective farm. Northwest of the settlement is a mixed forest, and to the northeast we find bush and meadows, while the remaining area is given over to plowed fields. To the east is a small hill, to the south a river flows, and to the west there is a railway branch and abridge across the river. A railroad runs from west to southeast through the settlement, connecting the farm community with the railway station and the city. To the north a dirt road runs from the collective farm to the neighboring village.

In order to successfully complete this assignment, the student must know how to interpret the conventional signs and orient the map from the standpoint of a person reading it. He must also know how to determine the compass points and correctly orient the depicted objects relative to these directions. If the further problem of determining the distance between objects is posed, it is then necessary to use conventional scale notation.

Thus, orientation based on the human body, which is the ontogenetically earliest form of orientation, serves as a foundation for the system of reference not only in real (physical) space, but also in geometrical space. This is clear both in educational as well as professional activity.

In many instances, orientation based on the human body makes it possible to successfully perform an activity, though it may have an adverse effect on the solution of problems whose objective content requires a transition to other systems of reference. Let us consider an example. In order to read different types of text and conventional representations, the individual must take a definite, fixed position and read from left to right, top to bottom. This ordinary method of dealing with text is so well-established that it can be carried over to reading various scales, instrument panels, geometrical figures, and so on, without the need for special teaching (B.F. Lomov [1966]; W. Woodson and I. Conover [1968]; J. Metzler and R. Shepard [1971, 1974]; L.A. Cooper

[1975]). Students also maintain this method in reading perspective diagrams. They perceive perspective representations on a sheet of paper as an arrangement with respect to the fixed position of an observer. A left view, therefore, is often mistaken for a right view, since it is placed on the right side of the sheet of paper relative to the observer.

In terms of psychological nature, these mistakes result from the fact that perspective representations establish an arbitrary position from which the object is observed, while students replace this position by another position which is unambiguous, more familiar, and well established for them. Experience has demonstrated that these difficulties can be overcome only by teaching them specialized procedural techniques that lead to a method of obtaining a particular type of representation (A.D. Botvinnikov, 1965).

These facts indicate that orientation based on the human body constitutes the foundation on which various systems of knowledge of the spatial properties and relations of objects are formed and methods of manipulating spatial images are created in a natural way.

But people use other systems of reference, in addition to orientation based on the human body. In many types of mental and physical activity, it is routinely necessary to switch to other frames of reference that are apparently abstracted from the body. Children are capable of this transition at an early age (two to three years), when they can reproduce spatial relations which reflect not their position relative to some system of objects, but relations between the objects themselves. For example, when the child draws a narrative picture (regardless of his graphic skills), he takes some object as the basis and arranges all the other objects relative to it (nearer-farther, around, next to, etc.). Here he apparently abstracts from his own position and takes an arbitrarily selected point as his reference point.

When they move on to geometrical space, students must not only rely on the human body, but are often also forced to abstract from it. Thus, to determine the spatial distribution of geometrical objects they often use as their initial reference point not the observer, but rather an abstract, arbitrarily selected element (point, segment, angle, etc.) relative to which all the other elements are distributed in space. This is particularly vivid when images of geometric objects are based on conventional graphic representations (drawings, diagrams, graphs, etc.). For example, the position of any geometric figure in the plane is determined in a selected coordinate system. In various two-dimensional representations, any geometric element with known coordinates may be taken as the reference point. For example, the position of any point on a number line, as well as in a coordinate plane, is defined by the coordinates of this point. The location of the observer relative to it is of no importance.

Under these conditions, the formation of spatial images displays its own distinctive nature. This is mainly because the individual must abstract from an existing natural system of reference, which is also firmly "bound" to the individual, and switch to a second specified or arbitrarily selected frame of reference. This transition is based on the use of different systems (frames) of reference, and the position of the individual may be ignored.

Mathematics makes use of other systems besides the rectangular coordinate system, e.g., the polar system. Physics makes wide use of spherical, cylindrical, and other coordinate systems. Many spatial displacements treated in modern elementary mathematics courses are carried out without respect to the initial position of the observer. These displacements, defined as "reflections of the plane onto itself," are based on the relative position of figures. The position of the observer has no essential significance. The basic difficulties encountered in descriptive geometry courses arise because the student must change his base of reference, mentally overcoming the limits set by the trihedral angle open to the observer, and representing the position of geometric figures in other octants.

Similarly, in geography other coordinate systems are widely used besides those based on the human body. Spatial images are formed on the basis of cartographic projections such as cylindrical, conical, and azimuthal projections, besides the rectangular coordinate system adopted for determining the position of objects on a topographic map. Furthermore, the location of an object on a map is related to the "movement" of two dimensions in the plane, whereas on a sphere we presuppose the concept that motion there is unbounded in all directions.

Images derived from a geographic map differ from topographic images in that their creation requires a variety of different frames of reference, rather than just one. Any point on a map may be taken as the origin of reference. For example, to determine the geographic location of a city, it is important to know its location relative to other objects, as well as in terms of latitude and longitude. It is unimportant whether a person reading the map has determined his own "standpoint." However, map images, as F.N. Shemyakin has remarked, may be converted into topographic images if the person has determined his standpoint. Even topographic images may reflect the individual's position relative to the objects surrounding him, or may be based on the relative position of various objects ("travel map" and "survey map" in Shemyakin's terminology [1940]).

The process of learning how to read a geographic map requires not only a transition from one system of conventional designations to another; it is equally important to understand the different systems of reference. Both topographic and geographic maps are conventional representations of individual portions of the earth's surface taken in a particular cartographic projection. In this respect, they differ from a globe, the shape of which reproduces the earth's surface without requiring projection onto a plane. Moreover, in a geographic map the position of any point depends upon other objects, regardless of the position of the person who is reading the map. For example, a student who wishes to determine on a map the position of Voronezh may say that it is south of Moscow and north of Volgograd, giving its latitude and longitude.

Thus, the use of various graphic representations in a geography course requires not only learning the meaning of conventional designations, but also switching over to other systems of reference. The mathematical foundations of spatial orientation also vary. A rectangular coordinate system may be used to create a topographic map, and a spherical (longitude and latitude) grid to create a geographic map. It is often necessary to rely on other systems of reference as well when working with geographic maps. This need creates difficulties for students.

"In geometrical space," writes Shemyakin, "we are free to take in our minds any point as the origin of the coordinate system and relate it to any other point. Our own personal perceptions of physical space operate on an entirely different principle. Of necessity, one point is expressly picked out: the place where we are located and from which we perceive the world around us. There are also specially 'marked' directions, such as the pair 'up-down,' which is imposed upon us by the earth's gravitational field. This point serves as a natural origin of the coordinate system underlying our perception of space. We may replace it by another point only if we first abandon our previous position in space. It is by virtue of the pair of directions that we perceive the world around us relative to the position of our body, represented in its normal or vertical position, perpendicular to the horizontal plane of the earth's surface" [1968: 20].

These examples attest convincingly that in order to learn, students must simultaneously employ various systems of reference, which stand in highly complicated "competing" relations to each other. The use of a particular coordinate system requires the manipulation of spatial representations of differing psychological character. It is easier to deal with representations in a rectangular coordinate system, since such a system largely reproduces the natural orientation in the two- and three-dimensional space to which man is accustomed. Switching to other systems means that our existing, highly accustomed representations must be readjusted considerably. In such a transition, it is necessary to create representations based on novel systems of reference not reinforced by experience which are adequate for the given system.

An individual's ability to use different systems of reference to orient himself in space, for these reasons, is regarded by many researchers as an index of creative activity. The ability to switch from traditional representations based on experience in solving standard problems in a system of rectangular projections, to novel and unusual representations that require a different system of reference has been exploited by D.B. Bogoyavlanskii [1968] to create a special experimental method, called the "creative field" method. Subjects who play chess well on an ordinary rectangular board are asked to play in a cylindrical field. Despite the fact that the set of pieces and rules of play remain unchanged, under these conditions even experienced chess players experience considerable difficulties. This may be because chess positions are usually thought about and the moves mentally represented in a two-dimensional plane bounded by the edge of the chess board. Cylindrical chess forces the player to switch to a different frame where the mental distribution of pieces on the chessboard presupposes an ability to utilize a cylindrically-shaped coordinate grid. Interestingly, subjects may attempt to overcome their difficulty by mentally unrolling the cylinder into a two-dimensional figure, i.e., creating its evolute, and then return all the figures to their ordinary spatial position, after which they succeed in playing the game.

Studies by B.M. Blyumenfeld [1948] demonstrated experimentally that in solving chess problems, subjects principally utilize an image of the position, (i.e., the spatial position of one particular chess piece relative to the system of all the others) rather than an image of a particular piece *per se*. They achieve the same rate of success in solving chess problems using various substitutes in place of the actual chess pieces, e.g., chips, pebbles, buttons, etc. The player solves a problem by rapidly finding a correct spatial combination of the pieces as he mentally shifts them around. Of course, this presupposes a vivid image reflecting the dynamic spatial relations among the pieces. Creating a spatial image of the initial position, along with the ability to retain it in memory and mentally utilize it, allows experienced chess players to play chess games simultaneously on several boards and solve complicated chess problems based on an analysis of a conventional representation of the position of the chess pieces. The same law comes into play when creating "geometric" images. The well-known Russian mathematician D.D. Mordukhai-Boltovskii [1908] placed special emphasis on the fact that memory in geometry is basically memory of the relative position of lines and surfaces, or parts of them.

We must emphasize that the vertical/horizontal construction of a coordinate system, which causes the perception of real and geometric

(Euclidean) space to merge, is not the only possibility; there exist other systems as well. For example, much of modern mathematical and physical knowledge is based on spherical, rather than planar, representations. In this case, the coordinate grid is generated by curves, rather than straight lines.

People must frequently abstract away from body orientation and switch to other systems of reference in their professional activity. By perceiving conventional graphic models (three-dimensional diagrams, instrument panels, scales, dials, etc.) of real working parts, rather than the parts themselves, the machine operator mentally represents the status of the part he or she must regulate. The spatial distribution of real objects is generally not the same as the distribution of their conventional substitutes. The machine operator must be able to imagine clearly the real spatial distribution of parts based on their spatial distribution in a diagram. For this purpose, he must translate ("recode") the conventional semiotic form of signals into images of working parts (or the processes they engender). The basic problem is not so much to decode the conventional designations representing the parts as to determine their relative position in space, and thereby create vivid visual images of a "real place" (e.g., the control section of a shop, railway, electrical transmission system, etc.). This spatial orientation is realized indirectly through a system of signal codes. That is, the images in a conventional diagram reflect only approximately the actual distribution of mechanical parts. The machine operator must repeatedly relate a dynamic image of the diagram to a representation of the real parts so as to prevent any "discrepancy" from arising between them. For these purposes, railway transportation dispatchers frequently travel those portions of the line which they are responsible for regulating at a distance. This custom insures that they will be able to form correct spatial images formed on the basis of a remote-control system of conventional signals.

Thus, spatial orientation requires that the individual not only determine the actual situation, but also create dynamic spatial images based on a variable reference point. This is particularly clear in the work of an aircraft pilot. Correct orientation of the aircraft requires that the pilot be able to conduct observations of ground objects, as well as to note the readings on instruments rapidly and correctly. Orientation derived from instrument readings may conflict with orientation based on ground objects. When the pilot orients the aircraft with respect to ground objects, the orientation scheme lies outside the aircraft, on the ground. When he flies using only the various instruments as reference, the situation changes abruptly. The center of orientation is displaced psychologically to the aircraft cabin. The pilot judges the position of the aircraft in space by means of the instrument readings, rather than by direct impressions from his perception of ordinary ground objects. The instrument readings provide information about the aircraft's spatial orientation in coded form. As conditions change, the pilot must not only note the instrument readings at once and decode them, but also create an abstract mental picture. The act of reading instruments must take into account both certain spatial coordinates and the pilot's own visual position relative to the instruments. In contrast, the flight plan is based on other coordinates, derived, for example, from a determination of the aircraft's position relative to the earth, which may not be observed visually.

A person who is accustomed to conditions on earth, and therefore takes the position of his own body as the initial reference point and distributes all objects in space relative to his body, finds himself in a problematical situation when this customary reference point ceases to exist. This is convincingly demonstrated by data gathered by Soviet cosmonauts. Whenever the cosmonaut is in free fall in a space lab or in space flight, he is forced to orient himself in space as a function of the objects around him or the cabin walls. Under conditions of weightlessness, the position of his own body is no longer fixed, and therefore it cannot serve as an initial reference point for orienting himself in space. In fact, he must actually determine the position of his own body. The reference objects available for this purpose include the walls of the cabin, as well as any objects rigidly fixed in the cabin and relative to which the cosmonaut may determine the position of his body. This process of "reorientation" is not undertaken immediately. It requires a lengthy period of adaptation to weightlessness and different forms of exercises whereby the cosmonauts learn to deny the ordinary reference system and switch to a different system.

According to a number of Soviet cosmonauts (A. Nikolaev, P. Popovich, and others), spatial orientation based on the fixed position of one's body is so well-established that even in the absence of gravity the individual continues for some time to comprehend the basic directions of "down-up" relative to the vertical position of his body. In their book, A.A. Leonov and V.I. Lebedev remark that "in putting the spaceship in orbit, the cosmonaut must clearly imagine the position of the spaceship relative to the terrestrial horizon and the direction in which the ship is traveling. Once he is aware of these data and has incorporated the ship into the orientation of the body, he can begin the maneuver" [1971: 98].

Spatial orientation is even more difficult when the cosmonaut leaves the vehicle and takes a space walk. He encounters not only free fall, but also "unoriented" space. Once he leaves the spacecraft, his psychological representations of his position relative to the spacecraft cabin are destroyed and he is forced to assume an entirely new orientation based solely on his visual perception of the surrounding space. "In order to teach the cosmonaut how to orient himself on a space walk, he should first be given a coordinate system, where one base point is the spacecraft, together with its longitudinal and lateral axes. In this coordinate system, the spacecraft serves essentially as the lowermost point. This representation is instilled in the course of flight training" [1971: 98]. Thus, orientation in outer space requires a conversion to novel systems of reference, and this entails the formation of spatial images that differ from those created as part of one's orientation on the earth's surface.

Thus, in various types of educational and professional activity the individual must regularly switch from a fixed system of reference to other systems either selected arbitrarily or specified by the conditions governing the activity. This transition requires the development of spatial understanding. Various forms and levels of transition from the human body to other systems of reference may act as unique critical points in the development of spatial orientation, whether in theoretical or practical space. As S.L. Rubinshtein has pointed out, "the transition from a fixed frame of reference (coordinate system) to a system based on a freely-mobile reference point constitutes the core of the general development of spatial understanding" [1946: 237].

A variety of frames of reference are used to solve graphic problems, and constant transition from one frame of reference to another enriches and influences each. However, the predominant use of some one particular frame of reference (most often the human body) often impedes successful problem-solving. This is particularly clear in descriptive geometry, where it is necessary to use several frames of reference simultaneously (one based on the human body, and others based on certain reference points specified by the conditions of the problem, or based on completely arbitrary reference points). Specialists have observed that it is precisely this circumstance which is responsible for the basic difficulties in problem-solving; these difficulties are difficult to overcome even through the teaching process.

The predominant use of a particular frame of reference is characteristic of certain lines of development of spatial thinking. In the course of ontogenesis, each line of development is perfected and enriched at the expense of other lines. We can identify three basic trends, within which systems of reference develop and are perfected: 1) expanded opportunities for orientation based on the human body both in physical and geometrical space, attributable to the use of an arbitrarily varied position in space (visible or imaginary), along with fixed positions; 2) enriched methods of varying the observation point, when the reference point is not the individual, but some other object; 3) the use of any theoretically specified and arbitrarily selected reference point.

Let us consider this point in greater detail. In the course of ontogenetic development, body orientation undergoes changes which lead to more arbitrary use. The child first reproduces a particular spatial situation (creates a mental picture), based on his own real location. As the child grows, he learns how to alter his position mentally and, accordingly, create different spatial pictures (for example, imagining a 90- or 180-degree revolution). The child's ability to alter the position of his body arbitrarily and, on this basis, create different spatial images, is developed through instruction.

The same line of development is followed with older children for orientation in graphic representations of real objects, as well as in systems of real objects themselves. By means of graphic representations, students may try to conceive of the relative position of depicted objects in space in terms of the human body. They perceive graphic representations located in front of them. As E.N. Kabanova-Meller has remarked [1971], "in creating a spatial image from a drawing, the student locates it mentally in some specified or imaginary plane (i.e., projects it onto the blackboard, a sheet of paper, or the surface of a desk). This act of projection is intended to reflect the actual position of the observer. In teaching students how to apply methods of orthogonal and parallel projection methods in mathematics and mechanical drawing, the teacher should take into account the human body and show students how to modify it mentally.

The line of development represented by human body orientation exists alongside the formation and development of other systems of reference in which the position of any object (thing or geometric entity) may be taken as the reference point, so that the position of the child's body is abstracted. The child is surrounded by moving, interacting objects, not by fixed objects. In order to correctly orient himself in space, therefore, it is often important that the child takes the position of one object situated among other objects as the reference point, thereby establishing various spatial relations among the objects, adapting himself to these relations and modifying and altering them.

Analyses of children's drawings conducted by O.I. Galkina, V.S. Mukhina, N.P. Sakulina, and others have demonstrated that it is sometimes more important for the child to depict in his picture the interaction of one object with other objects, rather than representing this object in a fixed position relative to himself. For this reason, the child may try to represent not just a girl, but a girl running, playing ball with other girls, and so forth. Children's typical perceptual dynamism helps them make elementary transitions to different systems of reference, and arbitrarily alter the position of the observer. Furthermore, the free transition from three-dimensional to two-dimensional representations and vice versa may be observed, where they have to compare representations and recognize the object depicted.

It should be emphasized that children demonstrate the ability to arbitrarily change their reference point when operating with spatial relations at a very early age. This ability is determined by the very nature of the perceptual process. Any normally developing child recognizes objects not by viewing them passively, but rather by using them actively. When he uses different objects in his practical activity (play, work), the child regularly observes that, depending on the reference point he selects, the object may appear to change in external appearance, and may become enriched with various details previously hidden from his perception. When he manipulates an object, the child gains a better understanding of its structure (the relation between its parts) by learning about its function. Intuitively, he begins to understand that the same object may display various relations between its parts, depending upon the conditions of the perceptual process (the observation position). This emerges quite clearly from children's drawings. In her analysis, N.P. Sakulina writes that "in observing the child's first attempts to create graphic images, we may establish not only two-dimensional frontal and profile representations, but also those which combine representations of the object from several points of view" [1971: 95].

Psychological studies (by N.P. Linkova, O.I. Galkina, N.P. Sakulina, I.S. Yakimanskaya, and others) have shown that preschoolers and children in the early grades have no trouble learning to create a perspective drawing using a method of projection. Their analysis of the object from three distinct points of view (from in front, above, and the side) corresponds to their habit of manipulating objects in the course of playful, representational, and creative activity. They intuitively distinguish the functions of the two types of representation quite easily, that is, the picture and the diagram, and their potential of each for representing objects and conveying shape, proportion, and structure. The child appears to turn the object about mentally, so that he faces each of its sides in turn, selecting as his point of reference the side from which it is easiest to identify the complex structure of the object.

Let us consider an interesting study carried out by A.D. Botvinnikov [1968] which illustrates this point. Third- and fourth-graders were asked to make a diagram and a picture of some object (a box, birdhouse, dollhouse, stool, sled, glass, etc.). In the space under the picture they were asked to describe the shape of the object, while above the diagram they were to write down everything they knew about the diagram. Although nothing was said about how to select the object to be depicted, most of the students drew a doll house, a box, a stool, or a birdhouse, clearly because of their experience from using these objects in art and crafts classes. Before giving the assignment, the teacher made sure that the students knew enough about the basic geometric figures and simple three-dimensional shapes (the cube, parallelepiped, cylinder, cone, etc.). They were also introduced to the basic concepts of evolutes and methods of creating an evolute, and had learned to represent simple elements in perspective and depict objects in two and three dimensions. However, the curriculum included no special exercises involving comparative analysis of diagrams and pictures.

What did the experiment show? The object was distributed spatially in various ways in the pictures drawn by the students, with 50.2% of the students representing the object in its most natural position. For example, the bird house was depicted in the way it is usually seen (fastened to the top of a tree). The house was depicted basically in a frontal view (30%) or obliquely (46%). Nearly 75% of the students depicted the objects in three dimensions. A two-dimensional representation was given by only 23.3% of the students.

From their diagrams, it was apparent that 25% of the same students were fully ready to learn how to create a diagram, indeed, before being taught how. The diagrams also showed that the students were able to understand the basic attributes of the method of projection. In certain instances, an overhead plan or view of the object was created, while in others, a frontal representation. In the third group, the object was represented obliquely or simultaneously in two projections, though no order in their arrangement nor any projective relation was observed.

Botvinnikov emphasized that students in this age group have no trouble distinguishing a picture and a diagram not only visually, but also in speech. In their responses, they point out that "a picture conveys lines in the order in which we see them in front of us, " whereas "a diagram conveys lines as they might be seen from above or from the side." Some of their answers pointed out that a picture gives us a representation of length, width, and depth, whereas a drawing supplies only length and width. Most of the answers expressed in various ways the thought that "a diagram is an outline of the object."

These data show that young schoolchildren display considerable ability at using a variety of frames of reference under the influence of various activities (play, classroom, crafts, drawing, and building and design). At a rather early age, they have already learned everything they need to know in order to abstract from the human body and assume dynamic and diverse points of reference, which may include not only the individual, but any other object. Moreover, the observation point may be varied arbitrarily.

This age also seems to be the most sensitive for learning the projective method, whether central, parallel, or rectangular projection, and for developing projective representations, a factor which is insufficiently taken into account in practical teaching. Systematic instruction in projective methods begins only in grade 7 (at the age of 13-14). The dynamic perception characteristic of children at this age is held back by the teaching process simply because students are accustomed to working with prepared representations, e.g., geometric diagrams, pictures, diagrams that reproduce objects in an arbitrarily selected, but strictly fixed position. Moreover, instruction is restricted to two-dimensional representations which reflect only a single view (i.e., the frontal position in the plane). Practice at working with these representations makes it difficult to learn drafting and solid geometry in the later grades, when it is necessary to again switch from two-dimensional to three-dimensional representations.

We should emphasize that before entering school, children can easily switch from three-dimensional images to two-dimensional images, and vice versa. They have no difficulty recognizing a real object projected onto a sheet of paper (in a picture book), or a cinema or television screen. This basic experience is almost never used, since in the process of learning students work for long periods of time entirely within a system of three-dimensional representations or a system of two-dimensional representations. Thus, in the elementary mathematics course, students deal basically with two-dimensional representations (e.g., two-dimensional geometric drawings, diagrams, and graphs). In addition, the method by which these representations are created is never explained. The concept of "projection" is introduced much later, though geometric drawings reflect nothing other than distinctive projections of bodies and objects in the plane.

In view of the foregoing, it is clear that students assume a single definite, strictly fixed, but often arbitrarily selected point of view, whereas the acquisition of many systems of knowledge requires the dynamic application of several groups of different systems of reference, rather than just one. This is most obvious in the case of mechanical drawing, engineering subjects, and descriptive geometry, where it is routinely necessary to switch systems of reference, abstracting from the human body and assuming diverse points of reference. These reference points include not only the objective features of objects, but also their relative position in space. In many cases, it is necessary to switch from such points of reference to more abstract and theoretical systems, in which the center consists of any specified or arbitrarily selected geometric figure (point, line, plane, curved surface, etc.). It also turns out that the three basic directions in which systems of reference may be changed in solving many spatial (graphic) problems, are also the most obvious directions.

The student's psychological preparation for different various educational and professional activities requires, as we have tried to show, the routine adoption of different systems of reference, which may or may not be related to the human body. The basic difficulties faced by students include: 1) the use of different systems of reference to create spatial images; 2) a shift, where necessary, from the customary system of reference that is well-established based on empirical understanding of space; and 3) a transition to another system based on the mathematical understanding of space. Quite often the curriculum does not take into account these individual difficulties. It is no accident, therefore, that with the wide variety of classroom problems in the different school subjects, students' development of spatial thinking (particularly its dynamic side) remains at a comparatively low level.

A transition from the perception of real space to geometric space requires a change in the system of reference. While he remains within the empirical system of reference, the individual can never understand the theoretical content of the notion of geometric space. As we have attempted to show, students may utilize different systems of reference even within a single subject. In solving graphic problems, they are regularly required to change the point of reference, using abstract geometric figures, rather than exclusively real objects, as their starting points. However, the ability to establish and make use of spatial relations remains unguided for a long time in the process of instruction. There is no special curriculum designed to teach this ability. In particular, there is no classification of objects which reproduces in its very structure the various types of spatial relations which make up their component parts. There is no well-established and scientifically-based system of exercises which might be used to teach students how to arbitrarily alter their reference points and use different coordinate systems based on their characteristic properties.

Indeed, we have found in the educational psychology literature no sufficiently comprehensive and systematic study of the most effective conditions for switching to specified or arbitrary systems of reference. In teaching practice, these transitions are carried out by the student empirically, and sometimes without regard to their psychological features. Not only in school, but also in institutes of higher education, students know nothing about the classification of the various coordinate systems and are unaware of the function and characteristics of each system. The different types of representation are often used exclusively based on their objective content, without any analysis of the methods used to construct them.

Studies have shown that instruction does not give students clear notions of the possible types of representation, although they use them constantly to learn about various topics. As they are introduced to the types of representation, students learn, as a rule, the characteristics of each type of representation without comparing it to others. This naturally does not promote optimal development of spatial thinking in the educational process. A more effective course of development is possible, we believe, through a classification of the various types of spatial problems. The classification should reflect the requirements imposed on the use of different systems of reference based on an analysis of the characteristics of each system.

Our own studies, as well as others conducted under our direction, have established that the structures of spatial thinking (in terms of operational content) apparent in the process of solving mathematical problems (I.Y. Kaplunovich, 1978) and problems in descriptive geometry (V.S. Stoletnev, 1979) differ only in minor respects from each other. The introduction of a new mathematics curriculum has helped to narrow the gap between the content and the nature of the spatial transformations used in school geometry and mechanical drawing courses and the college descriptive geometry course.

Based on various material in school, students carry out generalized transformations (parallel and rectangular projection, rotation, central and axial symmetry, symmetry relative to a plane, etc.). The identification of common lines of development which enable the student to learn the basic types of spatial orientation through the use of techniques that can be applied to various school subjects and incorporate their psychological mechanisms is among the more important and promising goals of our study.

Spatial Thinking as a Variety of Representational Thinking; Spatial Thinking in the Classroom

We have considered the basic features of spatial thinking; let us briefly characterize them at this point. In its most highly developed forms, spatial thinking is manifested in the course of solving graphic problems, where the creation and manipulation of images is based on the use of various types of visual material. The psychological mechanism underlying spatial thinking is derived from representational activity. Representations make it possible to recode images, use different systems of reference, and manipulate various properties and attributes (form, size, relative position of objects in space) in problem-solving.

All this complex activity is realized primarily in representational form. The perception of various types of representations in solving graphic problems does not constitute an end in itself. Rather, it is always part of the solution of a particular problem, subordinated to the conditions of the problem. Moreover, the image that arises on the basis of a given representation undergoes repeated change in the problem-solving process, so that spatial thinking is, we believe, only one type of representational thinking.

Representational thinking deals not with words, but with images. Representational thinking is host to the reconstitution, rearrangement, and alteration of images in the necessary direction. In this type of thinking, images serve as the raw material and basic operational unit. Furthermore, images also make it possible to establish the results of any mental process. Of course, this does not mean that we do not use verbal knowledge in the form of definitions and detailed judgements and inferences. Unlike verbal discursive thinking, in which verbal knowledge is the basic content, representational thinking uses words only as a means of expression or interpretation of transformations already carried out in images. Moreover, representational and discursive thinking may each be used to solve the same problem, but in different ways. Let us explain this thought using an example from Rudolph Arnheim [1965].

Peter and Pavel are given the same problem: "It is now 3:40 p.m. What time will it be in half an hour?" Peter proceeds by recalling that half an hour is 30 minutes; therefore, 30 must be added to 40. Since there are only 60 minutes in an hour, the remaining 10 minutes are carried over into the next hour. Thus, Peter reaches the answer: 4:10.

Pavel solves the problem differently. From his standpoint, an hour is a round clock face, and half an hour is half of this circle. At 3:40, the minute hand forms an acute angle on the left at a distance of four five-minute marks from the vertical. Taking this as the basic position, Pavel mentally divides the dial in half and reaches the point two marks beyond and to the right of vertical. Thus, he obtains an answer and expresses it in the numerical formula 4:10. Both Peter and Pavel have solved the problem mentally, but Peter solved it intellectually, using quantities divorced from sensory experience. He reasoned according to rules learned from childhood, carrying out computational operations with numbers, that is, 40 + 30 = 70, and 70 - 60 = 10.

Pavel, however, solved the problem representationally. For him, a whole is a simple ultimate form, and one-half is half of this form; a temporal process does not represent an increase of an arithmetical quantity, but rather a circular motion in space.

This example illustrates the difference between representational and verbal discursive thinking. In representational thinking, the very movement of thought and the search for a solution are carried out through alternation and transformation of images and the derivation of new images. With this in mind, a number of researchers (V.N. Pushkin, 1967; L.L. Gurova, 1976; and others) believe it best to divide the logic underlying mental processes into two sub-types: verbal and representational. Verbal logic is established by replacing one set of judgements by another set expressed by means of definite laws underlying the structure of inferences. Representational logic is quite different. A representational strategy for the solution of a problem may be found generally based on visual material, and searches are carried out simultaneously in several, often quite unrelated directions. Elements of the visual situation may be examined in various relations and connections, not excluding accidental connections, thus often leading to unexpected results. The visual situation is "captured" all at once (L.L. Gurova, M.S. Shekhter, and others), such that recognition is not accompanied by detailed verbal reasoning, and conclusions are not stated verbally. The mental process based on visual images passes rapidly, as if abbreviated, and the solution seems to appear at once as a flash of insight. Therefore, the logic reflected in images that appear within short time intervals is treated as an intuitive mechanism (Y.A. Ponomarev, 1967; N.I. Polivanova, 1975; D.N. Zavalishina, 1968; and others).

In our treatment of the features of representational thinking, we must not forget that the very images which constitute the operational units of thinking differ substantially in terms of the mechanism by which they appear. The most important role in representational thinking is played by visual, auditory, and kinesthetic images.

Thinking by means of visual images, or visual thinking (R. Arnheim, G. Gregory, R. Holt, V.P. Zinchenko, and others) is considered a complex process of transforming visual information. It is realized as perceptual events which make it possible to create images corresponding to the initial visual material, manipulate these images, and solve problems in comparing, recognizing, identifying, and transforming images. Studies carried out by B.B. Kossov [1971] and M.S. Shekhter [1967] have demonstrated how complex, and often contradictory, the conditions are under which objects are recognized and their distinguishing features and relations identified.

Experimental data obtained by research in educational and engineering psychology indicate that the ability to manipulate images develops differently in different people, with persistent individual differences. In our studies (I.S. Yakimanskaya and A.D. Botvinnikov, 1968, 1972), it was found that some students experience great difficulty in shifting from visual (three-dimensional) representations to perspective drawings. Others find it difficult to shift from perspective drawings to conventional diagrammatic representations. A third group undertakes these shifts readily and freely. The subjects (60 people) were all placed under the same teaching conditions. They learned the various forms of graphic representation under classroom conditions at Moscow School No. 35, following our experimental methods. The same teacher handled all the classes.

Studies by B.F. Lomov, E.N. Kabanova-Meller, V.I. Zykova, A.P. Sorokun, and others have shown that students always vary in their ability to create visual images in different subject areas (mechanical, geometry, geography, etc.) and manipulate these images in the problem-solving process. The deepest study has been devoted to difficulties related to manipulating images in shifting from two-dimensional to three-dimensional images.

I.Y. Kaplunovich [1978] studied how students learn methods of geometrical transformation, a topic which has since been introduced into the school mathematics curriculum. This study discovered that a shift from two-dimensional to three-dimensional images entails considerable difficulties, manifested primarily in the students' ability to manipulate the images. A special instructional curriculum developed by Kaplunovich failed to eliminate these difficulties for certain students. Some had no trouble manipulating three-dimensional as well as two-dimensional images, so that the shift from one set to the other caused them no special problem. Others could successfully manipulate two-dimensional images, but could not carry out analogous mathematical operations (for example, rotation) with three-dimensional images. Drills used by Kaplunovich in individual work with the students resulted in some improvement, but largely in the case of images of the same type (two-dimensional or three-dimensional). Techniques designed to create two-dimensional images could not be transformed into methods for manipulating three-dimensional images, although the students did know how to carry out mathematical transformations.

Students may differ substantially in their ability to use visual material. Some students require a great many exercises using models and geometric objects, while others require some practice with conventional diagrammatic representations. Some students are able to shift rapidly and easily from visual pictures to projective and symbolic representations, while others find this a complicated task. Some students can solve problems based on symbolic representations even easier than problems based on visual pictures. These facts seem to indicate that the transition from one type of visual image to another is a "recoding" of the image, which presents significant difficulty. Far too little attention has been paid to the psychological nature of these difficulties.

The type of graphic representation depends in many ways on the method by which the visual image is created. If a person works for a long time within the context of a single type of representation, (e.g., a projective drawing), his perception of objects and ability to identify essential properties and relations will take place as though through the prism of this type of representation. It also defines the methods he uses to read and construct the properties and relationships. Thus, he develops his own distinctive method of viewing objects and real events. It becomes more difficult for him to use other conventional representation. This is particularly clear when the manipulation of a system consisting of a particular type of graphic representation constitutes the basic professional activity. For example, it is well known that the artist is usually not nearly as good at drawing graphs as is a draftsman. The methods of visual observation and the construction of diagrams and pictures, along with the requirements for the perception of nature, and the techniques of representation are far too different. What is important for understanding and constructing a picture (laws of perspective, light and shade, color, relation of figure and background, etc.) turns out to be not so important when dealing with perspective drawings.

In order to read and construct a perspective drawing, one must learn the various methods of projection used in the rectangular coordinate system, the rules for the construction of representations in other coordinate systems, and the conventional symbols used in a diagram. The conditions of the activity, the nature of the graphic representations it involves, and the requirements imposed on their manipulation promote the development of lasting, professionally important methods of seeing, and engender a unique style of visual perception. In addition, certain types of activity require the ability to simultaneously manipulate different types of representations. For example, the design engineer must have a good understanding of engineering drawings, works of art, as well as various diagrams, and be able to switch easily and freely from one type of representation to another in carrying out a given construction.

Analogous requirements are imposed on students in their study of school subjects. In acquiring knowledge, the student must often deal not just with a single type of representation, but simultaneously with several types (pictures, drawings, diagrams, maps, plans, etc.) each of which reproduces objects both with their particular attributes as well as in generalized and schematic form (the maximally conventional mode in two- and three-dimensional systems). Thus, in physics class students confront visual pictures of real objects, conventional diagrammatic representations of processes and events occurring in them, and structural formulas. In anatomy lessons, students must deal with full-scale models (three-dimensional representations) of the human body, diagrammatic representations of cell division, structural formulas of nucleic acids, and other conventional representations. Similar examples may be drawn from many other school courses. Moreover, in accordance with its scientific content and underlying logic, each individual subject may include representations that constitute a special subject of study. For example, students may use topographic and geographic maps, together with various conventional symbols in geography, or diagrams of parallel and series circuits in physics. Also prevalent are representations which do not comprise an independent subject of study, but rather act exclusively as visual aids and differ in content and type.

These facts indicate that as they learn, students constantly find themselves in situations where they must recode information obtained in pictorial form through the perception of various types of visual material. However, instruction merely acquaints students with the characteristics of individual types of representation, and never requires them to make a special study of methods used to transform images that arise in different types of visual situations. Students learn about various types of conventional representations and rules for reading and constructing them in the most general form only in the seventh-grade mechanical drawing course, even though they rely on this knowledge literally from their very first day in school.

It is this, we believe, which is responsible for the many difficulties students experience at every step when they have to deal with graphic representations and, using these representations, derive correct notions of the objects they are studying. These difficulties are encountered not only in school, but also in higher education, where reliance on various types of graphic representations is the basis for learning a large number of school subjects. For example, it is well known that students in the art and drafting departments of teacher-training institutions who are preparing to become mechanical drawing and art teachers often experience major difficulties when they switching from creating pictures to learning how to read and construct projective drawings. This transition requires not only the acquisition of a new system of knowledge, but also a reorientation to other methods of viewing objects and a different type of perception.

When creating a picture, it is necessary to rely on direct observation of a full-scale model and use knowledge of perspective, anatomy, and shadows. The size and shape of objects may vary visually, depending upon their remoteness and the observer's position relative to them. Therefore, in order to create a picture (compositional construction), it is very important to maintain a unified point of view.

On the other hand, in order to read and construct a perspective drawing, it is necessary to vary one's unified visual standpoint and consider the object simultaneously from three distinct points of view. This leads to an immediate and simultaneous "transformation" of images in three different dimensions as we pass from: (1) the full-scale object to a conventional diagrammatic representation; (2) from three-dimensional to two-dimensional representations ones, and vice versa; and (3) from a fixed reference point to other systems of reference, with an arbitrary change in the systems.

Using graphic representations requires complex intellectual activity. In fact, most often the graphic representation is used not just to create an image which corresponds to the representation, but also to transform it into another image. For example, from a reading of a functional diagram, a student may not only produce an image of this diagram (he could draw it from memory and make some changes), but also create a dynamic image of a moving object. The image of the diagram and the image of the object must be consistent, and this requires constant shifting from the static, two-dimensional representation, that is, the functional diagram, to a dynamic, three-dimensional image of a real moving object.

We have spoken of the transformation of images which arise within the framework of various types of visual situations, or within a single visual system. However, it is often necessary to manipulate images which arise simultaneously in different sensory systems, such as visual and auditory, as well as motor. Thus, a musician must think simultaneously in different images. A musical text which has been read is at once translated into images of an auditory melody, and vice versa. In music lessons, students are introduced to methods of visually perceiving musical signs and rules used in the construction of sheet music, and simultaneously learn to form certain relations between the image of musical signs and how they sound. An image of an auditory melody is always accompanied in the mind of the musician (singer, conductor) by an image of the movement of hands playing the instrument, leading the chorus, or performing various theatrical movements. We may observe here a constant transition from visual images to auditory and motor images, and vice versa, without which the activity of the actor and musician would be impossible. The psychological mechanisms of this transition have been made explicit in the system of K.S. Stanislavskii, and in studies by B.M. Teplov [1947], P.M. Yakobson [1958], and others.

Often the ability to transform images that arise in various sensory systems takes on vivid and enduring personality characteristics. The history of art offers many examples; this was true of the composers Rimsky-Korsakov, Scriabin, Chyurlenis, and others. In describing the creative ability of Chyurlenis, Gorkii referred to it as "musical painting," emphasizing thereby Chyurlenis' ability to transform auditory (musical) images into visual (artistic) images, and vice versa.

The use of images based on various sensory systems is an important aspect of representational thinking. By virtue of the specific conditions of human activity whereby images are formed and manipulated, we may observe the predominant use of images of a particular modality, a fact which, of course, does not preclude, but rather presupposes the participation of other modalities.

Let us note one more important feature which distinguishes representational and conceptual thinking. Unlike concepts, images reflect in their content relations and connections which are maximally dynamic, variable, and mobile. The conceptual world stands before us, seemingly abstracted away from everything accidental and insubstantial. The world of images is reproduced frequently in many different ways and in highly varied relations and connections. It is precisely here that the imagery manifests itself in all its factual multiplicity, movement, and variation, and for this reason we may discover (detect) new relations and connections. Because real objects are reproduced in the direct perception of reality, we may often establish the source or origin of various properties in the full richness of their factual manifestation.

Knowledge of objects developed to the level of concept guides the use of their properties and relations along a certain path, which does not ensure that we will obtain a new result. Conversely, if we avoid a system of well-established concepts, the opportunity to view the object in a new way often leads us to a real discovery. This is attested to by all the empirical knowledge of design engineering and artistic and graphic activity. Thus, certain design engineers, artists, and musicians with whom we have discussed this very topic have emphasized that knowledge they have accumulated in the form of conceptual systems often does not help, but rather hinders the creation of a new concept, since it orients them to the reproduction of the same system of relations, whereas the goal is actually to transcend this system and construct another system.

Representational thinking displays certain features and advantages which substantially augment conceptual forms of thought. In particular, many spatial concepts fix (or "crystalize") only the most stable or invariant properties (concepts of geometric shapes, attributes of figures).

Spatial images establish highly variable and dynamic spatial relations which reproduce both the linkage between form and size as well as methods of transforming, transmuting, and altering them.

The concepts and images employed in thinking constitute two aspects of a unified process. They make it possible, on the one hand, to establish real existence in its substantial definiteness, stability, and regularity, and on the other hand, to "capture" movement, alteration, and development. Therefore, the image and the concept each fulfill an essential and particular function in the cognitive process. Since it is more intimately and directly related to the reflection of reality, the image gives us knowledge not of individual isolated properties of this reality, but rather serves as an integral mental picture of an individual portion of reality.

The image, unlike the concept, reproduces not individual, isolated attributes and properties of an object, but necessarily also the relative position of these properties in space characteristic of a real object possessing these properties. This is particularly clear in the description of objects. For example, a person may know the distinctive features of a building and be able to reproduce them in the form of a verbal response by enumerating these features ("the building is made of wood, has five stories, is quite decrepit, has rotting boards in many places," and so forth), though in this case the spatial disposition of the building is not reproduced. The latter presupposes not the enumeration of individual, even essential, features of a particular object, but their necessary disposition in space. In that case, the description of the building takes the following form: "If we stand facing the front of the building, it appears as a symmetric, five-story structure. At the center is the entrance door. The left side of the building is quite decrepit, while on the right side of the front of the building can be seen traces of paint. Near the top, just under the roof there is a balcony, which gives this rather rundown building a degree of elegance," and so on.

It is clear from this description that, in the first case, rather fragmentary information about the outward appearance of the building is being reproduced from memory. The second case represents a clear mental picture, created through the selection of the reference point ("If we stand facing the front of the building...") and an explicit spatial distribution of the parts of the building in view of the initial reference point ("at the center, on the right, on the left, on top..."). The use of this type of description may act as a special diagnostic technique for differentiating the existence of verbal knowledge about an object and an explicit image of the same object.

Representational thinking can be divided into a number of varieties, based not only on the mechanism by which the images are created, but also on the very content of these images. For example, some images may reflect predominantly objective, real properties and attributes, while others depict more abstract geometric properties. Images may also reproduce various states of an object (i.e., structural and functional features, concealed processes and events). Of course, such a division of the set of images is to a certain extent provisional. In a real object these properties are inseparable. But in practical activity, as we prepare the object, we extract individual properties from its content and use them in accordance with the goals and purposes of our activity. Then either object or abstract geometrical attributes established by the image assume central importance, and this defines the content of the image.

Though it possesses all the characteristic elements of representational thinking, spatial thinking has its own distinctive features, related to the actual content of the images and the conditions under which they are created and manipulated. The basic operational units of spatial thinking are spatial images, which reflect only the spatial properties and relations of the subjective world, rather than all its properties and attributes. In its most highly developed forms, spatial thinking is formed within a graphic base, so that visual images are the most important. A shift from one set of visual images, reflecting spatial properties and relations, to another set is routinely observed in the solution of problems involving different types of graphic representations. Starting with these representations, there arise not only individual images corresponding to each representation, but also an integral system of images. The ability to think within the framework of these images constitutes spatial thinking.

The activity of spatial thinking is designed primarily not so much to create as to manipulate spatial images designed using different types of graphic base. This is ensured through the application of special techniques of representation and methods of recoding images. Since spatial thinking is one variety of representational thinking, it fulfills a specific function in cognition and in teaching. Spatial thinking enables us to distinguish spatial properties and relations from real objects and theoretical (graphic) models, and make them a subject of analysis and transformation. It is here that spatial thinking differs from other forms of representational thinking.

The basic and characteristic features of representational thinking (dynamism, recoding of images, manipulation of images to create new images, and so forth) are also the distinctive features of spatial thinking. In particular, in order to create a spatial image and manipulate it in solving problems (practical, professional, or graphic problems), it is important to select a three-dimensional system of reference. Note that the latter is not an important element in the creation of images from the standpoint of their objective real content.

We should emphasize that spatial thinking also occurs in practical activity, where it is not, however, an independent form of thinking. We might say that spatial thinking, when it occurs as a component of the process of solving many problems related to orientation in the world of physical objects and events, develops much earlier than representational thinking. This is particularly clear in ontogenesis. However, we will analyze only the most highly developed forms of spatial thinking, as manifested in the creation and manipulation of spatial images, and thus we will consider spatial thinking as part of the system of representational thinking.

Unfortunately, the number of studies devoted to the function of representational thinking in learning has decreased significantly in recent years. But because of the increased theoretical content of scientific knowledge, and the extensive application of modeling (especially graphic) methods in various fields of science, engineering, and industry, the role of representational thinking has increased, rather than decreased.

It is true that the nature and content of the images and the conditions under which they are created and transformed during human activity (problem-solving) has changed significantly. It has also become the subject of profound and comprehensive analysis by logicians, educators, and psychologists.

In analyzing the specific nature of spatial thinking, we must not forget that the reflection of spatial properties and relations in images occurs not only in man, but also in animals. However, one could hardly say that animals display spatial thinking in the forms we described earlier. The spatial images created by man in the course of his activity differ appreciably in terms of the mechanism by which they appear and the conditions under which they function from the images which arise in animals as they strive for spatial orientation. Let us consider this question in more detail.

Fundamental Differences in Spatial Orientation Between Man and Animals

We do not wish to present a comprehensive discussion of the complex differences in spatial orientation between man and animals, which have unfortunately been largely neglected in psychology. Instead, we will identify only those elements that are important for our analysis of spatial thinking and for understanding its essential nature.

It is well known that highly organized animals (e.g., apes) can solve quite complex spatial problems, both in ordinary day-to-day situations and under experimental conditions. Experiments in this area have been carried out by I.P. Pavlov, N.N. Ladygina-Kots, G.Z. Roginskii, N.Yu. Voytonis, N.A. Tikh, and S.L. Novoselova. This ability is demonstrated by the regular perception of the shape and size of objects by different animals (Roginskii), and the fact that animals display a highly developed process of interaction between visual, kinesthetic, and motor analyzers (Tikh, Voytonis, and others). Furthermore, various animals have the potential for perceiving the objective structure of an object and differentiating its constituent elements.

Experiments with anthropoids have shown there is a relation between the way in which spatial relations are perceived and the animal's individual experience and conditions underlying its organization (N.N. Ladygina-Kots, S.L. Novoselova, and others). In the course of the animal's physical and manipulative activity, there arise direct images of his perceived situation. This enables it to adjust its behavior in the surrounding space and plan its subsequent acts, i.e., control them. This enables the animal to freely orient itself in space in complex, variable situations, provides for a flexible response to variable conditions, and gives practical realization to the animal's orientation potential. Therefore, many researchers believe that apes have vivid perceptual images of spatial relations, which enable them to solve quite complex practical problems involving elementary construction, the use of small tools, and the transformation of surrounding space.

However, the use of spatial relations and their identification based on objects are determined entirely by the animal's biological needs and serve the realization of those needs. According to N.A. Tikh [1956], of all the potential forms of spatial orientation, animals can acquire the ability to judge distances most quickly and with the least trouble. This ability enables them to constantly adjust their spatial position relative to other objects and their distance from these objects, approach, change direction and their mode of travel, and so forth. Animals orient themselves above all relative to spatial attributes which help them adapt successfully to their environment. This adaptability is responsible not only for their ability to respond promptly and correctly to the situation before them, but also accumulate and preserve behavioral experience and remember it. The animal's perceptual images, which are directly implicated in practical activity, reflect not only the spatial properties and attributes of objects (shape, size, position), but also methods of influencing and manipulating these objects.

The full set of spatial relations may be divided into two basic categories, reflecting the particular "attitudes" of a living being to the objects in the environment and relations between these objects. Animals primarily acquire the first type of relation. They are much more successful at establishing spatial relations between objects and themselves than between objects as such. Experiments by N.Yu. Voytonis have shown that apes can hold a stick correctly in their hands and use it to reach a reward; this occurs independent of the position of the bait (to the right, to the left, above, below). Moreover, Pavlov's well-known experiments showed that Rafael the Chimpanzee had great difficulty in establishing spatial relations between objects. As a result, only after repeated trials could Rafael learn how to construct a tower out of boxes in the form of a pyramid directly beneath the reward. For this purpose, Rafael had to establish definite spatial relations between the individual boxes and the reward, rather than between himself and the boxes (which was irrelevant here). This indicates that, even in anthropoids, spatial relations between objects are much more difficult to establish than between an object and the animal himself. Voytonis' data provide valuable material for understanding the origin of spatial perception.

Images created by animals establish (consolidate and reproduce) the forms or modes of individual behavior within the narrow scope of their immediate environment. The animal's spatial orientation is subordinated to the basic goal of preserving himself as a biological entity. For the animal, spatial perception is mainly a matter of perceiving and evaluating surrounding objects relative to himself. In the animal's picture of the world (i.e., the distribution of objects in space), the position of the animal himself relative to these objects is of fundamental importance, serving as an idiosyncratic system of reference or starting point changing define all spatial relations. For the animal, space is a rapidly variable environment to which he adapts as best he can in light of changes primarily in the position of his own body. If this position is maintained while the relative position of objects in space changes, the animal seems to notice no change until he experiences a lengthy series of failures.

Other experiments by Voytonis [1949] revealed a highly interesting fact. Apes were taught how to reach a reward at the bottom of a well in the form of a narrow vertical box. They sat on the edge of the box, stuck a fork through the hole at the top of the box, lowered it, and reached the bait. But in one experiment, the position of the box was modified. The well was oriented on its side, so that the hole was now in the vertical plane, rather than the horizontal plane. To the experimenter's surprise, the apes continued to act as if the box was in its initial position. They sat on the well and poked the fork into the wall. Only after many fruitless attempts did they change their behavior.

Analogous experiments (under somewhat different circumstances) were repeated by N.A. Tikh. In analyzing the data, Tikh writes, "The animal's behavior is defined not only by visual or kinesthetic stimulants, but also by their reflexes in the cerebrum. Reflexes formed in both the visual and motor analyzers are so long-lived that they continue to define the method of action despite utterly different conditions" [1956: 15]. We find that this explanation fails to reveal the psychological mechanism underlying this behavior. In our opinion, the ape experiences difficulty in adjusting his behavior because the orientation derived from the body image is, for the animal, the most customary method of orientation to spatial relations, reinforced by all biological experience. Accordingly, the animal relates himself to other objects. Interrelations between objects themselves are no longer independent.

Animals do not separate or isolate themselves from their environment, but rather include themselves directly in nature. As they interact with their environment, animals orient themselves in space primarily in terms of their own positions. Even the tools they use are employed as simple extensions of their limbs. Thus, the animal's identification and subsequent manipulation of spatial relations occur mainly within the framework established by the body image. Their own positions in space are understood in terms of spatial relations between objects. A change in this position relative to objects means that the animal must relearn all the necessary spatial relations. The behavior of apes is stereotypical, in that they are unable to immediately transfer experience gained from established spatial relations to other conditions.

In man, particularly in the first year of life, the spatial orientation derived from the body image is also of paramount importance, though, unlike in animals, it develops under more variable conditions. We might attribute this to the fact that the child repeatedly alters the position of his body. Studies by B.G. Ananev [1955], N.I. Golubeva, V.V. Bushurova [1956], and others have demonstrated that the child gradually learns all the directions in space, first the left and right directions, then in front and above, next behind, and finally below. This sequence, Bushurova has remarked, is directly related to changes in the child's position, from lying on his back to lying on his stomach, from lying on his stomach to a sitting position, and then to a standing position. The ability to assume a vertical position helps the child acquire a definite picture of the world, a picture which differs from that of animals since animals derive their pictures from their own body positions in space. The vertical position also means that humans experience more varied relations in the space around them.

However, the essential point is that man's orientation in space is the result of a fundamentally unique relation to the world of things and events. From the very moment of birth, man is surrounded by a space consisting not of natural objects, but rather objects which have been transformed by social and historical experience, including the experience of their production, application, and improvement. Human activity is primarily formed in relation to objects. By manipulating objects, the child learns not only their distinctive features (shape, size, breadth, distance, etc.), but also the social function embodied in each object. Orientation derived from the body image and its modification and development proceeds under the decisive influence of the objective acts which the child masters under adult guidance. A dominant role in the child's determination of spatial relations is played by the functional asymmetry of the child's limbs in the course of objective activity. In the process of mastering objective acts (in play or interaction with other children), children learn how to distinguish between the directions of left and right, front and back, above and below, etc., and orient themselves in surrounding space based on the positions of their own bodies.

Emphasizing the enormous role played by objective acts in the process of acquiring functionally asymmetric hands, R.Ya. Lekhtman-Abramovich writes that it is precisely actions which involves two objects which give rise to a differentiation of the relative functions of the two hands, one becoming the guiding hand in activity, and the other assisting it by bringing objects closer to or holding them [1949: 27]. The importance of objective actions for the child's acquisition of spatial representations has been studied in detail from a number of different standpoints (B.G. Ananev, F.N. Shemyakin, A.Y. Kolodna, V.V. Bushurova, A.V. Zaporozhets, and others).

From the very first months of life, however, children learn to identify spatial relations based not only on the position of their own bodies relative to objects, but also entirely independent of these positions. This is promoted by adults' external organization of their activity. Without any training in scientific psychology, the people around young children learn very early how to amuse them with toys of varying construction, shapes, and sizes. They not only offer them these toys, but also show them how to handle them and discover their function in the course of objective activity (a rattle makes noise, a spoon is for feeding, etc.). In offering objects, the adult puts them together, takes them apart, puts one inside the other, and rearranges them, transforming and modifying their spatial arrangement relative to each other in every possible way. In this situation, the child remains immobile and can only attentively watch the adult's actions. Spatial relations between objects appear to the child as transformed and dynamic relations, rather than static relations.

Under the influence of this contact with adults, revealing the relations between objects, the child who is still unable to move on his own can already orient himself to the spatial relations between objects. Although he begins to move on his own only at 10-12 months, he can put together plastic bricks (or nested wooden dolls), and assemble and take apart toys and various objects which are structurally quite complex. The identification of spatial relations between objects may even outstrip the child's success at orienting himself in space during locomotion. This is particularly clear in the case of children whose locomotor organs have been destroyed. According to R.A. Voronova [1936], at the age of 8-10 years such children experience significant difficulties in determining above-below and right-left positions. In addition, they have a highly developed ability for playful activity in the course of which they can orient themselves correctly in terms of spatial relations between objects.

These facts indicate that because children are brought up in a social environment, they begin very early to orient themselves to the surrounding space, identifying not only the position of their own body relative to objects, but also the positions of objects relative to each other. The latter often is even more significant for the child, since as he transforms objects, he thereby learns how to interact with them. "The entire internal content and structure of his perception of things," writes S.L. Rubinshtein, "bears the imprint of the fact that these things are the objects of his activity... The development of social experience introduces into the development of human perception, understood as a social and historical essence, the individual's own characteristics, which may vary in the course of history" [1957: 98].

In children, spatial orientation arises under the influence of the demands of interaction, as well as activities which use objects. Here we also observe the very important fact that the child's body-image orientation begins to take on a social character. The child is forced to recognize his position through the eyes of someone else (an adult, a game partner). In order to have meaningful interaction with someone else, he is forced to take the latter's point of view, and this frequently requires a mental retranslation and abstraction from the position of his own body. It is precisely within the context of cognitive reflection that the child's spatial representations are created (M.V. Vovchik-Blakitnaya, A.Y. Kolodna, F.N. Shemyakin, A.A. Bodalev, and others). A number of studies (A.E. Kozareva, R.Sh. Karimova, A.A. Lyublinskaya) have shown that in children (unlike animals), projective representations are formed under the influence of adults and verbal interaction between children during group play and classroom activity. When the child plays with dolls which look like people or animals, he distributes them in space and changes their stance and relative position, abstracting from the position of his or her own body. Interestingly, the child starts by controlling the doll's actions, giving it a strictly defined position relative to himself, and moves the doll back and forth. The child then begins to control its movements by rotating it and placing it in the "mirror" position, ultimately irrespective of his own position.

F.N. Shemyakin's data [1940] show that children first acquire the ability to represent linear space, where the body image assumes primary importance. Only subsequently do they learn to represent maps (or visual space), where spatial relations between objects as such play the dominant role.

Interesting studies by Yu.N. Karandashev [1965] have shown how children learn about three-dimensional systems of reference. In one procedure, the experimenter walked in a circle with his face towards an immobile standing subject, who was required to determine right and left directions on the basis of the experimenter's changing position. In the course of the experiment, it was found that most children imitated the experimenter's movements, and shifted around in the direction of the required position. If this was not allowed, the children utilized vestigial forms of movements (maintaining their stance, they turned their heads, put their hands behind their back, etc.). Based on these data, Karandashev concluded that projective representations are acquired gradually by children. Constrained by the requirements imposed by the adult with whom he is playing, the child tries to abstract mentally from his real position and assume the position of his partner. Projective representations, in A.A. Bodalev's definition, are expressed in the individual's ability to compare himself mentally with another person, seeing an object through the other person's eyes. This requires the ability to abstract from one's own position in space and to shift to another system of reference (Bodalev, 1970).

With this in mind, it is clear that man's orientation in space arises in a completely different way than that of an animal. Even the natural mode of orientation based on the body image develops in the child through his physical experience, which is nothing other than his experience of interacting with objects with a definite social function and his experience of meaningful communication with other children. Under the influence of his social environment (requirements imposed by adults and his peers), the child must constantly abstract from his body-image orientation and apparently switch to other systems of reference. This fact is the key impetus to the development of the child's spatial orientation. We should add that man's activity in society constantly requires spatial reorientation and abstraction from the position of his own body.

A number of psychologists have recently carried out profound studies which confirm L.S. Vygotskii's hypothesis of the social nature of mental processes. These studies have demonstrated convincingly that the child's orientation in space (visible or represented) develops along with his objective activity, as he is taught human methods of realizing this activity. Through the creation and development of various types of activity (practical, educational, professional, representational, and design engineering, etc.), the child learns to speak and thereby acquires mankind's accumulated knowledge of the sensory properties of objects in the surrounding world, reproduced in the form of sensory models (A.V. Zaporozhets, 1963; P.Y. Galperin, 1965; L.A. Venger, 1969, 1976; and others). By means of special models, the child also learns about the spatial properties of objects, their shape, size, position, etc. An important role is played by the child's acquisition of methods for the spatial transformation of objects which reflect their functions in his activity (N.N. Poddyakov, 1977; S.L. Novoselova, 1978; and others).

Because of the children's inherent assertiveness and curiosity, they constantly transform objects as they interact with them. In play and classroom activity, objects become changing entities for the child, rather than remaining fixed and frozen. The child's relation to objects is not one of contemplation, but rather active transformation.

The identification and use of spatial properties and relations are most clearly manifested in complex forms of educational and professional activity. Here the production of articles is necessarily associated with man's constant reorientation relative to the objects of labor, and along with the constant change in the spatial relations between these objects. In the course of productive activity new forms and structures are created, as well as new methods of handling these objects. This requires flexible and variable methods of establishing different spatial relations, simply because mechanical parts are mobile, operational objects. The objects of labor produced by means of these parts vary in shape, structure, and spatial position in the course of a manufacturing process. The interrelation between their constituent parts also changes constantly.

Different types of transformations applied to objects in the course of man's cognitive and professional activity make it possible to discover internal relations between these objects which may not be established perceptually. In the course of producing objects and transforming them, man identifies the origin of spatial properties and relations, the transformations of shape, size, and position undergone by objects, and the relation of the parts to the whole. Before him emerge spatial relations, whether static or dynamic. Objects undergo transformations repeatedly, under highly variable conditions, and man learns how to apply active methods of modifying them. When generalized, these methods become a powerful source of knowledge about space and its properties and relations.

Objects are transformed not only during practical activity. Transformations may also be realized in the mind, beyond all perception of real objects, where these objects have in fact been replaced by their semiotic analogs. In reading a conventional graphic representation, man reproduces in images the spatial characteristics of objects and transforms them in the desired direction, creating in his mind new geometric shapes and structures, embodying them in drawings, pictures, diagrams, sketches, plans, etc. This transformation and embodiment of images through the use of graphic aids is possible only when the individual has acquired theoretical knowledge of various types of transformations and methods of realizing them, as well as laws of projection developed in various sciences (topography, cartography, descriptive geometry, mechanical drawing, etc.). The acquisition of graphic fluency not only improves the individual's ability to see and understand spatial relations, but also fundamentally enriches his store of techniques of spatial orientation.

The wide-scale application of graphic representations helps the individual acquire specifically human methods of orientation, associated with the constant transition from the perception of real space (the world of things and events) to graphic substitutes of space, and the use of three-dimensional and two-dimensional images (moving from solid objects to their projections in the plane). These factors affect man's ability to acquire complex and varied methods of spatial orientation, as well as form different systems of reference which may be arbitrarily selected and dynamically altered depending upon the content and conditions of practical or theoretical activity.

In determining spatial relations, man, unlike animals, does not use just the body image for orientation, which, after all, is common to all human beings; he also employs specialized methods developed in the different sciences which he has learned during objective, transformative activity. Social and historical experience has altered the way man views the surrounding space, so that he identifies spatial properties and relations required for the successful realization of objective activity, primarily work.

"The eye," writes Marx, "became the *human* eye precisely when its object became a social, *human* object, created by man for man. Therefore, the senses became conceptualized in their immediate use" (Marx and Engels, v. 42: 120). According to Marx, by comparison with animals man's perception is not simply more sensitive; rather it has an entirely different content and nature. The sensory acuity (vision, touch, hearing, smell) possessed by many animals is well known, and in fact helps them orient themselves successfully in the surrounding world and adapt to it. But stimuli which are essential to man are utterly insignificant to animals. "The eagle sees much further than man," noted Engels, "but the human eye sees much more in things than does the eagle's eye. Dogs possess a much finer sense of smell than man, but cannot distinguish a hundredth of the scents which man considers the defining attributes of many different things" [Marx and Engels, v. 20: 490].

Thus, in the course of his social and objective transformation activity, man learns specifically human techniques of spatial orientation which enable him to flexibly utilize different systems of reference. Man's manipulation of spatial relations proceeds both in physical space, as well as in geometric space, as a result of his acquisition of semiotic fluency, methods of representation, and projective techniques. Spatial relations inside objects which serve as the subjects of activity are identified in accordance with the goals of man's objective activity. The relations between man himself and the surrounding objects also change.

The principle differences we have examined in the conditions under which spatial images are formed in man and in animals lead us to conclude that the spatial orientation inherent to humans is social in its very nature. Even such a stable coordinate system as the body image is acquired by man under the decisive influence of teaching and instruction. It becomes quite diversified and may be readily altered once the individual has learned to speak and to engage in objective transformative activity. By linking his actions to those of other people (adults and older children), he masters an entire system of spatial relations. His body-image orientation varies constantly in light of his active interaction with objects. His orientation becomes increasingly complicated in various types of educational and professional activity.

Unlike animals, humans employ not only the natural orientation derived from the body image, but also theoretical methods of spatial orientation associated with human mastery of theoretical space and semiotic fluency, including graphic knowledge. This is what forces man to shift routinely to different coordinate systems, which he utilizes consciously and manipulates freely. Both utilization and manipulation are possible only with the acquisition of both theoretical and practical knowledge.

However, our description of this difference would be incomplete if we did not touch upon one more quite important aspect, that is, the mechanisms by which spatial images are created and manipulated. One such mechanism in man is representational activity. The most highly developed forms of this activity are utterly absent in animals. The appearance of images and their effective use are related intimately to the animals' immediate actions and are inseparable from them. Animals are unable to manipulate images, i.e., retain them consciously, plan future activity based on their use, predict the results of this activity, and generalize them in representational form. N.N. Ladygina-Kots, a leading student of mental activity in anthropoids, has noted [1959] that visual perception is highly differentiated in the chimpanzee, although it is still questionable whether chimpanzees display any representational activity.

A more definite conclusion was reached by S.L. Novoselova [1978] after an extended comparative study of the activities of anthropoids and very young children. Novoselova writes that "the image of an external object guides and orients the animal's physical activity relative to this object, though the image does not become a specialized ideal object of mental transformation for him. In the animal, the transformation of the object occurs only in practical terms, and not in the field of representation..." [1978: 78].

Man is characterized by the conscious and free creation of images and their manipulation in the problem-solving process. This is achieved through special techniques for the creation and transformation of images. In the course of learning to perform various types of activity and acquire different types of knowledge, man learns special methods that make it possible to create images, preserve them in memory, transform them with or without the use of visual aids, and obtain new images which differ from the initial ones. Thus, in Y.A. Ponomarev's terminology [1966, 1967] an "internal plan of action" inherent to man alone is developed. Unlike animals, man can work freely with images and repeatedly manipulate them mentally for prolonged periods of time, i.e., man can think in images.

These remarks lead us to conclude that in animals, spatial images, although highly differentiated and structurally complex, do not exist apart from their effective visualization. Independent forms of representational thinking are characterized precisely by the ability to manipulate images based on an aptitude for engaging in representational activity. This activity must be performed consciously and freely, relying on knowledge of and theoretical methods for mental activity which make possible the assertive, deliberate transformation of images determined by the requirements of a problem. The creation and modification of images occur through intellectual techniques that make it possible to conceive of: 1) the process and results of this activity; 2) the nature of its realization; 3) the general knowledge of modes of activity; and 4) techniques of implementing these modes (especially semiotic modes) and expressing them in language. It is in this sense that thinking in spatial images is not found in animals.

2

The Structure of Spatial Thinking

A Systematic Approach to Analyzing the Structure of Spatial Thinking

Extensive research in educational psychology has been devoted to discussing the creation and manipulation of spatial images. The principles underlying this activity have been investigated by analyzing specific occupations in terms of their content and the conditions essential for fulfilling the requirements they impose on man's psychological outlook. This issue has been seriously addressed in a number of studies designed to identify and describe the qualities of intellectual activity required by the professional for successful performance of his productive functions (V.P. Zinchenko, 1968; K.M. Gurevich, 1976; M.V. Gamezo, 1977; B.F. Lomov, 1966; V.N. Pushkin, 1965; V.F. Rubakhin, 1965; etc.).

The characteristics of spatial images and the mechanisms by which they are created have been studied in connection with the analysis of design-engineering activity (T.V. Kudryavtsev, 1975; N.P. Linkova, 1964; V.A. Molyako, 1968; B.M. Rebus, 1965; P.M. Yakobson, 1934; S.M. Vasileiskii, 1972; and others). This problem has been investigated in educational psychology most intensively as part of an analysis of the conditions that foster effective learning. It would be difficult to list all the works in this area. The underlying principles of spatial images have been identified in terms of the content of various classroom subjects and the diverse methods of teaching for various age groups.

Researchers have analyzed the acquisition of knowledge, habits, and skills (V.I. Zykova, 1958; E.N. Kabanova-Meller, 1950, 1954, 1962; B.F. Lomov, 1959; N.D. Matsko, 1975), called for the development of techniques for mental activity (E.N. Kabanova-Meller, 1968; L.V.

Vaitkunene, 1974), and studied the development of spatial imagination, (G.A. Vladimirskii, 1949; A.D. Botvinnikov, 1963; N.F. Chetverukhin, 1964) and the improvement of geometric vision (B.V. Zhuravlev, 1940; I.S. Yakimanskaya, 1959). A number of studies have concentrated on mechanisms for the solution of graphic problems, demonstrating that the productivity of their solution is dependent upon: 1) the awareness of mental operations (L.L. Gurova, 1976; Ya.A. Ponomarev, 1967; K.A. Slavskaya, 1968); 2) the methods of representation (B.F. Lomov, 1959, 1961; O.I. Galkina, 1956; E.N. Kabanova-Meller, 1958; I.S. Yakimanskaya, 1965); 3) the types of spatial orientation (F.N. Shemyakin, 1940, 1959; A.I. Fetisov, 1968); and 4) various features of design engineering and technological habits and skills (E.A. Mileryan, 1970; T.V. Kudryavtsev, 1964; V.V. Chebyshev, 1969; I.S. Yakimanskaya, 1962; and others). Special emphasis has been placed on the function played by visual aids in learning as part of the problem-solving process.

As we do not wish to give a detailed analysis of work in this area, we will now turn our attention to two circumstances which are important from our point of view. Even though quite a number of studies have discussed the creation and manipulation of spatial images, the literature contains virtually no systematic presentation of the content of spatial thinking and its structure. Furthermore, despite the intensive and multifaceted studies that have been carried out, the teaching process still lacks a psychologically-based technique for the formation and development of spatial thinking in students throughout the entire educational system (from elementary school to college).

In view of the great importance of spatial thinking for various areas of human activity, its development is utterly inadequate. This is demonstrated by the difficulties experienced by students in both elementary school and technical-vocational institutes and colleges when they try to create and manipulate images in their effort to solve classroom, design-engineering, and creative scientific problems. Spatial manipulation of artistic images is especially difficult. Sharp individual differences, many firmly ingrained, may be observed in spatial thinking; far too little attention has been devoted to the psychological nature of these differences.

The development of spatial thinking generally proceeds within the closed boundaries of a school subject (geography, geometry, drafting, etc.). Because of the specific content of each subject, spatial thinking must take on specific qualities. Moreover, because man's orientation in real space is derived from the body image, in the course of ontogenesis certain elemental (more general and universal) mechanisms are created; they may not only affect the success with which specific activities are learned, but may also hinder the individual's efforts to understand the various forms of theoretical space. Specific mechanisms are engendered on the basis of these quite fundamental mechanisms of spatial orientation and then further developed. The relation between these mechanisms has received inadequate attention in psychology.

For these reasons we have constructed a theoretical research model which enabled us to identify and evaluate experimentally the general logic underlying the development of spatial thinking in children, analyze its psychological mechanisms, and locate transitional (critical) points of development. We then turned to an investigation of the structure of spatial thinking. Our methodological approach was a systems method of analysis. In this method, a study of the structure of any particular event presupposes knowledge of its constituent elements, along with their interdependence and interrelation, complexity, and level of development. The systems method of analysis is now widely used to study mental events. A number of works describe the essence of this approach: I.V. Blauberg and E.G. Yudin, 1973; M.S. Kagan, 1974; A.N. Leontev, 1975, 1976.

The systems method assumes that the "specific nature of any complex object (system) is not exhausted by the characteristics of its constituent elements, but rather is primarily rooted in the type of relations and connections between the individual elements" (Blauberg and Yudin, 1973: 168). It presupposes an analysis of particular events whereby a process is conceived of in terms of the interdependences of its constituent components, in terms of their hierarchy. The event may be studied in terms of its various relations and connections, dynamically, developmentally, and variationally. "The proper interpretation of a complex dynamic system," writes Kagan, "requires linking together its three planes of investigation, the objective, functional, and historical planes, which we must regard as necessary and sufficient methodological components of the systems approach as a whole" [1974: 22].

As the systems method has developed within the framework of Marxist-Leninist methodology, it asserts that a scientific understanding of every element of a system can be attained only when it is considered in the dynamics of the system as a whole, as one moment of the dynamics. "Every level," emphasizes Leontev, "may take effect only by means of techniques achieved at lower levels, and such understanding is uniquely correct, enabling us to discover the internal dynamics of a system and its various transformations. Of course, a system is not an additive creation, not only in not being the sum of its individual elements, but also in that it is not generated from mechanically stratified levels" [1976: 145]. Adopting a systems method in a study presupposes a special conceptual apparatus to make it possible to describe particular objects and events in more integral units. In fact, the application of the systems approach to the study of spatial thinking has made it possible to consider this form of thinking as an integral, multi-level creation, a particular form of activity, engendered through various mental processes (perception, memory, imagination, and the necessary involvement of speech).

Spatial thinking, understood as a form of representational thinking, is based on expressive activity occurring in diverse forms and at various levels. Two levels of this activity may be singled out: the creation of the image, and its manipulation or use. Within each of these two levels we may identify various types of images and means of creating and manipulating them, as conditioned by definite concrete conditions.

Such an approach to the analysis of spatial thinking may help us describe its structure, "resolve" this complex whole into its constituent elements, determine hierarchical relations, and reveal relations between the various levels of development of the individual elements and the system as a whole. Let us now turn to a description of the structure of spatial thinking in light of these features of spatial thinking.

Description of the Structure of Spatial Thinking

As we have already noted, spatial thinking is considered here as a multi-faceted, hierarchical whole, and essentially multi-functional. It is a specific form of mental activity which makes it possible to create spatial images and manipulate them as part of the process of solving varied graphic problems.

The creation and manipulation of spatial images are closely interrelated processes. Each process is based on expressive activity, although the structure of this activity and the conditions under which it is realized differ in the two cases. In the first case, activity is aimed at creating a spatial image, and in the other, it is aimed at reworking the image, mental alteration and transformation in accordance with the particular problem.[1]

The conditions under which this activity is realized through reliance on graphical visual aids also vary. This, of course, does not imply that the creation of the image is an exclusively imitative activity. Indeed, the manipulation of images when abstracting away from the initial visual aid is always a creative process. But in any event, expressive activity is transformational in nature, although it is realized under various conditions and with varied subject matter. Let us consider this point in more detail.

In creating any type of image, especially a spatial image, the visual base on which the image first arises is subjected to a mental transformation. In order to manipulate and use images, it is often necessary to mentally alter the image that has already been created on this visual base. We should add that our identification of the manipulation of images as a special form of expressive activity which coincides with the process by which the image is created neither in content, conditions of realization, nor outcome thereby enables us to determine the basic function of spatial thinking. In keeping with our understanding of its characteristics, we understand spatial thinking as the free use and manipulation of spatial images created on various types of visual base, along with their transformation due to the requirements of a problem.

Of course, this delineation should not be considered absolute. Elements of the transformation of the spatial image may also be found in the course of its creation, and, similarly, the very manipulation of an image is aimed at the creation of a new image. However, our distinction between the process of creating the image and the process of manipulating it helps analyze both processes from the standpoint of the particular form of expressive activity they make possible. By distinguishing between them, we can delineate two closely interrelated creations, thinking in spatial images and representational thinking, in terms of their results and determine their interrelations.

The creation of images is possible because of the accumulation of representations that serve as the starting point and as necessary conditions for the realization of thought. The richer and more diverse the store of spatial representations, the more highly perfected the methods of creating representations and the easier it is to use images, since it is impossible to utilize what has not been learned and what is not at hand.[2] However, as our data demonstrate, the acquisition of the ability to apply techniques for creating spatial images from their graphic representation, no matter how effective and refined, still does not yield the ability to use these images successfully. This is quite clear, in that activity aimed at creating images is not entirely identical to that aimed at manipulating images.

This conclusion has been confirmed by a number of our experimental studies [1962, 1976, 1977], conducted using material from various school subjects (geometry, physics, painting, mechanical drawing, and technology). Two groups could be sharply distinguished among the individuals we studied (students in grades 5 to 9). Those in the first group experienced no special difficulty in creating images starting with specified visual aids (pictures, geometric and projective drawings, and diagrams), but found it difficult to transform them mentally based on a problem. Their difficulties may be attributed to an inability to retain the image in memory: it seemed to slip away, becoming diffuse and vanishing altogether. Students resorted to various techniques in order to retain the image in their memory, e.g., drawing imaginary lines in the air or tracing with their finger or a pencil the figure they had to transform mentally (rotate, cut, unite, etc.). Those in the second group did not experience these difficulties. They manipulated images in their mind easily and freely, without resorting to auxiliary graphic aids.[3]

These characteristics were quite stable. This is due to the fact that subjects who tended to create images successfully, but found it difficult to manipulate them mentally, preferred to solve problems in the classroom which require constructing drawings, using data given in the drawings and describing what is shown in the picture. Furthermore, these subjects performed this activity creatively and willingly, using material from various classroom problems, although avoiding as far as possible problems involving the transformation of an image, claiming that they do not know how to do this well. Students usually expressed their difficulty as follows: "We find it difficult to imagine how to transform an initial image, and what it will be transformed into, when we don't have a drawing to rely on." These students willingly agreed to work with the researcher if they could be convinced that he could help them overcome their continuing difficulties.

The identification of two types of expressive activity, aimed at the creation and manipulation of images, and the analysis of their psychological mechanisms demonstrate that we are dealing with distinct levels of development of spatial thinking. In psychology, any understanding of the mechanism underlying the appearance of different images still proceeds basically by ascribing them to distinct mental functions (perception, representation, imagination) which may be interchanged sequentially and independently. Differences between images may also be considered in terms of dynamic relations between sensory and conceptual components and their transformation, either individually or in general. There are two clearly distinct types of activity underlying the creation and manipulation of images: creative and imitative activity. This is expressed in the psychological classification of images into memory images and imagination images, which may in turn be divided into reconstructive images and strictly creative images. The creation of a new image in representational form is usually ascribed to imagination.[4] This understanding of the mechanism underlying the creation of the image is not supported by the experimental data accumulated since the 1950's. Fundamental studies by B.G. Ananev [1960], A.N. Leontev [1970], A.V. Zaporozhets [1960], V.P. Zinchenko [1969], L.M. Vekker [1967], and others have demonstrated that the sensory image, even at the perceptual level, is formed in the course of the individual's positive transformative activity. The structure of this activity arises through the acquisition of socially conditioned sensory standards (L.A. Venger, 1968, 1974; N.N. Poddyakov, 1977). It constitutes a system of actions (practical and theoretical) which combine dynamically, depending on the content of the sensory problem, the nature of the object to be perceived, and the individual's level of cognitive activity and understanding of these perceptual events. Organized perceptual activity based on definite methods of "surveying" the object and the application of a conceptual apparatus which make possible the multi-dimensional, multi-level perception of the object (B.V. Kossov, 1969; M.S. Shekhter, 1967; I.S. Yakimanskaya, 1961; and others).

The transition to the formation of an image based on a representation is associated with forms of perceptual activity as well as a variation of its governing conditions. This is a creative process, because the representation of the image occurs predominantly in the absence of the object, supported by transformative activity aimed at mental alteration of the perceived object (or data from past sensory experience). These mental transformations are realized through specialized representational activity, consisting in the arbitrary reproduction of the image and its mental manipulation in the course of solving a problem. This activity has as its basic content not so much the recollection of past perceptions (which serve solely as the initial material), as the mental transformation of these perceptions, leading to the creation of an image that differs from the visual material on which it was initially based.

A number of studies (A.D. Botvinnikov, 1968; B.F. Lomov, 1959; E.N. Kabanova-Meller, 1958; I.S. Yakimanskaya, 1962) have shown that the creation of an image from a drawing is made possible by representational activity, and it requires transcending the given representation. The creation of the image begins with the perception (or reconstruction by memory) of three representations of the drawing (front, top, and left views). But this perception (or reproduction) does not in and of itself insure the creation of an image. The image of an object created from a drawing, in fact, is not an image of the drawing itself (its three projections)—it is not the simple sum of these projections, nor is it the superimposition of three representations (as in photography). The creation of an image from a drawing presupposes the mental "aggregation" of each projection, with knowledge of methods of projection, superimposition, rotation, and coincidence, the ability to handle a system of conventional signs, and so forth. The same occurs when we wish to create an image starting with a picture, diagram, or graph, i.e., any type of visual aid.

Our analysis of the mechanism underlying the creation of an image at the level of perception and representation demonstrates that this process (in whatever form it is realized) is designed for the creation of a new image (relative to an initial image): it is founded on creative activity. But if we agree that the creation of the image, both in the perceptual as well as the representational process, is made possible through creative activity leading to the production of a new image, then what happens to imagination? In fact, in traditional psychology it is precisely imagination which has the "authority" to create the new. This factual and terminological difficulty was correctly noted by A.V. Brushlinskii [1970], who observed that if the new is created not only in imagination, what then is the specific nature of imagination? If imagination is to be understood as a special mental process, what is its content? This question may be answered, we believe, only through a study of the specific content of expressive activity and its levels of development. Let us now turn to an analysis of imagination.

Imagination is a process consisting in the use and manipulation of images given in representations. Imagination is also realized through expressive activity, which appears as independent, extensive activity realized under particular conditions. Imagination is based on preexisting primary images, without direct reliance on initial visual material (which can only hinder this activity). As a rule, it is based on the use of different types of images involved in the process of forming a new image, which is creative in its very nature. Thus, while a representation is the result of expressive activity and reliance on perception, imagination is a complex form of expressive activity carried out with maximal abstraction from the initial base, through multi-dimensional and repeated transformation of existing representations.

We should emphasize that expressive activity is creative at any level. The only differences are in the degree of creativity and the conditions under which the activity is manifested. The transformation of initial material for the purpose of constructing an image occurs at any level of expressive activity; only the particular mechanisms of this mode of creativity differ.

From this standpoint, our division of spatial images into memory images and imagination images seem inadequately justified, since it is founded, first, on the assumption that the image may be associated with some particular mental process, and second, on a delineation of images into creative and imitative. The creation of a new image and transformation of a perceived image are not distinctive attributes of the imaginative process. Imagination occurs at all levels of sensory cognition (perception and representation). The term "reconstruction of the image" should also not be identified with passive recollection of data from past experience which does not transcend sensory perception. This understanding of the nature of imagination, in contrast to other mental processes, is complicated by certain definitions still accepted in modern psychology.

Thus, representation is commonly defined as the reproduction of past perceptions, while imagination is understood as the transformation of past perceptions and representations (*Philosophical Encyclopedia* [*Filosofskaya Entsiklopediya*], 1969, v. 1). The difference between reconstructive and creative imagination is found in the degree of the individual's passivity and activity. "Reconstructive imagination," according to one psychology text, "does not transcend the limits of representational concretization of what is said in the text or given in the drawings. Creative imagination is found in the creation of a new image without any reliance on an image given externally" (*Psychology* [*Psikhologiya* 1962: 339-340). Indeed, we believe that expressive activity at various levels leads to the transformation of initial sensory experience. However, the difference (which may be quite substantial) is that the content and level of these transformations may vary, along with the conditions under which they occur.

By analyzing expressive activity within the context of its content and structure, it becomes possible, we believe, to resolve certain terminological difficulties encountered in the educational psychology literature regarding the application of such concepts as spatial representation and spatial imagination. Frequently, particularly in the teaching methodology literature, the same problem, e.g., reading a perspective drawing, is considered by some authors to be aimed at the development of spatial representations, while a second group believes that it is directed at developing spatial imagination. The objective complexity of the problem serves merely as a basic criterion of this difference. These terminological difficulties may be overcome only with a clear understanding that expressive activity must be ascribed to both representation and imagination, by virtue of its psychological content.

Let us consider the levels at which this activity may be implemented. Even in the process of perception, expressive activity displays its own elementary forms, although they are neither independent nor fully spelled out. It is directly involved in the perceptual process, subordinated to its goals and tasks, and is manifested in the ability to transform and interpret visual material mentally, identifying and retaining in memory individual elements of the perceived object, while ignoring other elements. Since it is an independent activity, expressive activity enters into the creation of the image through the mental transformation of its visual base. It has an explicit structure displayed in a definite system of acts and the sequence in which they are performed. Finally, it results in the creation of a representation.

A clear example of this type of activity may be seen in the creation of an object of spatial representation from reading a functional diagram. The creation of the image here depends on perception, but is not exhausted by it. In fact, in perceiving a diagram we start solely with conventional notation, a set of lines, and a certain distribution of these lines relative to each other and to the plane of the drawing. Based on these perceptions, we must transcend the diagram and view at a "mental glance" the objective reality behind the conventional notation, and conceive of it in a definite, real embodiment, not only in the static state, but also dynamically. For this purpose, we must carry out an entire chain of mental transformations, which constitute the content of expressive activity.

The perception of the initial visual material already contains all the essential elements for the creation of the image (the act of perception relies on a system of specialized knowledge), although the image itself is not given in finished form. The initial image must be created and the resulting image embodied in a picture or verbal description. The resulting image differs markedly from the initial visual material, and is a new image with respect to it. The fact that the image of a diagram or drawing is not the same as a diagram or drawing of the object is borne out by the difficulties experienced by students who have no trouble reproducing or describing a diagram or drawing from memory, but find it difficult to describe or draw the object.

In many cases, the ultimate images do not remain unchanged. They may be altered as desired in the problem-solving process. Here, expressive activity is aimed at transforming existing images, and not the initial visual base, as is the case in the representation process. These images are mentally transformed in several ways at the same time, especially when they are fully abstracted from the initial visual base and they are not directly based on this material. Expressive activity becomes an independent and rather complicated form of imaginative mental activity, performed predominantly without reference to perception, but with its own complicated structure. It consists of a series of acts aimed at the mental retention of the initial image and focusing various transformations of the image in the representation, carried out in view of the requirements of the particular problem: detailed, repeated operations with the image.

This activity is characterized by: (1) any special conditions underlying the creation of the image (abstraction from visual base); (2) the content of the expressive activity (the transformation of existing images); (3) the degree of complexity with which representational activity is performed (transformations are realized in the mind, from representations, and may constitute either repeated transformations or an entire system). It serves as an essential prerequisite for the solution of design-engineering, manufacturing, graphic, and art problems.

An example where this activity is quite clearly manifested is the solution of a manufacturing problem in which it is necessary to create sketches of manufacturing steps for machine-tooling a part in a given mode of production. In order to create sketches, the worker must first read through the technical documentation and drawings of a blank and a finished part. Then, holding an image of the initial blank in memory, he must mentally determine the shape, size, and position it may assume after the first and each successive work operation. This type of complex expressive activity, proceeding simultaneously in several directions and based on abstractions from visual aids, is typical of the process of imagination.

Manipulating images with arbitrary content is associated with their transformation. The direction of these transformations may be defined by conditions of the problem, which guide this process in a certain direction. Thus, in our example of the transformation of the image of a blank, the production process and conditions for tooling the parts are given. Production requirements developed especially for these purposes may be specified in a large number of engineering transformations requiring the transformation of mechanical parts. The search domain of these transformations is defined by a given problem, and the expressive activity itself is subordinated to the logic underlying the problem-solving process.

In other cases, images are manipulated under more arbitrary conditions; the direction of these transformations is not rigorously regulated by the conditions of the problem. This circumstance is found in many forms of creative activity (scientific, graphic, artistic, and pictorial). In solving creative problems, the domain within which the image is to be created is not specified ahead of time; often the very techniques for its creation are unknown, and there is no initial visual base which might be used to define the process in which images are created and manipulated.

The line of development and the nature of transformations realized representationally are dictated by the individual's personal situation, occupational interest, and efforts to express his emotional and representational relations to the world.

We have considered differences in expressive activity based on an analysis of the result of this activity, the conditions under which it is performed, and its structure. The level of development is manifested in its degree of detail, arbitrariness, and balance. In delineating the two levels of this activity, we have constantly emphasized that the manipulation of images is based on activity aimed at creating images, which are seemingly prepared in the very depths of this activity. Moreover, the manipulation of images becomes a complex form of activity with its own specific content and forms of realization.

The foregoing remarks also apply to the description of spatial images. The creation of spatial images starts with various types of visual base and proceeds through the mental transformation of this base. Spatial images are manipulated in graphic problems, frequently in abstraction from the initial visual base and subordinated to the goals of the problem. Spatial images may be transformed in several directions at once or in a highly selective manner, which is reflected in the structure of the images. This defines the complexity of the mental transformations, and thereby the structure of spatial thinking itself.

The Manipulation of Spatial Images

The full range of uses of spatial images may be reduced to three basic cases: a change in the position of the depicted object (type I), a change in its structure (type II), and a combination of these transformations (type III). Let us now describe each type.

In **type I** use, the initial image, which has been already created from a visual graphic base, is altered in the mind as part of the problem-solving process according to the conditions of the problem. These changes primarily involve the spatial position of the image and do not affect its structural elements. Typical examples include various mental rotations and displacements of a preexisting image both within and outside the plane; these manipulations can cause substantial modification of an initial image created from a visual base, which otherwise remains objectively unchanged. This type of manipulation of an initial image to change its spatial position is used to solve geometrical, graphic, and design-engineering problems.

We should add that techniques of mental rotation (displacement) can be used to create a spatial image. But in this case, they are applied to a representation (for example, a drawing) or to individual elements of a representation. In the process of manipulating the image, it is not so much the elements of the perceived object which change as the image created from it. Mental rotation is realized without direct reliance on visual aids. As an example, let us compare the following two problems.

1. Given a perspective representation (Figure 1), picture the object using this representation and draw a visual representation of it.

2. Given a visual model, picture the object it depicts. Then, turn it over mentally so that its various faces (W, H, V) are in front of you, and, from the given projections (A, B, C, D), find the position corresponding to the resulting transformation (see Figure 7). (One of the four projections is obviously false, and is included only to eliminate the possibility of selecting projections based on the number of faces; that is, there are three faces, but four projections.)

In the first problem we must create an image of an object from a finished drawing (see Figure 1). The second problem requires not only creating such an image, but also performing a number of mental transformations, i.e., manipulating this image. Naturally, if a student finds it difficult to create an image from a perspective drawing, he will have even

Figure 1

greater difficulty in trying to manipulate this image. Conversely, if a student is able to manipulate spatial images easily and freely, he will have no difficulty creating an image from a representation (of course, assuming that all other conditions are equal, for example, in knowledge, graphic habits, and methods of work).

In **type II** use, the initial image is transformed structurally under the influence of the problem. This is achieved through different transformations of an initial image created by mental regrouping of constituent elements, and by the application of various techniques of superimposition, addition (truncation), and so forth. With type II use, the image is altered so much that it bears little resemblance to its initial form. The resulting image is somewhat newer than with type I use, since the initial image here is subjected to a more radical transformation. Mental activity is also somewhat greater here, since all the transformations of the image are performed, as a rule, in the mind without direct reliance on a representation. These transformations and their results must all be retained in memory and "viewed" in a mental glance. Let us offer a problem that illustrates this type of transformation.

Given two isosceles triangles with congruent bases, create a figure which has an axis of symmetry if: (a) the two triangles are congruent; (b) the two triangles are not congruent.

The problem requires mental transformations of two-dimensional figures. Analogous problems, requiring, for example, the manipulation of three-dimensional figures, may also be given.

In **type III** use, an initial image is transformed repeatedly. The transformations form a series of mental events which follow each other in succession, each aimed at transforming the initial image in terms of structure and spatial position. Let us give an example of this type of problem.

1. Describe the set of points symmetric relative to a given point A and to all the planes passing through a given line.

2. What displacement results from the composition of two axial symmetries of a line?

These transformations are carried according to a certain logic, which explicitly specifies the content, nature, and sequence of each transformation. Such problems are frequently encountered in mathematics, mechanical drawing, and descriptive geometry.

A comparative analysis of the three ways of manipulating spatial images demonstrates that such manipulation may be applied to various elements in the structure of the image, e.g., its shape, position, or a combination of the two. This makes it possible to develop a series of indices for identifying the weakest points in the structure of the student's spatial thinking and adopting measures to eliminate them through the selection of specialized problems and exercises.

We believe that the various types of manipulation of spatial images identified here and their comprehensibility to students indicate the level of development of spatial thinking. Our studies have shown that the particular type of manipulation comprehensible to a student is rather stable in nature. It makes its appearance as part of the process of solving problems with varied content, such as the manipulation of varied graphic representations (visual, projective, conventional, symbolic), the selection of a particular method of problem-solving, and so forth. Experimental confirmation has been provided by specially organized studies carried out under our direction by I.Ya. Kaplunovich, I.V. Tikhomirova, and V.S. Stoletnev. Let us describe these studies briefly.

Kaplunovich [1978] attempted to identify the characteristic features of students' manipulation of spatial images when they attempt to solve problems requiring transformation of two- or three-dimensional space, as called for by the content of the elementary mathematics course. Using classroom material, Kaplunovich developed a set of exercises for testing sixth- to eighth-graders, in terms of their knowledge, habits, and skills. A total of 60 students were tested, each of whom did problems requiring the manipulation of all three types of spatial images.

Kaplunovich's data demonstrated that students may be differentiated quite sharply by their level of development of spatial thinking, a fact which is expressed in the predominance of methods of manipulating a particular type of spatial image. Of the 60 subjects, 36 successfully completed all the exercises involving type I use, 12 subjects could handle type II exercises, and only two students could handle all three types of use. Kaplunovich was led to conclude that the particular type of manipulation understood by a student is a reliable index of his level of spatial thinking.

Along with the three types of image manipulation, we have identified three corresponding levels of development of spatial thinking (low, medium, high). This index correlates highly with other indices, such as the flexibility with which spatial images are manipulated, the comprehensiveness of the image, image dynamism, generality, reversibility, and so forth.

Interesting data in this area have been obtained by I.V. Tikhomirova [1976]. She showed that the type of spatial image manipulation is the most stable index of the level of development of spatial thinking. In many students, not even lengthy (up to three years) and systematic work involving a series of individual exercises succeeds in "destabilizing" their accustomed type of image. Therefore, the ability to switch from one type of manipulation to another (in terms of ease or teaching pace) may in certain students serve as one more index of the level of development of spatial thinking.

Using material from descriptive geometry in the curriculum followed in a technical institute, V.S. Stoletnev [1978] developed a battery of problems in which students carried out all three types of transformations of spatial images. Let us give examples of these problems.

The first type of manipulation involves altering the spatial distribution of reference points relative to a fixed spatial image, as well as altering the spatial orientation of an image relative to given reference points. Type II manipulation is associated with a change in the structure of the spatial image with no change in its spatial orientation relative to specified reference points, and in type III manipulation, the structure of the image is altered along with its spatial position (for example, the introduction of truncated surfaces). In solving these problems, Stoletnev notes that the mental manipulation of spatial images becomes more comprehensive and elaborate, since the conditions of the problem include only the initial spatial image, while repeated and multi-dimensional alteration of this image is required to solve the problem.

Stoletnev's data demonstrate that students are differentiated consistently in their ability to apply various types of spatial image manipulation. Both strong and weak subjects experience the greatest difficulty in problems requiring type III manipulation. On this basis, we may suppose that this type of manipulation is the most reliable and explicit index of highly developed spatial thinking in students.

We should, however, emphasize that the various types of manipulation reflect special features in each level of development of spatial thinking under certain conditions, especially in solving graphic problems. Expressive activity displays a mediated, generalized character here, since it is based on the manipulation of graphic substitutes for real objects, rather than the objects themselves. This factor which indicates the special nature of the activity, i.e., the mental transformation of given representations and the creation of new images from them. The reliability of this index may be tested under more general experimental conditions, using problems that differ in content.

The use of this index in actual teaching presupposes an analysis of classroom problems in terms of the type of spatial image manipulation they require. Such an analysis would make it possible to evaluate all problems based on the requirements they impose on mental activity as well as their content. Our research in this area has centered on problems employed in the grade 6 geometry course. The evaluation of classroom problems for the desired type of spatial image manipulation can be used to rank the problems by degree of difficulty, systematize the sequence in which they are assigned to students, and, based on their solution, make a more objective assessment of the level of development of spatial thinking in students. Our early results in this area have been promising.

The manipulation of spatial images occurs beyond the realm of graphic activity. It is a special problem in practical geographic orientation, solving engineering problems, and various areas of creative activity. In our study, however, we wished to analyze only those types of manipulation which are typical of graphic activity and determine its specific nature. The opportunity to use certain types of manipulation to characterize the form of spatial thinking manifested in other mental and physical activities requires special study.

We have considered the basic types of spatial image manipulation encountered in solving practical problems of varying content. Identifying them in students of various ages (from elementary school pupils to college students) demonstrates that complex forms of image-expressive activity are far from accessible to everyone. The study of the real mechanisms which make it possible to manipulate images will help us understand the psychological nature of various difficulties and design reliable criteria for determining the level of development of spatial thinking.

Basic Indices and Conditions for the Development of Spatial Thinking from a Graphic Base

In our description of the level of development of spatial thinking, we noted that the type of image manipulation employed may serve as a basic index of the development of spatial thinking in graphic activity. To insure that this index is reliable, we also used two closely interrelated indices, the flexibility with which the image is manipulated and the comprehensiveness of the image.

Let us imagine that a student is fully capable of performing transformations involving one type of manipulation. In order to determine that this type of manipulation is not merely an accident on his part, it is necessary to ascertain how stable it is, i.e., that the student regularly carries out these transformations with different types of graphic material. An index such as "manipulability" may be used for this purpose. Moreover, the manipulation of spatial images presupposes that the student is capable of mentally transforming a given pictorial visual aid in three closely interrelated ways: by shape, size, and spatial position. The reflection of these attributes in an image that has been mentally transformed is characteristic of a comprehensive image. If students do not forget these attributes as they transform the image, the transformation will be successful. Thus, the comprehensiveness of the image becomes an important index of the level of development of expressive activity. Therefore, we take manipulation type, manipulability, and image comprehensiveness as the basic indices of the development of spatial thinking.

The image manipulation type is a method of transforming an image that is accessible to the student. The psychological nature of these transformations has already been described. This index helps us identify not only the specific type of image manipulation mastered by the subject at the time of the test, but also to trace its changing dynamics in the course of experimental teaching.

"Manipulability" indicates the degree of freedom with which the image is manipulated in view of the graphic base on which the image is initially created. This index helps us identify the regularity in the manipulation of images in terms of type of manipulation, independent of the nature of the representation. The freedom with which an act of manipulation is accomplished, manifested in the flexibility and speed with which the subject moves from one graphic representation to another and the unique way in which their content is "recoded" are typical of highly developed thought processes. Conversely, the tendency to restrict oneself to a single representation and the inability to recognize the same object in a different representation attest to an insufficient level of development of thought. This index makes it easy to establish whether a given type of image manipulation (for example, manipulation involving mental rotation) results directly from teaching (the teacher demonstrates how this must be done using specific graphic material) or is a manifestation of students' individual abilities, by virtue of which they perform similar transformations of different types of representations independently, at their own initiative. Of course, it is well known that the flexibility with which knowledge is transferred is one of the basic indices of mental development (N.A. Menchinskaya, E.N. Kabanova-Meller, N.F. Talyzina, and others).

A study by A.D. Botvinnikov and the present author [1968, 1970] has shown that students at different ages, but under identical teaching conditions, may be distinguished in terms of their ability to perform mental transformations of an initial image. Under experimental conditions, all the students were provided with identical knowledge regarding different types of representations (graphic, projective, conventional, diagrammatic), acquired a necessary store of graphic habits and skills, and, in this sense, were placed on an equal footing. However, sharp individual differences were discovered when the students were given the following problem: given a perspective drawing, picture the object, then rotate the object mentally in a given direction, and determine which of a series of conventional diagrammatic representations corresponds to the newly created image (different versions of this exercise were used). It turned out that for some students the type of representation was of little significance, as they had little trouble solving the problem with various types of graphic material. Other students, however, could solve the problem only by starting with one type of representation, most often an engineering diagram.

Thus, the extent of the manipulation of spatial images created in various forms of graphic material may be expressed, first, by the absolute number of representations in which this manipulation may be accomplished successfully, and, second, in the relation between different types of representations. Of course, it is one thing to move from one three-dimensional representation to another, or to a projective representation, and an entirely different matter to move from a three-dimensional representation to a conventional semiotic representation and vice versa. Naturally, these transitions may be accomplished only where the individual has acquired a definite system of graphic knowledge, habits, and skills, although experience in working with students has demonstrated that this is insufficient. It is also important to know how to create and manipulate images, using for this purpose various forms of graphic representations.

Studies have shown that even when students have been taught the concepts of various forms of graphic representation (drawings, pictures, sketches, diagrams) through a special curriculum, they still have varying ability to manipulate different types of graphic representations. Effective manipulation of spatial images depends largely not only on the type of visual aid, but also on the combination of objective and semiotic elements in the representation. For purposes of our experiment, we presented exercises that involved reading different types of representation (isometrics, drawings, and sketches) of various objects. Moreover, we also developed exercises involving different representations of the same object. In one case the object was represented by a perspective drawing, in a second case we combined conventional signs and a representation of a certain projection, while in the third case the object was depicted in the form of a conventional diagrammatic projective representation, in which the projections themselves were not given, rather only their semiotic substitutes.[5]

Our experiments demonstrated that some students have no difficulty moving from an objective to a semiotic representation, while others find this quite troublesome. Both groups were taught methods of handling graphic material under the same conditions. During the lessons they were shown a table of conventional notations, followed by exercises requiring the use of this table. Both groups completed the same number of classroom and test exercises and were given the same explanations by their teachers.

Thus, the ease and speed with which the individual moves from one representation to another, as well as the quantity of exercises and nature and extent of assistance required, may serve as indices of the flexibility with which the student manipulates images. We believe this index is especially important because it is highly characteristic of thinking. In solving graphic problems (design-engineering, manufacturing, projection), it is often necessary to deal with several representations, rather than just one—usually different types of representations—and to move from one representation to another while creating and manipulating images. The use of indices such as flexibility and the type of image manipulation makes it possible to measure the level of development of spatial thinking in two distinct dimensions: longitudinal (horizontal) and transverse (vertical). Their use for research takes into account the educational conditions of the teaching process and the analysis of the graphic problems which students must solve in geometry, mechanical drawing, and shop class.

Any description of the range of aptitude for the application of various types of image manipulations must take into account the amount of assistance required to make students understand exercises at higher levels of difficulty. Some students may be receptive or require only moderate assistance, e.g., prompting designed to help them reach a solution of the problem, while others, despite doing a large number of exercises, continue to "see nothing in space," as they themselves describe their difficulty.

In our attempt to evaluate the level of development of spatial thinking in terms of the flexibility and type of image manipulation, we have taken into account the content of the spatial image. Indeed, the student's success at manipulating the image depends largely on the content of the image, i.e., the extent to which it reflects all the spatial characteristics of the object. The feature of comprehensiveness has been used to identify the structure of the image.

The comprehensiveness of the image is understood to refer to the structure of the image, i.e., the set of elements, the relations between them, and their dynamic interrelations. The image reflects not just the set of elements (shape, size) occurring in its structure, but also their spatial distribution relative to a given plane or the relative position of the elements themselves. An analysis of the errors and difficulties that occur when students handle various types of graphic material in order to manipulate images demonstrates that students have no difficulty in indicating shape and size. At the same time, not all students correctly reproduce spatial relations (determining what is located in front, behind; below, above; to the right, to the left; nearer, farther; etc.) notwithstanding identical teaching conditions.[6]

There are a number of reasons for this. The shape and size of objects (or representations of objects) are the subject of exercises in lessons in mathematics, mechanical drawing, and vocational education. Students measure and construct geometric figures, model and produce products, and thus actively manipulate shape and size. The identification of purely spatial relations, on the other hand, is not the subject of any special instruction, but develops spontaneously. When solving a graphic problem in mechanical drawing or shop, students perform spatial transformations in their minds. Although these transformations are not treated as independent subjects of study, they are part of the solutions to other classroom problems.

Obtaining a correct idea of the shape and size of a depicted object is facilitated by knowledge of the system of conventional notation accepted by the State Bureau of Standards (for example, for round and square holes, diameter, angle of inclination, types of lines, and conventional notation of tolerances for the various geometric constructions). However, there is no such clear system of orientation that may be used to determine spatial relations; acquisition of concepts is a first step here.

Thus, the ability to identify and use spatial relations does not depend solely on learning, whereas the ability to identify the shape and size of a depicted object is mediated by a system of acquired knowledge and techniques and methods of action. For example, detailed explanations for the analysis of the shape of objects are given in the mechanical drawing course. According to teacher's manuals, the study of the shape of objects should proceed in the following way: "First consider it as a whole, and determine the approximate relation between the length, height, and depth. Establish whether the object is symmetric or asymmetric in shape, and then generally ascertain the special features of the upper and lower, and left and right sides of the model. Next start your study of these sides, considering all projections and indentations and determining their shape and relative position. In your effort to discover the shape and relative position of each part, you should not limit yourself to a simple review, but rather strive to determine by sight the size of the projections or holes you are studying and approximate the relation between their size and the size of the entire model. Once you have finished studying the model and its parts, give it another quick glance in order to improve your conception of the object as a whole."[7]

No such detailed recommendations are given for the identification of spatial properties and relations. The relative "independence" of this ability from specialized knowledge makes it extremely important for diagnostic purposes. It becomes an index of the least variable psychological feature of an individual, stemming from his spatial orientation.[8] It is well known that students following a the same school curriculum under identical educational conditions manifest differing levels of ability in spatial relations. Their ability level is quite stable, and is manifested when working with different types of material. Through special instruction, it may be successfully developed, although the rate and nature of the development are determined largely by the initial level; identification of the initial level is extremely important for properly individualized instruction. This holds particularly true in teaching graphic disciplines in high school and college. The dynamism of the image, as expressed in the ability to mentally establish changes in the content of the image, and arbitrarily vary the point of reference, serves as an important gauge of the comprehensiveness of the image.

Many students find it difficult to follow transformations carried out in space by a "mental glance." For example, Volodya S. (grade 7) remarked, "when I try to create an image, I first see the object to be pictured clearly before my eyes, but when I have to modify it or turn it around, I seem to lose sight of the initial image, in fact it almost becomes a blur and there is no longer anything I could picture." The ability to retain the initial image in the representation and manipulate it mentally is fundamental for the solution of graphic and mathematical problems (B.F. Lomov, V.A. Krutetskii, and others).

The dynamism of the image shows up in the ability not only to alter it, but also to discern the movement and displacement of objects in a static representation, as well as how objects can be combined and created. For example, it is important to visualize the path of current in a circuit, the transmission of motion in various parts of a mechanical device, the displacement of parts, and transformations applied to parts in a production process in order to make use of conventional representations such as electrical diagrams, assembly drawings, and production flow charts. These transformations must all be undertaken in "mental space," since graphic representations remain objectively invariant.

The second type of ability can be seen most clearly in solving problems in which one system of reference must be rejected and a new one selected. For example, in order to create a perspective drawing we must analyze the characteristics of the object from the front, from above, and from the left. The position of the observer who wishes to view the object changes as each projection is created. The same takes place when reading a blueprint. The ability to view the object from various points of view is a fundamental ability in solving many geometry, graphic, and topography problems, as well as practical problems involving terrain. S.L. Rubinshtein makes a special point in emphasizing that it is precisely the "free transition from a fixed reference point to a system with a freely movable reference point which constitutes the core element of the general development of spatial understanding" [1946: 272].

The indices of image flexibility and image manipulation, which find their reflection in the comprehensiveness and dynamism of the image, define the level of development of spatial thinking. They remain fixed for each student, and are manifested when the student undertakes different classroom lessons and uses different types of graphic material. Thus, we have every reason to assert that these indices reflect ingrained individual psychological features of the personality which may be developed through teaching, but only where teaching is specially organized to impart techniques for creating and transforming images. The level of development of these properties significantly defines the student's capacity for learning, i.e., the student's "susceptiveness" to or aptitude for the acquisition of specialized knowledge in the areas of mathematics, mechanical drawing, and other school subjects, together with his readiness (disposition or interest) for undertaking assignments in these areas.

Studies undertaken by M.G. Bodnar have shown that, even through systematic school lessons, it is impossible to eliminate or compensate to any great extent for the substantial individual differences in students' ability to manipulate spatial relations. Developmental differences here are less sharply expressed than individual differences. For example, we have been unable to discover any statistically significant differences between the second and fourth grades. Moreover, there are data which indicate that certain students in the younger grades exceed seventh and eighth graders in terms of our indices, since the accumulation of knowledge in and of itself does not guarantee the development of spatial thinking. These data seem to support the conclusion that, because of its structural complexity, the level of development of spatial thinking should be defined not in terms of just one index, but rather in light of the entire series of indices described above. It is also necessary to explicitly differentiate indices of the development of spatial thinking and conditions underlying their appearance in the course of teaching.

The acquisition of a special system of graphic knowledge, habits, and skills serves as a key condition without which spatial thinking could not develop. However, spatial thinking itself depends not only on the acquisition of special knowledge, but also on the structure of spatial images. Considerable research into developing spatial thinking in children has been conducted in recent years. New curricula have been introduced which have expanded considerably the amount of school work directed at helping students acquire effective techniques for the analysis of graphic representations and methods of representation. In mathematics, considerable emphasis has been placed on teaching students generalized techniques of performing geometric transformations.

The early grades incorporate geometric exercises involving the mental recomposition of a representation for the purpose of identifying figures formed through the union and intersection of elements of these figures. Exercises involving the generation of evolutes have also been widely used. In the senior grades, considerable emphasis has been placed on the ability to perform various transformation operations in the plane and in space through the application of such methods as central and axial symmetry, similitude, rectangular projection, and homothetic projection.[9] Major changes have also been made in mechanical drawing, which now makes extensive use of exercises requiring mental transformation of graphic representations with respect to the structure and spatial position of their constituent elements (A.D. Botvinnikov et al., 1977).

However, the manipulation of spatial relations still lags far behind the use of shape and size. Our studies have shown that students working in theoretical space bring into this space methods of orientation acquired in the analysis of practical (objective) space. The transition from practical to theoretical space requires not merely the acquisition of specialized conceptual tools, but also the formation of essentially novel methods of spatial orientation, although these methods are not identified explicitly nor assigned for study. For this reason students experience great difficulty when they are required to learn different systems of reference in which the reference point is not the position of their own body, but some other object, relative to which the entire system of orientation (the "spatial" picture) may change.

Our research, along with studies by other scholars (see N.P. Linkova, 1964), has shown that younger students are fully prepared for systematic knowledge about spatial shape and methods of representing it in the plane. Clearly, further in-depth research is needed to lay the foundations for teaching students how to correctly perceive representations of three-dimensional bodies and their two-dimensional shapes, and to use different systems of reference within the framework of various school subjects, even in elementary school.

The design of suitable drills based on a classification of the different forms of representations and types of transformation of representations has not only helped students gain a correct understanding of the fundamental concepts of space and spatial elements (e.g., plane figures, methods of creating plane figures, three-dimensional bodies, planes) in earlier grades, but has also played a major role in the development of their spatial thinking. Introducing students to the basic types of representations in the early grades has played an important role. When learning about various subjects, students encounter different types of graphic representations, although, as studies have demonstrated, they do not create the necessary generalizations. In fact, in our experiments, fourth- and fifth-graders solved an experimental problem using their intuition and practical abilities. The problem required the recognition of a visual picture and drawing, although they had not been given corresponding concepts that would enable them to consciously differentiate these types of representations (based on essential attributes).

Sensory activity, the basis for the development of spatial thinking, proceeds through several stages in ontogenesis. Children first learn to distinguish individual objects by their shape and size, and on this basis undertake the operations of comparison, generalization, and classification. Once they have identified one spatial attribute as dominant, children undertake a generalization of objects based on this attribute. For example, they may organize objects in terms of their geometric shape (round, square, rectangular, mixed, etc.), by estimating the relation between their size and angles. They attempt to make quantitative estimates of magnitudes, based on the notions of size differences ("greater-less"), height differences ("above-below"), length differences ("longer-shorter"), width differences ("wider-narrower"), and thickness differences ("thicker-thinner").[10] Often, they analyze objects with respect to a whole series of parameters simultaneously, since it is the combination of these parameters that defines the qualitative identity of the object. For example, in comparing square or rectangular objects (or representations), children may feel that geometrical figures differ whenever the sides are quantitatively different, even when the relations between the angles and the directions of the sides are the same.

The acquisition of a definite system of attributes is of crucial importance for evaluating various objects and representations of objects. In the process of social and theoretical experience, mankind has picked out from the full set of perceivable actions certain systems or natural series of shapes, colors, magnitudes, and other perceivable qualities of objects, which have been given verbal equivalents. As A.V. Zaporozhets has noted, once a child has acquired this type of system, he also acquires a set of measures or standards by which he can compare any perceived quality, give it a suitable definition, and find its place among other qualities. Studies by L.A. Venger, N.P. Sakulina, Z. M. Boguslavskaya, and others have demonstrated convincingly that the child's understanding of sensory standards enables him to differentiate objects qualitatively and manipulate them consciously in varied play, educational, and representational activity.

However, the formation of spatial thinking depends crucially on the ability not only to abstract attributes of spatial objects, but also to understand the relative boundaries between individual groups of objects and the potential use of a variety of closely interrelated criteria (e.g., shape and size, whose interrelation makes it possible to move from one group of objects to another in an analysis) when analyzing these groups. The relative nature of the spatial characteristics of objects can be attributed to the dynamic nature of objects, and the fact that they are constantly in motion, shifting, and being transformed. And the development of this important feature of spatial thinking has yet to receive the attention it is due. Meanwhile, students' understanding not only of the mode of existence of various geometrical shapes, but also their origin and the possibility of transforming them, is an important prerequisite for understanding the dynamism (reversing and interchanging) of spatial images.

In the course of ontogenesis, children continue to orient themselves in space for quite some time by distributing surrounding objects relative to the position of their own body. Orientation derived from the body image, which is an early developmental trend, substantially influences the formation and development of the entire system of spatial images. Since it is thoroughly established in their minds, it is transferred from physical action with objects to the analysis of geometrical space, creating major difficulties for students' understanding of geometry.

A central idea in the modern school geometry course is mapping of the plane onto itself. This notion presupposes the ability to visualize any plane and its set of elements which, under certain conditions, may be mapped onto itself. Starting with this notion, students are introduced to the basic transformations, such as displacement, rotation (central and axial symmetry), and rectangular projection. These transformations all presuppose the ability to create corresponding spatial images and manipulate them based on specified conditions. But the very concept of a "mapping of the plane onto itself" denotes that the elements of the plane change their spatial position relative to the initial plane, regardless of their position relative to the observer. Many students are unable to discard their customary system of reference based on the body image. We believe that this is the psychological reason for the difficulties some students experience when studying the basic ideas of modern mathematics.

Thus, the creation and manipulation of spatial images depends on a complicated system of knowledge of spatial properties and relations, along with specialized techniques for their perception and representation. But this is still insufficient. We also need complex, meticulous, and systematic research designed to understand how the child develops the ability to use various types of graphic representations and change his system of reference arbitrarily. This will require a fundamental change in the content and methods used in teaching a number of subjects (geometry, mechanical drawing, art, geography, as well as more specialized disciplines). Clearly, the psychological nature of many difficulties, particularly related to the comprehension of graphic activity, may be attributed to the fact that these changes have not been implemented to the necessary extent. It is thus clear, for example, why students make the common error of referring to a left view as a right view (noted by A.D. Botvinnikov, B.F. Lomov, I.S. Yakimanskaya, and others). With body image orientation, a side view is located on the right in a drawing if the plane of the drawing is represented in a rectangular coordinate system. But in creating projections of a drawing, the fixed position of an object (normally the main view) is taken as the basic system of reference, rather than the position of the observer. The top and left views are constructed relative to the position of the object.

Inadequate skill at carrying out a dynamic change of reference points often creates many difficulties in the study of graphic activity. Even in the preschool years, important prerequisites are present for development of the ability to arbitrarily shift one's observation point (system of reference). When the child manipulates an object in order to grasp its nature or make practical use of it, he seems to "lose" his unified visual position, and moves from a frontal view to a profile viewpoint. This creates the psychological conditions for the mastery of advanced methods of representation using the three basic planes of projection. A number of recent studies (N.P. Linkova, N A. Kurochkina, and others) have shown that with a suitable system of teaching, seven- and eight-year-old children are capable of conveying volumes in the plane and apprehending projective relations literally, although the this ability is delayed for some time under the current method of teaching.

Psychological studies confirm that before they enter school, children are already ready to apprehend geometric space. Moreover, the very nature of the child's perception allows him to arbitrarily shift his position of observation. The preschool and early school years are therefore a "sensitive period" during which all the necessary prerequisites for the development of abilities of spatial orientation are created. What is particularly important is that the ability to arbitrarily shift one's reference point is also founded here. This ability is of decisive importance for the development of spatial thinking.

In the course of teaching, spatial thinking develops along the following basic lines: (1) apprehending the arbitrary nature of the use of systems of reference; (2) development of generalized methods of creating spatial images and manipulating them, i.e., improving expressive activity; and (3) the acquisition of graphic "fluency" to help in manipulating spatial images exhibiting various degrees of particularity and visualization, and recoding these images in accordance with the requirements of graphic activity.

Realizing these basic trends in the development of spatial thinking in the teaching process presupposes the development of specialized experimental models. Some of these models have now been tested by us in work with students. In particular, we have studied how students undertake graphic modeling in mathematics lessons. For this purpose, we used exercises in which the basic properties of sets (intersection and union) were to be expressed in verbal, graphic, and symbolic form. A battery of exercises requiring the formation of an ability to alter one's reference point flexibly and dynamically was also employed.

Development of Spatial Thinking in the Learning Process

Spatial thinking is formed within the system of knowledge the individual must learn. Each school subject imposes by virtue of its content certain requirements on the development of spatial thinking. But we confront several important questions: To what extent does the logic underlying the teaching process correspond to the logic of mental development? Does the logic underlying learning correspond to the logic of the development of spatial thinking? Is it dependent on the laws governing this development? Let us consider these questions in more detail.

In the course of ontogenesis, spatial thinking develops at the heart of the forms of thought which reflect the natural stages of the individual's general intellectual development. It is first formed within the context of effective visual thinking. In its most highly developed and independent forms, it becomes a part of representational thinking. Forms of spatial thinking with higher theoretical content are created in the course of apprehending objective activity, and acquiring graphic fluency and a definite system of knowledge, habits, and skills.

What do these stages in the development of spatial thinking signify? To what extent do they reflect the content and general logic underlying its development? The manipulation of spatial properties and relations at the early stages of ontogenesis occurs primarily in practical-objective manipulative form. It occurs in space, within a three-dimensional framework, where the body image serves as the basic system of reference.

In learning about the world of things and events, children recognize the spatial properties of things and events largely by identifying relations of order, i.e., through the disposition of objects relative to each other, identification of their shape, and analysis of the features of this shape. By identifying shapes, it becomes possible to isolate an object visually, delineate it from other objects, investigate its objective properties, operate in accordance with its social function, and so forth. It is topological representations which serve as the basic source for the formation of spatial thinking in early childhood.

However, the rather early familiarization with pictorial (graphic) activity means that children begin to use spatial properties and relations within a two-dimensional system, and not only a three-dimensional one, i.e., in the plane, as well as in space; they routinely transform (recode) three-dimensional images into two-dimensional ones and vice versa, and use both types simultaneously. The forms of visual aids become more complicated and generalized as well. Visual material here may refer not only to real (three-dimensional) objects, but also their two-dimensional representations (pictures, color illustrations and pictures, hand sketches, etc.).

A variety of different projective spatial representations are based on this. Major changes take place in the systems of reference, which become more varied and more closely regulated. Body image orientation becomes decisive for establishing spatial relations and dependencies. Moreover, other systems of reference in which any object whatsoever (material or ideal) may become the initial reference point, rather than just the individual himself, may also be created based on this orientation. Psychology identifies this stage in the development of spatial thinking as marked by a shift in methods of orientation and a transition from "travel-map" images to "survey-map" images, in F.N. Shemyakin's [1940] terminology.

Spatial thinking develops further in ontogenesis along the lines of greater complication of all forms of spatial orientation, their enrichment with theoretical content, and the greater complication of problems which require the transformation of a visual situation by means of its perception or representation of repeated and multifaceted manipulation of spatial images. These factors combine to create the conditions necessary for the acquiring a variety of habits of construction, computation, and measurement. Metric representations that make it possible to use such special properties as distance, breadth, length, and width also develop. It then becomes possible to solve problems in computing the area of two-dimensional figures, determining the volume of complex bodies and surfaces, and transforming various geometric forms through objective or graphic modeling. The visual aids used become more highly conventionalized, schematized, abstract, and symbolic. Such is the general logic underlying the development of spatial thinking in ontogenesis.

Let us now see in general how spatial thinking develops in the course of teaching. For this purpose, we will analyze three basic lines of its development: (1) the transition from three-dimensional space to two-dimensional space (from solid to plane figures), and vice versa; (2) the transition from graphic representations to conventional diagrammatic representations, and vice versa; (3) the transition from a fixed reference point to an arbitrary or specified reference point. Our analysis of numerous school subjects (geometry, mechanical drawing, geography, descriptive geometry, vocational education, etc.) demonstrates that the system of knowledge used in these subjects takes insufficient account of the objective logic underlying the development of spatial thinking, and often contradicts it. Let us take a look at the facts.

As we have already noted, the teaching process does not adequately insure a smooth transition in the development of spatial understanding. Topological, projective, and metric representations which serve as the foundation for spatial understanding are formed often in complete disregard of their development in ontogenesis. In the course of instruction, students at first primarily use metric representations, and then projective representations. There is no trend threading its way through the different school subjects that could reflect the general logic underlying the development of spatial thinking, as well as the specific nature of an actual sphere of reality (mathematical, geographic, etc.).

Many studies have shown that students who begin the systematic course in geometry have more highly developed spatial (three-dimensional) representations than planar (two-dimensional) representations. In the early grades, however, the child's ability to "work" simultaneously in the plane and in space is inhibited by the fact that students are accustomed to working solely with two-dimensional representations. The rich store of experience, accumulated from manipulating real (solid) objects seems to be suspended once they start plane geometry, since the content and logic of this subject entails the exclusive use of two-dimensional representations. Numerous experienced educators have noted this fact and recommended that from the very start, the mathematics teacher must "constantly emphasize" that the two-dimensional figure is a special case of a three-dimensional figure, and from the very beginning of the plane geometry course treat the point and line, and later more complicated figures, as situated arbitrarily in space and lying in different planes (G.G. Maslova, 1964: 47-48).

In the use of spatial relations, the concept of a projection serves as the fundamental concept for the transition from the plane to space and vice versa. In various school subjects (particularly mechanical drawing and geography), students are first asked to grasp this concept empirically and intuitively, and only subsequently through its scientific content. Resorting to such a method in introducing a concept of such fundamental importance in the development of spatial thinking can be attributed only to the insufficient importance attached to psychological laws.

Experimental studies, particularly by the present author, have demonstrated that even young schoolchildren are fully prepared to learn this concept and make extensive use of it in solving classroom problems. However, they are acquainted with the theoretical content of this concept only in grade 7, i.e., virtually at the end of primary school, a policy which is an unwarranted hindrance to the development of projective representation in children. Students do not have to sufficiently realize that any plane figure is a unique projection of a solid body. Moreover, the constant use of two-dimensional representations leads to over-attachment to a fixed observation point.

The development of spatial thinking is also hindered by the fact that there is no unified classification of the various types of graphic representations. Each school subject employs its own classification and defines its own requirements for the use of graphic representations, which are often unique to that subject. Problems in which students must select a graphic representation on their own or compare several representations based on an analysis of their objective content and visual features almost never occur in actual teaching.

Thus, many school subjects incorporate a variety of spatial transformations, although the psychological techniques used in realizing them have received little study. Therefore, even though they are similar in terms of logical content, they prove to be heterogeneous in terms of psychology, which is responsible for many difficulties. Let us demonstrate this using geometrical transformations as an example.

In mathematics, such transformations as rotation or central symmetry of the plane are considered quite similar, and nearly identical in terms of results. From the psychological standpoint, however, they are quite different. In performing a central symmetry, students must generate a linear displacement, whereas for a rotation they must displace a point in the plane along an arc of a circle; of course, this changes the psychological content of the transformations. In terms of results, the two operations are identical, although they are different in terms of the process by which the result is attained.

There are several instances in which the same geometric transformation is taught twice in the mathematics course. It may be performed first on figures, such that these figures are displaced within a single plane (plane geometry), and then, moving outside the plane, it may come up with three-dimensional, rather than two-dimensional shapes (solid geometry). Such an "artificial" division—from the psychological standpoint— is due to the complex nature of mathematical objects, although of course it corresponds to nothing essentially new in terms of the mental events which make up these transformations. Our observations have shown that elementary school students often perform spatial transformations more creatively and originally than older students. This is quite understandable. They are not yet accustomed to performing transformations exclusively in the plane. There is still much to ponder here for improving techniques of teaching mathematics.

Let us offer a comparative analysis of the content of courses in mathematics, mechanical drawing, and descriptive geometry. The basic notions studied in these courses are the related transformations of parallel rectangular (orthogonal) projection, rotation, various types of symmetries, and so forth. But these transformations are studied in terms of the specific nature of each individual subject, within the closed borders of its content. It must, however, be borne in mind that these transformations are performed by the same student in the study of the different subjects. He develops his own logic to guide his performance, and from the very start (often before receiving any systematic instruction) creates general methods of operation. As our experiments have demonstrated, third- and fourth-graders perform elementary symmetry transformations on their own initiative, both within the plane and in space. In performing a rectangular projection, they discover the dynamic nature of perception and learn how to arbitrarily shift their reference point and observation position, i.e., they easily and quickly acquire all the necessary psychological mechanisms which enable them to undertake spatial transformations of given mathematical objects. Unfortunately, however, in the course of teaching, these already highly polished mechanisms are not only not used, but even disrupted for no good reason, and despite them other mechanisms are constructed, dictated by the logic and content of each school subject.

Clearly, as a preliminary study before systematic instruction (using the case of elementary but highly significant examples), it is necessary to nurture mental operations in students which have "genetic priority" (in V.V. Davydov's terminology) and serve general purposes in terms of the psychological technique of realization. Studies carried out by I.Ya. Kaplunovich [1978] have shown that the psychological content of many geometric transformations is not identical to their mathematical content. Often, mathematically complex operations are simple from the psychological standpoint, and vice versa. The divergence between the mathematical and psychological content of these operations, we believe, is also the reason for the many difficulties students have when performing spatial transformations, a fact which complicates the development of spatial thinking.

The psychological content of various spatial transformations, along with their close relations to one another, is of great significance for determining optimal paths for the development of spatial thinking. Results of studies in this area, we believe, may help determine the proper sequence for studying various transformations and classifying them in different ways. In our study of the unity and differences of the psychological mechanisms underlying spatial transformations, we have found considerable opportunity for improving the teaching process and supporting a unified development for spatial thinking.

We have considered how the transition from the plane to space and conversely may be undertaken in the teaching process. Now let us see how the transition to different systems of reference may be accomplished. The same tendencies hold here. To a great extent, students spontaneously shift from a fixed reference point to an arbitrarily selected (or specified) point. Of course, this cannot help ensure optimal development of spatial thinking. What are the main problems here?

First, the various school subjects involving the creation of spatial images and their manipulation utilize different coordinate systems (rectangular, polar, spherical, etc.) and different methods of projection. The features of each coordinate system—what is shared by all and what is distinctive to each—and the way each affects man's general system of orientation in theoretical space, however, have received inadequate attention. Second, the full variety of problems involving spatial relations may be divided into two large groups on psychological grounds. The first group contains problems with varying specific content in which the spatial position of the observer is of prime importance, e.g., problems involving the reading and compilation of topographic terrain maps.

The second group consists of problems in which the position of the observer (subject) is not of prime importance for the spatial relations; for example, we may cite problems in physics in determining the velocity, path, or trajectory of two or more interacting objects. Unfortunately, the psychological aspects of the problem-solving process are not always taken into account when determining the nature and level of complexity of these problems, analyzing reasons for difficulties encountered in solving them, and so forth. Educational problems need to be classified by psychological criteria, since only this would make it possible to decide upon a sequence for their presentation. Such a sequence could radically alter many indices of the development of spatial thinking, both age-group and individual indices. Let us discuss briefly a number of examples which illustrate this important point.

In a study we have carried out with the assistance of a number of mathematics teachers, all the problems in the teachers' aid for grade 6 geometry (V.A. Gusev and G.G. Maslova, Moscow, 1975) were grouped according to the three types of spatial image manipulation. Many mathematically simple problems, it turned out, required more complex types of image manipulation, and vice versa.

Therefore, the sequence for the presentation of these problems was modified. To test the effectiveness of this criterion, two classes, one control class and one experimental class, were selected for comparison. In the control class, the problems were given in the lesson in the form presented in the teacher's aid. In the experimental class, they were used in a newly developed sequence. Comparison of the results showed that the creative element in solving the problems was higher in the experimental class than in the control class.

These data indicate that a classification of problems in terms of psychological criteria may increase the efficiency of learning, as the material is organized specifically to stimulate students' mental activity. Searches for such criteria will be carried out in our studies in the future. In particular, the use of various types of graphic representations (graphic illustrations, drawings, conventional semeiotic sets of symbols) as a visual base for the problem-solving process may also help group problems by their degree of difficulty. Clearly, other criteria are also possible.

We have considered complicated and ambiguous relations between the teaching process and the development of spatial thinking in children.

Teaching can promote mental development only where it affects mental activity directly, transforming and guiding it in a selected direction. Teaching must be organized to impart techniques for intellectual activity and the real mechanisms of such activity; only in this way can it become a developmental factor. S.L. Rubinshtein expressed the nature of this relation in its most general form: "External causes act only through internal conditions."

The development of spatial thinking in children still proceeds at too low a level. No scientific system guides this development through knowledge of its psychological features. Furthermore, as we have tried to show, we make no use of the spatial abilities students have already developed. There is an acute need for a scientific system for the development of spatial thinking in the learning process, beginning with the preschool years. Such a system must create a unified line of development of spatial thinking.

3

Designing a Method for Diagnosing the Level of Development of Spatial Thinking

Principles for the Development of Diagnostic Techniques

The study of the structure of spatial thinking and the identification of the content and level of development of spatial thinking in different people are important not only for resolving many issues in the area of elementary teaching, but also in analyzing the occupational activity in different professions and laying a firm foundation for differentiating people for purposes of vocational guidance. For this reason interest in the design of rigorous methods of diagnosing spatial thinking has recently increased.

In this area, Soviet psychology proceeds by assuming that the design of any diagnostic technique must be based primarily on a careful and comprehensive investigation of the mental trait to be identified and evaluated.[1] Only a study of the structure of the trait and its content and conditions of formation and development in specific activities can identify rigorous indices of the development of the property and design objective criteria for measuring it. This ultimately defines the choice of diagnostic tests, the organization of surveys, along with the proper use of the data obtained.

By their very nature, diagnostic techniques must serve as clinical techniques. Their basic purpose is not so much the evaluation of the ultimate result of the tests with respect to quantitative indices, but a qualitative analysis of the process by which this result is obtained, based on the structure of the trait under consideration. For an objective identification of the level of development of spatial thinking—or any other property of the personality—it is important to avoid testing individual, isolated qualities (symptoms), but rather to analyze the integral structure (syndrome) of thought by studying the content and functions of each element of this structure, the nature of the interrelations between these elements, and their level of development. Moreover, such techniques should identify the individual's potential aptitudes (not just his present abilities) for solving diagnostic items, based on actual achievements as well as the potential for improving them through the teaching process. In other words, diagnostic techniques must make it possible to measure "zones of proximate development," in L.S. Vygotskii's terminology. The individual's receptivity ("susceptibility") to teaching, i.e., his capacity for learning, is considered by many psychologists an important index of mental development (B.G. Ananev, A.A. Lyublinskaya, N.A. Menchinskaya, Z.I. Kalmykova, and others).

The standardized tests which are widely used abroad for evaluating "nonverbal intelligence" (spatial aptitude) commonly include various visual and spatial tests. Created based on artificial material (abstract geometric symbols), these tests help identify such aptitudes as visual acuity, keenness of observation, and quick-wittedness as they are manifested in the visual evaluation of interrelations between figures (points, lines, angles), the systematization of figures (comparison of series of geometric symbols, with the student supplying the missing symbols based on some general attribute), in selecting or eliminating "redundant" interrelations in the course of completing a set of geometric symbols based on certain attributes, in the discovery of logical relations between geometric figures and their individual elements, and so on. These tests require various mental acts, such as comparison, establishing visual and spatial relations, generalizing graphically specified attributes, mentally modifying geometric objects, etc. These mental acts are realized differently by different people, which determines the individual's success or failure in finding a solution.

Analogous tests, interesting and cleverly made, may help identify certain individual psychological differences between people, although they cannot reveal the psychological nature of these differences. As is well known, even the same result (objectively correct and achieved at the same time intervals) may be attained through different mental acts (methods of organizing mental acts), a fact ignored by specialists in standardized testing. Standardized tests establish not so much the process by which a solution is found, but rather the number of steps in the process. This limitation of techniques based on standardized testing has been pointed out by specialists in the area. For example, G. Eysenck [1972] emphasizes that tests based on numerical, verbal, and graphic material designed to measure intelligence quotients are capable of describing intelligence only in one, purely quantitative respect, i.e., in terms of the speed of mental processes; this latter quality defines to a great extent the subject's success or failure. The qualitative aspect of mental processes falls entirely outside the scope of analysis, since the subject's speed at solving problems depends on other parameters of the personality, such as persistence, self-criticism, interest in completing the exercise, etc., all of which are totally ignored.

Tests designed to measure "nonverbal intelligence" are based on an interpretation of spatial thinking and a collection of individual isolated aptitudes that follow one another in actual spatial thinking. These aptitudes are usually understood to include visual acuity, the ability to evaluate lines (angles) for size and spatial position, the ability to modify figures visually, and so forth. Undoubtedly, these are all important abilities which make it possible to perform various perceptual actions, but they do not exhaust the content of spatial thinking, even though they constitute its foundation.

The visual and spatial tests used extensively abroad are used to measure the individual's ability to establish various spatial relations based on visually specified objects (such tests have been created by Y.I. Raven, V. Koss, E.R. Kettle, J.H. Ryskop, R. Amthauer, Y. Skal, J. Vonkomer, F.E. Rybakov, and others). These tests, however, lack higher-order problems that would require not merely the visual comparison of representations (figures, symbols, number series, etc.), but also the manipulation of images based on these representations (mental manipulation, use, and modification of images, and the creation of new images). Indeed, this constitutes the essential content of spatial thinking. Tests based on graphic material often take the form of a homogeneous series of gradually more complicated figures, although the problems that may be solved by means of these series do not vary in principle. The content of these problems is monotonous and does not change to reflect the different activities involved in the creation and use of spatial images, because the design of these problems is not founded on a qualitative analysis of the structure of spatial thinking.

Furthermore, these tests can be completed without any special knowledge; they consist largely of problems that require quick-wittedness (intellectual grasp). The tests usually contain abstract geometric symbols and signs whose use does not presuppose the application of a system of knowledge or the development of complicated abilities. This ensures essentially identical conditions for all subjects, but at the same time significantly reduces the range of application of the tests. As they are based on artificial material, they cannot serve as a suitable model of educational and occupational activity, since there is nothing directly related to them. Thus, it is very difficult to judge the real abilities of students on the basis of these tests. Knowledge and accumulated experience exert a positive influence on success in taking tests and engender interest and emotional readiness for completing them, which, unfortunately, is not taken into account in their design. Together, these facts limit the potential use of currently available visual and spatial tests for identifying the level of development of spatial thinking and lead us to search for new principles of creating such tests on a different theoretical basis.

Our research was aimed at developing a diagnostic technique which would make it possible to objectively identify and evaluate the level of development of spatial thinking in children as it develops in the course of learning. We succeeded in creating such a technique, using indices based on a theoretical model of the structure of spatial thinking and tested in a large-scale experiment including over 2,000 students of various ages (grades 3-10).

The following basic indices were used: (1) success at creating a spatial image corresponding to a graphic representation; (2) types of image manipulation; (3) manipulability; and (4) image comprehensiveness, i.e., the extent to which it reflects a variety of characteristics (shape, size, spatial distribution, breadth).

In describing the degree of success at creating a spatial image, we took into account features of the graphic base within which the image is formed in the most creative way possible (visual picture—conventional drawing—diagram), as well as image dynamism, i.e., its variability and the possibility of creating an image when the representation is shown for varying lengths of time. The complexity of image manipulation was evaluated by the following three types of spatial transformations: (a) modification of the image in terms of spatial position (mental rotation, displacement, etc.); (b) mental transformation of the image structure through rearrangement of individual elements, using techniques of superimposition, unification, dissection, etc.; and (c) simultaneous modification of the spatial position and structure of the image. **Manipulability** is reflected in the ease with which visual information is "recoded," making it possible to create images based on various types of graphic material with the same degree of freedom. The **comprehensiveness** of the image reflects the presence of the basic spatial characteristics in the image (these indices are described in more detail in Chapter 2, section 4).

These indices enable us to evaluate the level of development of spatial thinking and the stability of its individual characteristics from a developmental and individualized standpoint. It is well known that spatial thinking develops in different ways in different students, even under the same teaching conditions. This shows that the structure of spatial thinking includes components which do not develop uniformly under the effect of teaching. The investigation of these components is of particular interest. The indices which characterize these components are actually the indices of mental development. They reflect, in L.S. Vygotskii's words, the "formal effect of learning," i.e., new constructs in the structure of thinking developed in the course of acquiring knowledge, habits, and skills based on the individual prerequisites of mental development.

The indices of the level of development of spatial thinking are also closely interrelated to each other. For example, manipulation type is determined largely by image comprehensiveness, i.e., the extent to which the image structure reproduces changes in shape, size, and spatial position. Both of these indices enter into the notion of manipulability, i.e., in the freedom with which an image created from different types of graphic base can be manipulated.

The internal similarity of these indices results from the fact that they are based on a qualitative characterization of the structure of representational activity. They make it possible to analyze and evaluate methods of representation accessible to students (flexibility with which the methods may be used, visual impact, primary manipulation of shape, size, or spatial relations, arbitrary variation of reference point, etc.).

After deriving these indices from diagnostic testing, we compared them to such "vital" indices as academic success rates in corresponding subjects (geometry, mechanical drawing, art, shop), as expressed in grades; interest in lessons in particular school subjects (attraction, indifference, or even distaste towards the subjects); predictions of students' future in light of these indices (selecting a particular college or technical institute); analysis of reasons for difficulties in these subjects, etc. For this purpose, we used questionnaires, discussions, lesson observations, teacher characteristics, and student comments.

Basic Requirements for Diagnostic Problems

Diagnostic problems were designed in accordance with indices of spatial thinking. In terms of content, these problems: 1) must be comprehensive, i.e., must incorporate the various psychological factors which reflect the level of development of expressive activity; accordingly, they must be graduated by level of complexity (by the type of transformation carried out on the basis of these indices); 2) must make it possible to identify not just the ultimate result of the problem, but also the process of attaining it; such problems must also be brief and should not require a great deal of time for their solution, nor should they be too closely bound to specific curriculum material; and 3) must be based on various types of graphic material and primarily require manipulation of the shape and size of represented objects and their spatial relations.

The use of such material for designing diagnostic problems has enabled us to describe spatial thinking adequately with respect to indices of interest and, moreover, made these problems educational in terms of content. Graphic representations used in geometry, mechanical drawing, and shop classes served as the testing material. The problems called for the most typical techniques of creating and manipulating spatial images employed by students in their study of mathematics and mechanical drawing (rotation, revolution, superimposition, translation, orthogonal and parallel projection, etc.). The problems also included all the basic types of manipulation described above, forming a definite series, starting from simple transformations based on perception to more complex transformations carried out mentally, which also defined a sequence for the presentation of the tests. The nature of the initial graphic base and its degree of generality and conventionality were taken into account.

By assigning various problems to the same student, we were able to establish not only his current level of development of spatial thinking, but also specific tendencies in his development. These tendencies were expressed in receptivity to assistance from the experimenter, the speed and ease with which the student shifted from one level of problem-solving to another (spurred by this assistance), the regularity with which image-expressive techniques were applied and transferred to other types of problems based on different graphic material, the predominant use of one specific type of visual support, and so forth. In terms of content, the problems were novel and unusual for the students, seemed interesting to them, and elicited active search for a solution. It was thus possible to identify the student's real potential for the manipulation of images.

Since the problems identified not so much the student's current store of knowledge, habits, and skills (this, of course, is taken into account) as the level of development of spatial thinking, their basic content consisted in the performance of various spatial transformations required by problems, and not just the recollection of an image based on a graphic representation.

The problems were adapted for working with students in different grades, and could also be used with students under various teaching conditions. Because of the way they were created, the problems did not take a great deal of time to complete, and likewise required minimal knowledge and skills. If necessary, students' knowledge and skills may be easily brought up to standard.

In order to equalize the conditions of the experiment, we spoke with each student in order to determine his familiarity with knowledge needed for successfully completing his problems before giving them to him; thus we evened out the effect of knowledge on the problem-solving process. If in the course of this discussion it was discovered that there were gaps in any student's knowledge, the missing knowledge was at once supplied by the experimenter through direct prompting or by reminding the student of his past experience. Thus, before beginning the tests all the students had at their disposal the necessary store of knowledge.

We selected problems that would not require complicated graphic work with drafting tools, since they make it take much longer to do problems. Moreover, graphic activity is often performed in such a way as to conceal precisely the property which we wished to identify and evaluate. To identify a student's aptitude for mental manipulation of images in its "purest" form, we attempted to eliminate as far as possible the effect of his or her knowledge and graphic habits on the test. Imagine that we are testing two students, one of whom is able to think "spatially" quite readily, quickly creating and manipulating a corresponding mental image from a representation. But because of insufficient understanding of graphic techniques, there are inaccuracies in the resultant representational form, and much time must be spent on completing the drawing. Another student has difficulty creating and manipulating the spatial image ("I don't see anything in space," he may say to point out his difficulty). But once this student has acquired drawing habits, he can successfully solve a number of problems; e.g., he can solve a problem requiring the completion of a third projection from two given projections if he knows the graphic rules for constructing a basis for projective relations, thus reconstructing a representation of this projection without first having a clear visual image of it. The second student may even take longer than the first student to solve the problem.

This example demonstrates that the difficulty in identifying the individual features of two students in terms of a chosen index may be attributed to factors whose effect we tried to even out in the design of the problems. Often, an identical result (in this case, the performance of graphic activity) conceals totally different processes of attaining it; we believe that identifying these different processes is of great diagnostic value. In order to highlight this process so that individual image-expressive aptitudes could be seen with maximal clarity, we attempted, on the one hand, to provide a content which would fix this process and on the other, to develop methods of establishing the content without resorting to the complex graphic knowledge and habits of mechanical drawing for this purpose.

Problems using graphic material (geometric and projective drawings, engineering diagrams, sketches) could be done on paper using simple techniques understood by all the students: drawing elementary geometric figures by hand (triangles, rectangles), completing standard tables, adding cross-hatchings to a model, applying well-known symbolic notation, and so forth. Because of these simple techniques, our subjects did not have to perform complicated graphic work to solve the problems and we were able to objectively establish the process by which each problem was solved (the types of errors, difficulties, etc.). Moreover, this made the problems wittier, more standardized, and applicable for use with well-known material, and also enabled us to use more uniform methods to process the resulting data and apply quantitative analytic criteria.

Techniques for the Use of Diagnostic Problems

The diagnostic tests we will present here consist of series of problems. Ten such problems were developed, broken down in terms of developmental degree of complexity. Each such problem displays all the basic indices described above.

The sequence of the problems, along with instructions for solving them, are rigidly determined. Special emphasis is placed on the development of units of measurement of completely solved problems, as well as units which may be used by the experimenter to monitor the process by which each problem is solved. This is especially important, inasmuch as the problems consist of the manipulation of images, and, as is well known, it is quite difficult to monitor a process that takes place in the mind. Self-testing methods have been developed for each type of problem, based on a preliminary analysis of the content. The methods are provided to each student, along with instructions which annotate the content of the problem. Because the instructions are isolated, the instructor is able to establish the course of the problem-solving process and describe it in terms of definite quantitative indices. The time spent by the student in solving each problem is also recorded. This helps create conditions for standardizing the experimental design, and guarantees that the results will be comparable with respect to a number of particular indices.

A model or key solution, i.e., the most correct and optimal solution, was developed for each problem. By comparing this standard to the student's solution, it is possible to establish allowable tolerances for deviation from the standard in each student's solution. Let us now give the actual problems, along with a brief description of the procedure used in solving them.

Problem 1. Identify the Simple Polygons in a Drawing

Directions. Look at the drawing (Figure 2). Determine what polygons may be found in the drawing, and how many of each. You need not draw each polygon; instead just write down its alphabetic label and give it a number corresponding to the sequence in which it occurs. Different polygons may be obtained by combining elements of the drawing in different ways. Try to identify all the polygons as completely as possible. Start to work.

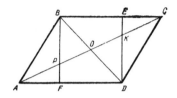

Figure 2.

Analysis of the Solution. From this drawing, it is possible to identify 24 polygons (twenty triangles and four quadrilaterals, including two trapezoids and two rectangles). This can be achieved not only through visual identification of directly observable figures, but also by applying various conceptual analytic criteria which make it possible to mentally rearrange the different elements of the drawing and thereby identify more and more quadrilaterals. The range of identification is determined by writing down on paper in a conventional notation the total number of polygons and the sequence in which they are found. As an example, let us consider the solution to the problem by sixth-grader S.A. (identifying quadrangles in Figure 2):

1) △*APF*, 2) △*ABP*, 3) △*ABF*, 4) △*ABC*, 5) △*ACD*, 6)△*AKD*,
7) △*AOD*, 8) △*EKC*, 9) △*KDC*, 10) △*EDC*, 11) △*PBC*, 12) △*BOC*,
13) △*OKD*, 14) △*ABD*.

This example shows that S.A. employed precise analytic criteria. In scanning the drawing, he systematically moved in a clockwise direction from the lower left point to the upper right point. He started with point *A* as his initial point of reference, and by means of this point identified eight triangles, then using point *C* he identified five more triangles. The two extreme symmetric points of the drawing now became his reference point. However, he did not identify all the polygons (he found 14 out of a total of 20 triangles). He found no quadrilaterals (trapezoids and rectangles) whatsoever. Thus, by establishing the process by which the problem is solved, we can judge the degree of creativity displayed in the problem-solving process.

The actual completion of the problem is judged according to three basic criteria: (1) the geometric features of the polygons found; (2) identification capacity—the number of polygons found; and (3) the sequence of identification. The subject's identification capacity is defined as the ratio of the number of polygons found to the total number in the model solution. The index may be computed by the formula,

$$V = \frac{\Sigma_n}{N}$$

where N is the number of polygons given in the drawing, and Σ_n the total number of polygons found by the subject (with values in the range). The sequence in which figures are identified from the drawing may be judged from the ordinal number of each figure. Its geometric characteristics are established in the symbolic and alphabetic notation.

The problem was tested on 1,000 subjects. Because of its simplicity, it could be used with subjects in different age groups, and it did not require complex systems of knowledge. On the average, it took eight minutes to complete the test. The test served as a good tool for differentiating subjects by ability to transform a given drawing mentally, using for this purpose various analytic criteria (sensory and conceptual). Different versions of the problem were used in order to adapt it to the age of the subject. Different versions took the form of the same problem with different types of graphic material, using both two- and three-dimensional figures.[3]

Problem 2. Find the Intersection of Three Figures

Directions. Look carefully at the drawing and find the intersection of the three figures (circle, triangle, and rectangle) (Figure 3). Once you have found the intersection, shade it in by hand using a pencil or assign it a suitable letter.

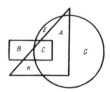

Figure 3.

Analysis of the Solution. Solving the problem requires the student to mentally overlay three plane figures (circle, triangle, rectangle) by means of superimposition, thereby determining their relative position in space. The material is based on two-dimensional representations of geometric figures, along with projections of a group of solids of revolution. Varying the complexity of the problem by means of the number of objects and the methods of representing them), we were able to create different versions, each of which may be presented to a particular category of subjects based on their age and past experience. The correctness of the completed problem was checked by analyzing the contour of the shaded plane of the drawing. Various attempts at a solution were also determined. The mean time for solving the problem was 4 minutes 22 seconds. The problem was tested on a large group (600 subjects).

Problem 3. Establishing Similarities and Differences between Illustrations

Directions. Look at the illustration and state: a) whether there is any difference in Figure 4 between diagrams 1 and 2, and if so, what it is; b) which of the planes in Figure 5 (a, b, a_1, b_1) are closer to you, and how you determine this. Give your answer to the first question in writing (briefly); in answering the second question, write down the names of the planes, for example, a is closer than b, a_1 is closer than b_1.

Analysis of the Solution. Depending upon the reference point (the angle of view) adopted, the pair of diagrams in Figure 4 may be perceived as identical or as different. The flexibility and correctness with which the

Figure 4.

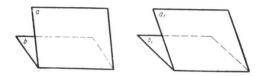

Figure 5.

diagrams are compared are determined from an analysis of the criteria used by the subject. The problem can be used to identify what the subject prefers to rely upon, direct review of the desired relations or logical reasoning based on graphic knowledge. The mean time for completing the problem was 5 minutes 4 seconds. The problem was tested on 100 subjects.

As an example, let us give the solution produced by seventh-grader M.V. "These diagrams (Figure 4) may be thought of as different or the same, depending upon what we wish to see in them," declares M.V. "No, excuse me, they are different. In fact here (pointing to diagram 2 of Figure 4) there are invisible outlines, which means that it is three-dimensional... Aha, one figure is two-dimensional, and the other is three-dimensional. There is the first difference. Let us look further. If we look at the outline, it becomes clear that both figures are hexahedrons. This is what they share. And how do they differ? One (diagram 1 of Figure 4) is a hexagon with diagonals that intersect at the center, while the other (diagram 2) is a cube. If the point of intersection of the diagonals is mentally 'stretched' up towards us, we no longer have a two-dimensional figure, but a three-dimensional one, in the form of a roof over a small box, and if we straighten it out, we have a plane six-corner star which can be considered a projection of a hexagonal prism..."

This example shows that M.V. referred to a rather large number of attributes, which enabled him to pick out what was common and different in the two visual representations. He displayed a degree of perceptual dynamism, evidenced in his ability to arbitrarily shift points of reference. However, many students gave answers which were less complete and elaborate than in our example. These answers were graded by the number of attributes identified by the subjects (some found one or two attributes, while others five, six, or even more), and by the qualitative distinctiveness of their approach to the solution. The technique used in solving the problem was also taken into account. For example, it was found that students may solve the problem correctly using different techniques. Some may establish a difference between the figures using purely visual means ("I can see it, but can't explain why"), while others give a detailed, reasoned answer that explicitly identifies conceptual attributes for comparing the illustrations ("plane," "projection," "shift in reference point," etc.).

Problem 4. Determining the Relative Position of the Elements of a Diagram

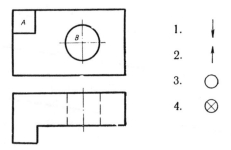

Figure 6.

Directions. Look at the drawing in Figure 6. Using this drawing, visualize the object and its constituent parts (*A* and *B*). Decide how these parts are arranged relative to the observer. Once you have visualized the object from its representation, determine the spatial position of elements *A* and *B*, and give your answer, using for this purpose the notation beside the figure. These symbols have the following meanings: 1) projection toward us; 2) projection away us; 3) open hole; 4) closed hole. In order to do the problem, the subject must write down the proper sign. The problem does not require graphic work involving the construction of a drawing.

Analysis of the Solution. The problem outwardly resembles an ordinary school exercise in reading a drawing. Unlike the latter, however, it does not require creating an expressive image of an illustrated object as a whole or describing its shape and size. Instead, the subject must establish spatial relations between only two elements of the rectangular plate depicted in the drawing: the hole and the square projection (whether the hole is open or closed one, whether the projection is on the front or back of the plate).

Of course, in the course of determining the spatial position of these elements ideas about the shape and size of the elements arose, although these ideas did not become a special subject of analysis, but remained in the background, based on which spatial relations could be used in "pure form," a result which was of major diagnostic value. Other analogous versions of this problem were also used.

In order to determine how these relations are established in these problems, we avoided the common procedure of asking the student to create an drawing from the diagram, and instead asked them to fill in a special table of conventional symbols (a table was designed for each version of the problem). This made it possible to judge objectively how subjects represented spatial relations between elements depicted in the drawing, what errors they made, and what difficulties they experienced, without requiring them to make graphic constructions. (Diagrams represented objects with various degrees of complexity.) This problem and its different versions were given to students in grades 7-9 who were already

familiar with the rules for reading diagrams.[4] The mean time for solving
the problem was 3 minutes 34 seconds. The problem was tested on 102
subjects.

Problem 5. Comparing Representations by Mental Rotation

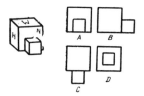

Figure 7.

Directions. Look at the representation of a model in Figure 7. Turn the
model around in your mind so that each sides faces you in turn, and tell
which of the views (*A*, *B*, *C*, or *D*) corresponds to the position of the
model where we see face *W*, *N*, or *H*? Is it possible to see it as it is depicted
in *A*, *B*, *C*, and *D*? You do not have to redraw the views. Turning the
model around in your mind so that it assumes one position after another,
correlate it with the corresponding representation and write it down in
this form: *N-A*.

Analysis of the Solution. The problem material was a three-dimensional representation of an object and a diagram of the same object. In
order to select the correct representation, the three correct projections of
the object were complemented with an incorrect one (*D*). The problem
was aimed not just at reconstructing an image from a diagram, but also
for rotating and correlating the image with given representations (the
rotation is realized outside the plane). The mean time for solving the
problem was 4 minutes 18 seconds. An experiment showed that the
problem is understandable to students in different grades. It was tested
on 60 subjects (students in grades 4-9 and adults). As an example, let us
give a correct solution of the problem by seventh-grader S.R,: *N-A*; *W-C*;
H-B.

Problem 6. Recognizing an Object by Comparing Different Representations of It

Directions. Determine how many different objects are depicted on the card in front of you (Figure 8). Consider the illustrations carefully, and determine which of them show the same object and which show different objects. Find and place in parentheses the numbers corresponding to identical objects.

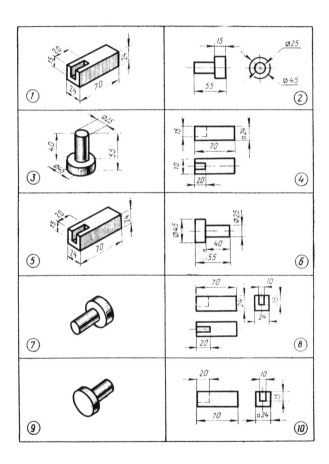

Figure 8.

Analysis of the Solution. The problem calls for the mental correlation of 10 different types of representations (drawing, diagram, sketch) of two objects. It also determines the subject's ability to create an image from various representations, and checks the flexibility with which he manipulates images. It is accessible to students who are familiar with the various types of representations. The mean time to solve it was 5 minutes 24 seconds. The problem was tested on 254 students (it was designed by Botvinnikov).

After receiving the test card (Figure 8), the student must look at it carefully and answer questions arranged schematically. For this purpose, each student is given the following special answer sheet:

Problem	Answer
1. Give the numbers of the isometrics and the drawings.	
2. Tell me which attributes you used to distinguish between drawings and diagrams.	
3. What is the difference between a drawing and a diagram?	
4. How many different objects are depicted on the card? Find and place in parentheses the numbers of the identical objects.	
5. Which attributes did you use to select illustrations of identical objects?	
6. Explain how an illustration of the same object can be distinguished correctly, i.e., starting with a drawing, find its diagram, or starting with a diagram, find its drawing.	
7. Are the objects labeled 1-4 and 2-3 identical? Justify your answer.	
8. What is the difference between illustrations 7, 9, and 3?	

In responding to the questions, the student not only establishes the results of his own actions, but also discusses them in detail, which makes it possible to identify his available criteria for selecting and comparing representations. This also makes it possible to establish individual approaches to solving the problem and analyze their psychological nature.

Problem 7. Mental Construction of Figures from Given Triangles

Directions. Given four congruent right triangles (Figure 9). Mentally create the following figures from these triangles, using all four in each case: a triangle, rectangle, rhombus, trapezoid, hexagon, and a parallelogram which is neither a rhombus nor a rectangle. How many different figures can you create? In completing the problem, recall that each figure you have created must contain all four triangles. Do all your trials on paper. The result must be given in the form of a figure drawn by hand.

Figure 9.

Analysis of the Solution. Constructing figures from other given figures requires a number of different mental transformations, e.g., unification, superimposition, rotation, and the convergence of figures both within the same plane and outside it. The initial figures must be combined as stated in the problem. Students have the greatest difficulty in making the hexagon.[5] The mean time for solving the problem was 11 minutes 40 seconds. The problem was tested on 60 subjects of different ages. As an example, we present in Figure 10 the solution by S.V. (a fifth-grader), including both correct and incorrect attempts.

Problem 8. Mental Transformation of a Given Representation

Directions. In trapezoid *ABCD*, *K* is the midpoint of side *A* (Figure 11). Imagine that the trapezoid is cut along line *KC* and that triangle *CBK*

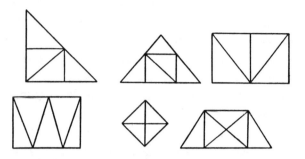

Figure 10.

Is rotated about point K so that segments KB and KA coincide. What figure does the trapezoid turn into? After you have finished the problem, construct a diagram and show which points will coincide.

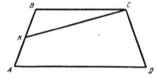

Figure 11.

Analysis of the Solution. The problem calls for the creation of an image from a diagram by a group of mental transformations (a "cut," rotation, and superimposition). As a result, the subject produces a new image which reflects these transformations. There are two solutions to the problem. The mental rotation may be realized through central (Figure 12) or axial symmetry (Figure 13). The problem is also interesting because it enables us to identify the ability to "see" the compatibility of elements of an image in different planes (in this case, the front and rear planes). Moreover, solution of the problem requires the ability to carry out the mental transformations both within the plane as well as outside it, which is extremely important for mastering not only the school course in mathematics, but also descriptive geometry in college. As a result of these transformations, the initial trapezoid becomes a triangle *CDF* in the first case (Figure 12), and a hexagon $DCKAF_IN$ in the second (Figure 13). The mean time for completing the problem was 9 minutes. The problem was tested on 50 subjects.

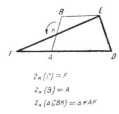

$$Z_K(C) = F$$
$$Z_n(B) = A$$
$$Z_n(\triangle CBK) = \triangle KAF$$

Figure 12.

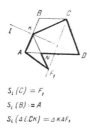

$$S_L(C) = F_I$$
$$S_L(B) = A$$
$$S_L(\triangle LCK) = \triangle KAF_I$$

Figure 13.

Problem 9. Constructing the Image of a Machine Part from an Analysis of Its Production Chart

Directions. We are given a drawing of a metal blank (Figure 14) and a description of its complete production cycle. In a cylindrical part measuring 62 mm in diameter and 100 mm in length, a hole is created according to the technique indicated in the production chart.

Determine how the part is processed. Create a mental image of the part and a diagram of it. For this purpose, visualize its outer view based on the diagram of the metal blank. Then try to imagine what changes in the shape, size, and spatial position it will undergo in the course of machining. Then imagine the final configuration of the part. Give the results of these transformations in a diagram. A model solution is given in Figure 15.

Production Chart

Operation	Assembly	Step	Assembly Sequence of Steps
1	A		Clamp billet in 3-jawed chuck
		1	Drill hole 24 mm in diameter and 100 mm in length
		2	Bore hole to 32 mm in diameter to depth of 55 mm
		3	Bore hole to 41 mm in diameter to depth of 22 mm
		4	Bore a 40-mm diameter bevel measuring 2 x 45° all around

Analysis of the Solution. The problem material consists of a diagram of a structurally simple metal blank. The diagram was complemented with instruction charts giving a description (verbal or graphic) of which transformations were to be performed. Once they had done them in their minds, the subjects could then visualize an image of the finished part. These transformations were performed simultaneously with respect to three features (shape, size, and spatial position). It was necessary to mentally trace the dynamics of these changes and fix them in the image. The repeated multidimensional transformation of "intermediate" images led to the final result, also in representational form.[6]

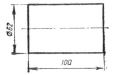

Figure 14.

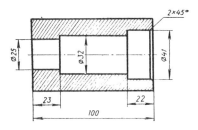

Figure 15.

The graphic material used in the problem consisted of diagrams of metal blanks, sketches of the manufacturing steps, and working diagrams of the parts. Using this graphic material, the subjects were supposed to perform a number of mental transformations and thereby complete the problem. Different versions of the problem were developed, distinguished by the graphic material employed, although with the same psychological content. In each version, it was necessary to imagine an image of the finished part from a drawing of the metal blank. In their various versions, these problems were presented to groups of subjects from different age groups and with varying amounts of educational (or professional) experience. The time it took to solve the problems varied as a function of their degree of complexity, although it did not exceed 15 minutes, since the computational part did not have to be performed, that is, it was only necessary to create a correct image and fix it as a sketch. The problem was tested on 75 students in the grades 8-10 and 100 students at a technical institute.

Problem 10. Create an Evolute of a Manufactured Item from a Model
Directions. Given a drawing of a shaft collar (Figure 16). Using this drawing, visualize the collar in full view and draw a diagram of it.

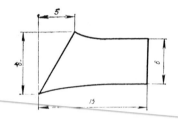

Figure 16.

Analysis of the Solution. In this highly simplified case, the subject must mentally supply the other half of the collar, connect it to the visible half, and picture the object as a whole, indicating correctly its shape and size. The mean time for solving the problem was 10 minutes 12 seconds. The problem was tested on 165 fourth graders. More complex versions of similar problems were also used; for the brevity's sake, we will not give them here.

Thus, all 10 problems reflect different types of manipulation of spatial images;[7] although created from different types of graphic material, all of them can be used to evaluate manipulation type and flexibility, along with image comprehensiveness, since they require constant manipulation of the shape, size, and spatial position of represented objects. From an analysis of these problems, it is clear that they impose different requirements on the level of image manipulation and, in their very content, reproduce different types of manipulation. For example, type I transformations are required in problems 1-5, type II in problems 6 and 7, and type III in problems 8-10. The problems were systematized and made into a book containing, besides the problems, all illustrations and instructions for the solution of each problem.

The description of the problems demonstrates that all of them call for the mental creation and manipulation of images. The problems include different types of image manipulation (from the simple to the complex) and make it possible to evaluate various abilities that contribute to the structure of the aptitude for thinking spatially: the ability to reinterpret diagrams, using for this purpose various analytical criteria (perceptual and categorical); the ability to vary one's reference point and see the movement of objects from static representations; the ability to create different transformations of an initial image (by rotation, superimposition, unification, etc.); the ability to convey in the image not only shape and size, but also the dynamic spatial distribution of its individual elements; and so forth. The different versions of the same problem make it possible to determine the student's "receptivity" to assistance and ability to transfer previously solution techniques to new problems.[8]

Experience shows that the problems can be used in a variety of situations, and that solving them requires relatively simple techniques. The time it takes to solve each problem averages 3-5 minutes. Problems with have several different versions take longer to complete, although their solution time does not exceed 10-15 minutes (cf. problems 7, 8, and 9). The development of special units for each problem that to establish the result (and in some cases, the process of obtaining it) help standardize data processing methods, and ensure uniform testing conditions. The problems were used with familiar material, which made it possible to identify certain developmental elements in their solution.[9] They also made it possible to differentiate students' ability to mentally perform various spatial transformations. In our experience, 95% of the students regarded the tests as novel and interesting. The problems had not been encountered in their ordinary classroom activity in the precise form in which they were tested. Let us now give several examples of such assertions by the students.

"The problems are interesting, since you have to do a good job of thinking and visualize everything in your mind properly." "The problems aren't difficult, in fact they are interesting. They seem kind of unusual and enticing. They are kind of familiar, for example, problems 1 and 6 are also found in geometry and mechanical drawing, but there it is necessary to apply rules, while here we just have to imagine." "We don't do problems like these in class. Of course, the girls who had already solved them talked about them at recess. I thought I had to recite certain theorems and rules, but it turned out that it wasn't so much a matter of remembering, as of visualizing how to perform the transformations."

The distribution of problems in terms of their mean solution time is given below. These times were derived on the basis of the solution times of 100 subjects from different age groups. The shortest solution time was found with problem 4 (3 minutes 30 seconds), and the longest with problem 9 (50 minutes). The distribution of the other problems in terms of solution time is as follows: problem 4: 3 minutes 34 seconds; problem 5: 4 minutes 18 seconds; problem 2: 4 minutes 22 seconds; problem 3: 5 minutes 4 seconds; problem 6: 5 minutes 24 seconds; problem 1: 8 minutes; [10] problem 8: 9 minutes; problem 10: 10 minutes 12 seconds; problem 7: 11 minutes 40 seconds; and problem 9: 15 minutes.

These quantitative data show that, first, the problems could all be solved within a comparatively brief time (3-15 minutes), and second, that the solution time reflects their difficulty, as is confirmed by a qualitative analysis. The longest mean solution times are found with those problems which require more complex spatial transformations. Thus, the most difficult problems were 7, 8, 9, and 10, and their solution times were the longest (11 minutes 40 seconds, 9 minutes, 10 minutes 12 seconds, and 15 minutes, respectively).

The distribution of the problems in terms of difficulty, as expressed in the amount of time spent in solving them, also coincides with the subjects' own evaluations as they did the problems. Thus, 50% the subjects regarded problems 7, 8, and 9 as among the most difficult ones; problems 1, 2, 4, and 5 were regarded as the simplest. This permits us to assert that the ordinal rank of correctly solved problems by solution time can serve as a quantitative index of the level of development of the student's spatial thinking.

In using these problems for diagnostic purposes, we ranked them in terms of various criteria (objective and subjective difficulty, solution time), and determined a common sequence of presentation of the problems. This sequence is important when using the problems in group experiments and for guaranteeing unambiguous results. For diagnostic purposes, we presented the problems strictly in the sequence in which they are described above (from one through ten). This is important for identifying the level of development of spatial thinking. The sequential transition from problem 1 to 2, to 3, and so forth, signals gradually more complicated problems from the standpoint of the requirements imposed on the mental manipulation of images. Thus, problems 1, 2, and 3 require the ability to manipulate dynamic spatial images based on the perception of graphic representations (by altering one's reference point). Problems 4, 5, and 6 require that subjects abstract from initial representations and manipulate images created on the basis of these representations by applying different spatial transformations.

Problems 7, 8, 9, and 10 require the ability to simultaneously manipulate several different types of representation (isometric diagrams, geometric and projective drawings, stages in sequence). Different mental transformations are carried out simultaneously (in terms of shape, size, and spatial position). Therefore, within the context of other conditions, the ordinal number of a problem is of great importance for describing the student's ability to perform mental transformations of spatial images.

Experimental Evaluation of the Diagnostic Methodology in Practical Teaching

In applying our technique for diagnostic purposes, we wanted to determine whether it was possible to differentiate students by the characteristics described here, and also how the data obtained compare to other indices. Our evaluation was organized in the following way. The subjects were 30 eighth-graders at Boarding School No. 72 in Moscow. The students were all the same age and were placed under the same teaching conditions. An individual lesson was conducted with each student, while he solved all the diagnostic problems described above. The sequence of problem presentation and requirements imposed by the problems were the same for all subjects. No additional explanation was given (other than those called for in the instructions). Therefore, all subjects were under the same conditions during their solution of each problem. No preliminary information about the subjects' grades in school was provided. The results obtained for each subject were processed for: 1) the mean solution for each problem; 2) the number of problems solved per unit of time (30 min); 3) the correctness of each solution (compared with the model solution); 4) the number of correctly solved problems as a percentage of the total number of problems; and 5) the numbers of problems the subject solved correctly. We should add that since the problems were conducted individually, the quantitative indices were complemented with an analysis of typical errors and difficulties. The most interesting problem-solving techniques were also identified.

Each subject was then asked to complete a questionnaire to indicate: 1) his grades in geometry, design, mechanical drawing, and shop; 2) his favorite subject; and 3) his most typical difficulties in geometry. The students' responses to the questionnaire were supplemented by discussions with their teachers and tutors. These discussions were aimed at identifying the reasons for each subject's difficulties in geometry and mechanical drawing. For purposes of evaluating spatial thinking, geometry is the most "symptomatic" of all the subjects in the mathematics cycle, since spatial relations arise in a highly diverse set of problems in the geometry course. For this reason, the student's grade in the course becomes one of the basic indices for us. Finally, once these data had been obtained, we compared the results of our test problems with certain "real-life" indices, and thereby verifying the reliability and correctness of our technique.

The "diagnostic" and "real-life" indices were comparable for several reasons. First, the diagnostic problems were distributed by level of complexity based on a theoretical analysis. The level of complexity of a problem was determined by the type of image manipulation (from simple to more complex, depending on the qualitative character of the actual manipulation). This index correlates with others, e.g., manipulability, comprehensiveness of the spatial attributes reproduced by the image, and image dynamism. This made it possible to evaluate the level of complexity of a problem with respect to not one, but an entire series of indices whose correlation was determined by a qualitative analysis of the structure of spatial thinking.

Second, each of our indices was evaluated with respect to its stability by developing and applying various versions of the problems in our experiment. Third, once the experimental problems had all been distributed by level of complexity, we were able to experimentally identify the degree of creativity displayed in students' problem-solving based on a number of qualitative and quantitative indices (the solution time, the number of problems solved per unit of time, the percentage of correct solutions, types of problems solved correctly by the subject, the number of promptings from the experimenter, the type of visual aid, and so forth). Fourth, by establishing the level of spatial thinking with respect to a number of indices (we used approximately 12), we were able to correlate our indices with certain real-life indices, e.g., interest in forms of activity (educational, occupational, play) where the manipulation of spatial images constitutes an independent problem: the degree of success in solving the problems; the subject's effort to independently develop his aptitude for solving spatial brain teasers, and so forth.

These factors together made it possible not only to evaluate the reliability and correctness of our technique, but also to use it for qualitatively describing the typological (developmental and individual) features of the student's spatial thinking. This helped us distribute the subjects into the three basic groups, which we will now describe briefly.

The first group included subjects who displayed the highest degree of creativity in solving the test problems. They solved all the problems quickly, easily, and with flexibility. The average time spent on each problem was at most 3 minutes 6 seconds to 4 minutes 9 seconds, with a high percentage of completed problems (80-90%) and correct solutions (8-9 out of 10 problems). These students successfully handled problems at varying levels of complexity, requiring the manipulation of different types of images. They also displayed a high degree of manipulability, as shown in the freedom and ease with which they used totally different representations, both visual and conventional. Typically, even where they lacked knowledge, they had no trouble with the problems, orienting themselves rapidly in the initial representations and regrouping individual elements in their minds. They were distinguished by their effort to find the most economical methods of solving the problems and the flexibility with which they moved from one problem to another, as well as their spontaneous use of various problem-solving methods. These subjects described all the problems as easy but interesting, requiring not so much knowledge as quick-wittedness and resourcefulness.

In their manipulation of spatial images, they handled shape, size, and spatial relations with an equal degree of creativity, and utilized various reference points to establish these relations. Changes in the reference point made at the experimenter's request caused them no special difficulty, but rather were received with interest, arousing independent desire and effort to transform images, yielding highly mobile and dynamic new images.

In comparing our data to the real-life indices, we found that the students in this group had average grades (a "B" average) in the corresponding subjects. Interestingly, in response to the question, "What is your favorite subject?", nine of the twelve students in this group listed geometry, mechanical drawing, shop, and design, and only three mentioned literature, biology (anatomy), and history. In response to the question about their difficulties in subjects which require highly developed spatial thinking, they usually declared that they did not always learn theorems by heart, forgot graphic rules, and so forth, but had no difficulty whenever it is necessary to "visualize" or find desired relations in a drawing or mentally transform a preexisting spatial image in solving a problem. Most of the students in this group found the experimental problems interesting, and expressed a desire to continue working along these lines in the future. All of them asked us to talk to them about their spatial thinking and help them improve it.

The second group of subjects consisted of students who on the whole were able to handle many of the problems, although their speed and the quality of their performance differed substantially from the indices of the first group. The mean time spent on solving each problem increased significantly in these subjects (to 5-6 minutes), and the overall percentage of completed problems fell to 60-70%, although the percentage of correct problems out of the total number of problems completed remained quite high. They displayed a low level of creativity in solving problems 7, 8, and 9 compared with the subjects in the first group.

The increase in solution time derives from a number of reasons. On the one hand, compared with the first group, the students in this group solved the problems with great care, showing a deliberate desire for accuracy and precision. They carefully checked their completed solutions several times, and worried about making mistakes and giving incorrect responses, which was not exhibited at all by students of the first group. Moreover, they displayed a different approach to the problems which could be termed "reasoning." While the subjects in the first group established the necessary relations in the diagrams quickly "on the spot," the subjects in the second group tried to replace direct observation of these relations by a chain of reasoning, relying basically on knowledge and paths of logic. This is particularly clear in problems 3, 4, and 7. For example, while students in the first group defended their method of solving problem 3 by claiming that "that's how they saw it, that's how they visualized it," students in the second group attempted to base their response on rules or theorems that they knew. Let us consider an example. In determining which of two planes is closer to the observer, Tanya P. (grade 7) said, "I think *a* is closer to us than *b*. Of course, there is a dotted line, and we know that dotted lines show an invisible object or a hidden part of it. So plane *b* lies behind plane *a*."

Even though the subjects have enough knowledge, they still have considerable difficulty whenever they have to perform mental spatial transformations. This is confirmed by the fact that the subjects in this group regarded problems 6, 7, 8, and 9 as interesting, although the most difficult. The percentage of problems solved correctly fell sharply. We should emphasize that the subjects in the second group had no difficulty creating images from drawings and were well aware of the differences between conventional representations.

Their main difficulty arose when it was necessary to manipulate spatial images, vary the reference point, and transform spatial relations. Here the following fact is quite clear. The subjects in this group found it difficult to dynamically vary a preexisting image. Once the image was created from the initial graphic base, they tried to preserve it in this form in every way possible. If it was necessary to manipulate the image, i.e., mentally alter it in some respect, the image disappeared, according to the subjects, became "blurred," and seemed to dissolve, which often led to its total loss. The subjects utilized various auxiliary techniques (not always rational ones) to make it easier to "retain" the image, but it was not always possible; this made them uncertain of their completed solutions. The students in this group willingly took advantage of the experimenter's assistance, but were too embarrassed to talk about their difficulties, possibly because they lacked a clear awareness of them and could not describe them.

The results obtained from our tests, compared with the real-life indices, indicated that none of the students in this group regarded geometry or shop as their favorite subjects; two of the twelve students did cite design. The other ten students named biology (anatomy, zoology), algebra, chemistry, Russian, and geography as their favorite subjects. Their mean grades in subjects which require graphic preparation varied from "B" to "C". In assessing their own difficulties in these subjects, the students usually remarked that they assiduously memorized all the rules, but could not discern the necessary spatial relations quickly. The mental manipulation of preexisting images presented special difficulties to them. Their verbal responses fully confirmed the objective data obtained from our problems.

The students in this group participated in our experimental research willingly, but were shy and timid, uncertain of their abilities and afraid to make mistakes in solving the problems. In their work, they often resorted to various auxiliary techniques, e.g., keeping their pencil in the portion of the illustration in which they were working, covering their eyes in order to visualize the spatial transformation they were mentally performing, readily utilizing any promptings from the experimenter, and willingly switching to cardboard models and physical manipulation of the represented objects. They tired quickly and lost interest in their work, although they outwardly appeared to continue thinking about the problem and did not overtly give up on it.

Comparison of these two groups of students made it possible to evaluate the diagnostic value of our technique. It also demonstrated that school grades are of insufficient diagnostic value, since they may be a symptom of the extremely varied indices. Grades of "B" were obtained by subjects in both the first and second groups who had very different ability to manipulate spatial images.

The third group included students who found it difficult to solve the majority of the problems. In these students, the mean problem-solving time ranged from 6 minutes 28 seconds to 9 minutes 20 seconds. The percentage of completed problems was in the 30-40% range. Typically, their methods of attacking the problems also differed sharply from the methods used by the students in the first and second groups.

The students in the third group attempted to solve the problems stubbornly and with a low level of independence, particularly in problems with complex content. They were able to solve only problems 1 and 2 (and different versions of them) on their own, without assistance from the experimenter, but even in these problems their level of creativity was quite low. For example, in problem 1 they found a comparatively small number of figures (50%) or, alternatively, described the same figure several times without noticing this fact. This attests to the difficulties they experienced when they had to change reference points and regard the representations from different points of view (problems 3 and 4). They found it particularly difficult to complete problems where they had to mentally manipulate spatial images. They were able to solve problem 7 only by means of cardboard models of triangles, and only when these models could be physically manipulated. The students first stacked them, forming the desired figure, and then sketched in the desired outline. In problem 6, they regularly confused the number of objects and number of representations. Each version of the problem was perceived as a new problem, even if only the drawing changed. It was also typical that they regarded more than half of the experimental problems (7 out of the 10) as difficult, although they regarded them as interesting since they had not encountered them in their lessons.

This group included students who regularly achieved average grades in geometry and mechanical drawing (particularly in geometry). As their favorite subject, three of the six students cited physical education, and the others named history and literature. These are either students with a keen interest in the humanities or poor students with no particular interest in schoolwork (or only in physical education class).

In analyzing their difficulties, these students remarked that they saw nothing in space. They were unable to employ conscious representational techniques. They regarded geometry and mechanical drawing classes as difficult and uninteresting. In response to the experimenter's remark that they should try to complete the test "imaginatively," many of them declared, sighing deeply, that "no matter how much I study, I still won't do better than a 'C'." They completed the experiment without special interest or desire. Once they were familiar with a problem, they made one or two stabs at solving it, and then stopped. They accepted the experimenter's help willingly, but were unable to make full use of it. They found it difficult to analyze their difficulties on their own or talk about them.

These facts show that by applying our technique for diagnostic purposes, it becomes possible to differentiate students with respect to these abilities. The three groups we have identified correspond to different levels of development of spatial thinking (which we may refer to provisionally as high, medium, and low). Thus, we have every reason for claiming that our technique makes it possible to "diagnose" difficulties in the development of spatial thinking in certain students, analyze the psychological nature of these difficulties, and on this basis, design a program of individualized remedial work (determining the nature and quantity of educational help, the content of practice exercises, they conditions under which they should be presented, etc.).

However, a number of issues still require refinement and further improvement. In particular, we need a finer differentiation of the real-life indices, refinement in the content of school evaluations, a deeper analysis of reasons for difficulties in geometry and mechanical drawing, an understanding of their psychological nature, and so forth. Since there were different versions of each experimental problem, our technique made it possible to determine not just the level of development of spatial thinking, but also its stability. However, since the number of different versions of each problem varied widely (from one to ten), it was difficult to achieve a reliable assessment of how stable the level of development of spatial thinking was as a whole from any one problem. Improvement in our technique along these lines is required.

For the time being, we may be certain that in terms of its basic trends, design principles, and results of experimental evaluation, our technique is fully adequate to diagnose the present level of development of spatial thinking formed through graphic activity. Furthermore, because of scientific and technical progress, graphic activity is playing an increasingly important role in the overall structure of educational activity. The postsecondary (professional) school, along with the secondary general-educational school has acute need for such techniques today.

We must not forget that because of the specific nature of its content, each school subject mandates its own set of distinctive requirements for the development of spatial thinking in students. Therefore, it would be particularly interesting to design modified techniques for identifying and evaluating the current level of development of spatial thinking within the framework of a particular school subject. Such techniques have been developed by I.Ya. Kaplunovich and V.S. Stoletnev, working under our general supervision. Let us briefly describe these techniques.

Kaplunovich [1978] attempted to develop a method of diagnosing the structure of spatial thinking based on a theoretical interpretation of this structure. His purpose was to determine psychologically-based methods of nurturing this structure in teaching mathematics. Starting from the assumption that optimal development of spatial thinking (with respect to the indices we have considered) may be achieved by building up its structure, i.e., essentially the homomorphic group of affine transformations in mathematics, Kaplunovich designed a scheme for analyzing the structure of spatial thinking in the form of a matrix. In this matrix, the geometric transformations in the plane and in space included in the mathematics curriculum (grades 4-9) are laid out along the vertical axis, and the level of comprehension of these transformations, as determined from three types of manipulation of spatial images, is placed along the horizontal axis.

This technique made it possible to identify poorly developed elements in the structure of spatial thinking in certain students, and determine the primary direction of remedial work with them (selection of exercises, their sequence of presentation, the technique to be followed, etc.). It was found that students could be differentiated with respect to the three types of manipulation of spatial images corresponding to levels of development of spatial thinking. In his study, Kaplunovich employed a diagnostic technique he developed to give a description and qualitative specification of these levels with respect to a number of indices (the complexity of mathematical operations comprehensible to the students, and the arbitrariness, generality, awareness, and dynamism with which they are carried out).

In particular, it was found that the first or lowest level of development of spatial thinking lacks a number of mathematical operations in its very structure. The operation of rotation creates particular difficulties. Kaplunovich remarked that this is because in all other operations (parallel translation, homothety, symmetry, parallel and orthogonal projections), the displacement of objects occurs along straight lines, whereas in a rotation objects move along the arc of a circle; this movement presents greater psychological difficulty. Thus, a rotation involves not linear, but angular measurement, and mental manipulation of the operation is far more complicated.

The most highly developed, third level of spatial thinking comprises not only individual transformation operations, but also systems of operations. Moreover, all the operations are performed creatively, consciously, dynamically, and with generality. This factor serves as an index of elaboration of the structure of spatial thinking with respect to these qualities.[11]

Kaplunovich's technique consists of a series of experimental problems by means of which it is possible to identify the student's current level of development of spatial thinking—that is, give a qualitative and quantitative description of this level—and evaluate its stability and receptivity to teaching. Use of this technique with students of various ages has shown that the level of development of spatial thinking, as defined basically by the type of image manipulation comprehensible to the student, is very stable. This type of manipulation can be "shaken" only by means of a specially organized teaching program which takes into account the actual difficulties experienced by students in manipulating images.

Kaplunovich's diagnostic technique can be used to reveal the individual structure of spatial thinking and its level of development in individual students. The technique makes it possible not only to evaluate, but also to nurture spatial thinking effectively through mathematics teaching. The technique is quite flexible, and so it may be used under both classroom conditions (to evaluate students' work, tests may be differentiated by degree of complexity), as well as in individual work with students aimed at developing their spatial thinking.

A second version of this technique that identifies the level of development of spatial thinking in college students has been developed by V.S. Stoletnev [1979] using material from the course in descriptive geometry. By analyzing the specific nature of this subject, together with the requirements and conditions governing the manipulation of spatial images, Stoletnev developed a classification of classroom problems by their level of complexity. The classification was based on the identification of methods for spatial transformations used in descriptive geometry and the various types of orientation (relative to oneself, or relative to any abstract system of reference, e.g., a point, a line, or a plane). The method takes into account the characteristics of graphic representations which define the conditions of problems. Using a collection of problems and exercises compiled by Stoletnev [1977], it is possible to identify the level of development of spatial thinking by means of the indices described above. Application of this technique with college students yields interesting data on the psychological nature of individual differences in spatial thinking, and helps to improve instruction.

The above discussion demonstrates that our indices of the level of development of spatial thinking are of diagnostic value. In the future, analogous techniques should be designed for courses in geography, mechanical drawing, design, and shop, wherever the development of spatial thinking is a key condition for effective learning.

Age-Group Differences in Problem-Solving Involving Spatial Transformations

Experience gained from teaching indicates that students' spatial thinking varies according to age group. This is clear from the following points.

1. The individual's store of spatial images is enriched as he grows and accumulates knowledge, abilities, and skills. The images become richer and more dynamic in content, which makes it easier to recode them. While students in grades 4-7 use the same geometric objects and graphic representations that their teacher employs in the course of a lesson and are given in their textbook, students in the grades 8, 9, and 10 often use several different versions of a representation and independently select visual material.

2. Students in the upper grades actively manipulate three- and two-dimensional images. They use different representations of both plane geometric figures and solid bodies. However, as is well known, considerable difficulties are caused, we believe, by existing teaching techniques. Students in the early grades primarily use two-dimensional representations in mathematics, and all required transformations are performed by displacing figures within the same plane. But then in the

upper grades, when they move from two- to three-dimensional geometry, they are required to manipulate three-dimensional (spatial) representations outside the plane in space. It is difficult to wean the student from his previous and firmly consolidated techniques of manipulating primarily plane (two-dimensional) representations.

3. As students grow, their attitude toward the use of visual aids for performing spatial transformations changes. In solving a problem, students in grades 4 through 7 first try to make a diagram using colored pencils, colored chalk, various types of lines, and so forth, in order to isolate spatial relations. Students in grades 8, 9, and 10 utilize these aids far less often, and usually only when they find it difficult to solve a problem.

The techniques for employing visual aids also vary. As a rule, students in grades 4 through 7 attempt to apply models of geometric bodies, drawings and simple diagrams in solving graphic problems. Students in grades 8 to 10 use a variety of sketches, schematic outlines, conventional notations, and projective drawings as their basic visual aids. Students first gain experience in working with various types of representations and thus learn about forms of representation, and subsequent instruction enables them to isolate (abstract) certain spatial properties and relations and establish them in the form of abstract diagrams.

However, as has been shown in a number of studies (M.E. Botsmanova, E.A. Faraponova, G.G. Mikulina, I.S. Yakimanskaya, and others), reliance on concrete visual aids is not so much an age-group characteristic of younger students as the result of current instructional methodology. The organization of the process of learning in a number of school subjects still rests upon the belief that thinking in the younger student is visual and concrete, and for this reason constantly requires graphic illustrations.[12] In geometry class, the presentation of any problem must include a visual representation, even though this does not help students develop abilities for solving problems imaginatively. The student is not given the responsibility to select his own form of representation, while in certain cases it is even necessary to avoid any representation and solve the problem mentally, with no reliance on graphic activity.

From this standpoint, therefore, we believe that age-group differences depend primarily on the teaching methodology. However, under the typical school conditions of mass education these differences are generally quite marked.

4. Students in the upper grades typically make conscious use of representational techniques. Unlike younger pupils, they can talk about them, evaluate their effectiveness, and analyze the difficulties they encounter when attempting to solve problems that require the manipulation of spatial images (I.Ya. Kaplunovich [1978]). As they grow older, their ability to transfer previously learned image-expressive techniques to new problems increases (L.V. Vaytkunene, I.V. Tikhomirova, M.G. Bodnar), and their ability to use generalized techniques grows. Senior students also try to analyze their own representational activity and identify their strong and weak points, which may be attributed to the heightened introspection typical of students in the upper grade. While younger students are primarily oriented to the ultimate results of their manipulation of an image, older students show greater interest in the process of attaining this result, attempting to master the most effective expressive techniques (I.S. Yakimanskaya [1978]).

Everything we have said indicates that age-group differences may be expressed all throughout our indices. We have been interested in how the indices of the level of development of spatial thinking we employed in our research varies with age. For this purpose, we studied the dynamics of age-group differences, and determined how the individual's approach to solving problems which require the manipulation of spatial images changes with age, and how school experience (accumulated knowledge, abilities, and skills) help improve expressive methods, thus making it possible to carry out transformations in the plane and in space. We used three groups of experimental techniques: 1) the diagnostic technique described above; 2) tests consisting of collections of problems and exercises requiring three types of manipulation of spatial images;[13] 3) tests within the ordinary curriculum designed to evaluate the student's ability to create and manipulate spatial images, apply various graphic representations, and perform spatial transformations. The tests also required students not only to perform the transformations correctly, but also to be able to talk about them. This provided us with information for establishing age-group differences and analyzing their psychological nature.

In order to investigate the dynamics of the age-group differences, we placed students from various grades (grades 4-9) under experimental conditions. Experiments involving the same technique were conducted in different years, during 1960-1964 and in 1968-1975. This made it possible to compare the results obtained with students of the same age, but during different periods of instruction (at a 10-year interval). A total of about 1,000 subjects participated in the experiments (500 in 1960-1964 and 479 students in 1968-1975).

The experiments were carried out both in groups and with individual students. In the group experiment, students from different grades were given written tests designed by us. The tests contained problems which we regarded as diagnostic, but at the same time also included problems found in the ordinary curriculum.[14] The tests were given systematically to students in the same grade throughout the school year in mechanical drawing and mathematics classes. They were given by the teacher following a specially developed curriculum (some of the experiments were conducted together with Botvinnikov[15]).

Each written test was planned in advance, and teachers were informed ahead of time of its purposes and problems. The teachers were given detailed instructions as to the presentation of experimental problems in the classroom (as part of the written test), and methods of monitoring the course of problem-solving. The students had to solve the problems in written form. Their work was analyzed according to previously developed criteria and evaluated together with the teacher, and the resulting grades were reported to the students.

The experimental problems were given in a specific sequence according to their complexity. In the diagnostic problems, the sequence of presentation corresponded to the number of the particular problem; the written test problems were presented in increasing order of complexity. From the number of any problem solved by the student on his own, we were able to judge his level of development of spatial thinking. Finally, our analysis and evaluation of the tests took into account not only the ultimate result, but also the process by which it was attained, using objectivized solution attempts, the number of versions used, the percentage of problems solved, the time spent on the problem, the type of problem the student handled most creatively, and so forth. These elements together made it possible to process data in terms of both qualitative and quantitative indices and obtain statistically significant results.

The 1960-1964 written tests were given in schools in Moscow, Odessa, Riga, Rostov-na-Donu, Vitebsk, Erevan, Volgograd, and Elektrostal. The 1970-1978 tests were given in schools in Vilnius, Podolsk, and Moscow. We are grateful to the teachers for giving us the opportunity to collect the information and obtain data on the dynamics of age-group differences.

In written tests given to students of the same grade, we were able not only to judge the quality of the problems solved and rank them by degree of difficulty, but also to follow the dynamics in the same student's solution of various types of problems at different stages of the teaching process. For this purpose, we systematically administered written tests to students in grades 4-10 at one Moscow school over several years. In analyzing tests completed by the same students and observing their progress as they advanced from grade to grade (from grades 4 to 8), we were able to make a long-term study of the overall course of development of spatial thinking in children placed under identical conditions (taught by an experienced mathematics teacher who also acted as the class tutor and participated in organizing and conducting the experimental tests).

Thus, we designed experimental work for students of various grades combining longitudinal and cross-sectional methods, and obtained reliable data on a particular group of students. Besides systematically analyzing written tests completed by students in these grades (once or twice a month), we used results obtained from their participation in mathematical contests, as well as marks given the students by their class tutors on the basis of a special questionnaire designed by us.[16] Some students in these grades participated in individual experiments conducted by I.Ya. Kaplunovich (grades 7-9) and by I.V. Tikhomirova and L.M.

Yampolskaya (grades 4-6). Data obtained from students in these age groups in a single school were complemented with information derived from written tests taken by students of the same age at other schools.

In our study, we tried to insure that the experimental conditions were uniform. For these purposes, we presented the problems in a strict sequence based on their type. Within each type various versions were given, and their complexity was also taken into account. Let us give several examples of written tests.[17]

Grade 4

1. A tourist traveled along the following route: he walked forward 100 m, turned left and went 50 m, then again turned left and went 50 m, went forward 50 m, and then turned right and went 50 m. Draw and compute the path the tourist travels.

2. Count all the triangles in the diagram in Figure 17.

3. In Figure 18, segment *BD* is shared by 7 figures. What figures are these? Identify and write them down.

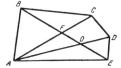

Figure 17.

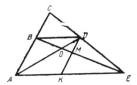

Figure 18.

4. Cut a rectangle 9 cm long and 4 cm wide into equal parts that can make up a square.

Grade 5

1. $[AB] \cong [CD]$ (Figure 19). What translation will map $[AB]$ onto $[CD]$ such that $A \to D$ and $B \to C$?

Figure 19.

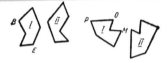

Figure 20.

2. Figure 20 shows two pairs of equal figures. Which points of the second figure in each pair correspond to points B, E, P, M, and O of the first figure? Label them.

3. What is the intersection of the two sets in Figure 21?

4. Construct two angles with a common vertex such that their union is a straight angle and their intersection a right angle.

5. Construct right triangle ABC, where A is the vertex of the right angle. Extend the bisector of angle C to its intersection with $[AB]$ at point D. From D, extend ray DE to its intersection with $[BC]$ at E such that $\angle ECD \cong \angle CDA$. Prove that $\triangle CBE$ is a right triangle.

Grade 6

1. Given a quadrilateral whose diagonals are 6 and 10 cm, compute the perimeter of the quadrilateral formed by the line segments connecting sequentially the midpoints of the sides of the quadrilateral.

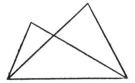

Figure 21.

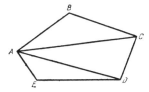

Figure 22.

2. What figure is the intersection of the following pairs of figures: 1) triangles *ABC* and *ADC*; 2) triangles *ABC* and *ADE*; 3) pentagon *ABCDE* and triangle *ACD*; 4) quadrangles *ABCD* and *ACDE*; and 5) triangle *ABC* and [*CD*] (Figure 22)?

3. Prove that parallelograms *ABCD* and *DKBL* share a common center of symmetry (Figure 23).

4. In △*ABC*, draw two lines *AD* and *AE* from point *A* to side *BC*, such that *AD* forms an angle congruent to *C* with [*AB*], while *AE* forms an angle congruent to *B* with [*AC*]. Prove that △*ABC* is an isosceles triangle (Figure 24).

Grade 7

1. Given trapezoid *ABCD*, where [*AD*] ∥ [*BC*]. Line segment *KL* is constructed through point *K*, the midpoint of side *DC* such that [*KL*] ∥ [*AB*] and *L* ε [*AD*]. Prove that $S_{BLDC} = S_{ABL} = 0,5S$ ABCD.

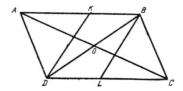

Figure 23.

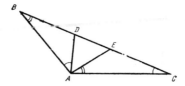

Figure 24.

2. How can we measure the distance between the inaccessible vertices of two angles by means of axial symmetry?

3. What figure is formed by the set of all midpoints of a line segment of a given length whose endpoints move along the sides of a given right angle?

4. The midpoints of sides BC and AD (points M and N) of quadrangle $ABCD$ are connected to its vertices. Prove that $S_{AMD} = S_{ABN} + S_{NCD}$ (Figure 25).

5. Given acute triangle ABC. Draw altitudes AA_1 and BB_1. Determine how many similar triangles are thus formed.

6. $ABCD$ is a quadrilateral whose diagonals AC and BD are perpendicular to each other such that $|AC| = x$ and $|BD| = y$. Find the area of quadrilateral $ABCD$.

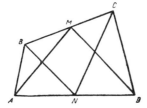

Figure 25.

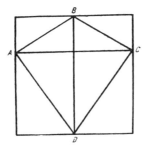

Figure 26.

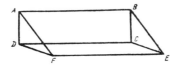

Figure 27.

7. Quadrilaterals *ABCD* and *ABEF* are both parallelograms. Prove that quadrilateral *DCEF* is a parallelogram (Figure 27).

It is clear from the content of the problems described above that their solution requires the mental transformation of given graphic representations, along with a series of mathematical transformations (symmetry, rotation, homothety, parallel translation, etc.). In the same way, problems were selected for grades 8-10, as well as mechanical drawing problems, although we will not give them here because of their complexity.

Let us briefly analyze the data obtained from a mass experimental study of subjects of various age groups. To make these results more comparable, we will show how the subjects completed diagnostic problem 1, which required that they determine the number of polygons depicted in a drawing (an example of the problem is given in Figure 2). Various versions of the problem were used. Two- and three-dimensional representations of various geometric figures (angles, line segments, polygons) and solids (cubes, prisms, cylinders, and pyramids) were presented, but it was always assumed that the same problem was to be solved, that is, determining the number of elements specified by the problem. The problem was varied for difficulty, and could be used with students of various ages with suitable material.

For these purposes, we used the following versions of the problem:

Grade 4. 1. Determine the set of line segments in the diagram in Figure 28. 2. Determine the set of angles in the diagram in Figure 29.

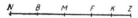

Figure 28.

Grades 5-6. 1. Determine the set of triangles depicted in the diagram in Figure 30. 2. Determine to which polygons [*ED*] belongs. Give them alphabetic labels (Figure 31).

Grades 8-9. How many edges and faces does a prism have? Give the number (Figure 32).

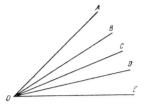

Figure 29.

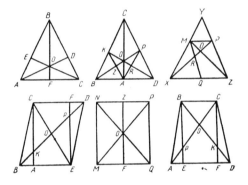

Figure 30.

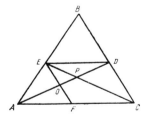

Figure 31.

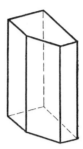

Figure 32.

By using problems that differed in terms of material but were identical in terms of psychological content with subjects in various age groups, we were able to identify several different methods of analyzing graphic representations and types of mental manipulation. Three groups of subjects were identified, each distinguished by a particular problem-solving method.

The first group of subjects (268 students), consisting primarily of fourth- and fifth-graders and certain students in grades 6-8 (7%) analyzed the diagram by carrying out practical operations with it. The subjects divided the diagram into the parts that could be obtained if it was folded in half along some line, or if part of it was cut out and the rest discarded. For example, subject Serezha M. (grade 4) analyzed the diagram in Figure 33. In deriving the figures by the method described earlier, the students did not identify, for example, triangle *AOD* (Figure 33). When the experimenter asked why she had not found this triangle, student Lyuba V. (grade 5) responded, "But we have cut this triangle into parts and it no longer exists." At the same time, we should note that in geometry it is extremely important to know how to identify polygons according to various criteria and mentally combine them according to various attributes. For this reason, the students in this group also failed to find the initial polygon, since it had been cut apart.

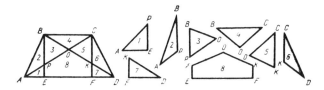

Figure 33.

The subject's analysis of the diagram was limited, as a rule, to identifying only the common elements, without finding the overlapping elements. This is also reflected in the number of figures found (the extent of their analysis). For example, in the diagram in Figure 33 it is possible to find 22 triangles, whereas these subjects could find only 8-12 of them. They found no figures formed by union or intersection, i.e., figures covered by or touching their own plane and sharing common elements (line segments, lines, parts of the plane).

What basic varieties of this method of analyzing representations were observed with the students in this group?

1. The students undertook simple imitative operations, reproducing part of a drawing by tracing out individual lines and parts of lines in its plane. Here, they still fail to clearly express the spatial identification of the figure and delineation of one part of the figure from another. The very first elementary form of analysis—the division of a whole into parts—is still performed incompletely. Indeed, this is how fourth-grader Larisa A. analyzed the drawing (Figure 34).

2. The subjects traced individual elements of the drawing, so that each isolated element is nothing other than the initial drawing with some part cut out. An example of this method of analysis is given in Figure 35.

3. Approximately 75% of the subjects in the first group analyzed the diagram by apparently splitting it up. Then the original figure can be reformed by bringing the parts back together. Here we find a sequential mental "dissection" of the diagram and the identification of its parts (see

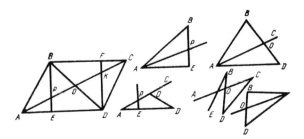

Figure 34.

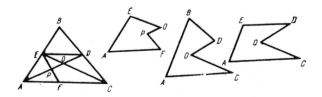

Figure 35.

Figure 36). The spatial position of the isolated parts seems to recapitulate the position in the initial drawing.

These varieties of this analysis (let us call it a practical analysis) indicate that students in this group exclusively utilized limited criteria in their analysis of the diagram. They found it difficult to alter the diagram, as is apparent in the first version of the analysis, which basically proceeds according to the single criterion of dividing the diagram into parts which can then be easily isolated in space.

The absence of clearly expressed criteria is also apparent from the analysis of the diagram. Many students dissect the diagram in a non-sequential manner. Their eyes seem to wander over the diagram. When they accidentally focus on some element, they pick it out it, attempting to

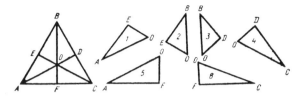

Figure 36.

prevent it from passing out of their field of vision. In reading the diagram, they repeatedly pick out the same parts without noticing that they have already done so. For example, triangle *AEO* (Figure 36) is picked out three or four times. Without picking out some element in their minds which could then be taken as the reference point, i.e., without abstracting a specific attribute or criterion for analysis, the students are therefore unable to verify which figures they have already found and which they have not.

Other subjects in this group sequentially divide the whole into parts, although the direction of their analysis (the sequence by which they identify line segments, angles, and polygons) proceeds primarily from right to left (clockwise). After they have glanced over the outline of the diagram (its extreme points), they begin to divide it into parts, picking out only elements that can be obtained by breaking down the initial figure in a definite sequence. When they give their completed test to the experimenter, they say, "I'm finished, I don't know how to cut it any further." Typically, they try to rely on various practical aids, turning the drawing around in their hands, trying to cut out individual figures from paper, and drawing a circle around the figures with their pencil in the drawing (where it has not been cut up).

From the composition of the diagram, they identify only those elements which catch their eye upon first glance, without completely identifying everything that could be formed through the union or intersection of the elements. They find it difficult to transform the diagram in their minds so that first one, then another figure moves into their field of vision in an orderly fashion, through the successive incorporation of various figures. The subjects of this group display a kind of rigidity in their analysis of the drawing; they do not arbitrarily replace analytical criteria and reference points, as can be seen not only from the present problem, but also from a number of others (3, 5, 7, etc.). The limited ability of this group of subjects for problems requiring mental transformation of visual aids is clearly attributable to inadequate development of techniques for the analysis of graphic representations, in particular, geometric diagrams.

We should emphasize that the problems given to the students corresponded to their educational experience. They all had the necessary knowledge of geometry and were able to differentiate polygons (triangles, quadrilaterals of various shapes, etc.). However, their mental transformation of the visual material was highly limited, which indicates, first, that their perceptual actions were insufficiently developed, and second, their methods of representation were too transient. The students did not interpret the drawing from the standpoint of geometric concepts, but instead guided their analysis exclusively by the practical criterion of dividing a whole into parts. They undertook no specific geometric analysis of the drawing.

The second group of subjects (486 students) primarily consisted of sixth- and seventh-graders (68%). These subjects typically made a more detailed analysis of the representations. They had already transcended the stage characterized by the mental repetition of practical analysis, but had yet to obtain better techniques. Consequently, this group can be referred to as intermediate. These students carried out their mental reconstruction of drawings more purposefully than those in the first group, although within highly constrained limits. In identifying the elements of a drawing, they were guided by a variety of criteria; e.g., in applying a practical criterion, they did not restrict themselves to it, but utilized other criteria as well, basing their analysis first on one line and then another, grouping around the line all the figures it was part of. The diversity of their analytic criteria was manifested in the number of polygons found.

The subjects in this group correctly identified more polygons than those in the first group (from 8-12 figures in the first group vs. 14-16 in the second). By contrast to the students in the first group, no undivided elements were left over. These subjects identified both individual elements as well as groups of elements, and not only sequential groups of elements, but also groups with common elements. For example, they found triangles *AOB*, *DOC*, and *AOD* without forgetting to draw the initial polygon *ABCD* (Figure 37). Some students began their analysis of the diagram with this polygon, while others concluded by identifying it. Their use of various analytic criteria affected the way in which they solved the problem as a whole; thus, they scanned the diagram more rationally and more purposefully, and explicitly identified any change in reference point. The subjects first employed a criterion for successively identifying sequential elements, obtaining eight polygons (cf. Figure 37, 1-8). Then, using lines *BE* and *CF* as the basis for their analysis, they obtained three more polygons (9, 10 and 11), and finally used point O to form three more polygons (12, 13, and 14).

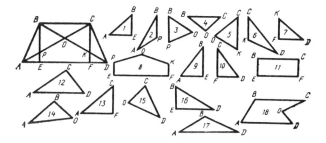

Figure 37.

The subjects in this group did not engage in repeated identification of the same elements of a diagram, which was typical of the students in the first group. Because they were guided by explicit and diverse criteria, they were able to determine which elements had already been found and which had not. However, their identification of elements did not specifically follow geometric criteria (for example, the identification of polygon 18 in Figure 37), although they moved on to this type of analysis after having already found all the basic elements.

Because they employed diverse analytic criteria, the subjects in the second group found it difficult to retain them in their mind and use them in various ways. They searched for ways of doing so in the visual aid. Once they were given the drawing, they shaded in first one part of it, and then another, so as to make their analytic criterion more "visual." Some students penciled in a line for this purpose, since it constituted a generatrix for the group of figures, while others held their finger over part of the plane, and so forth. For example, sixth-grader Galya P., a subject of this group, described his difficulties in the following way: "I look for the necessary element, but as soon as I look away to pick up the pencil, for example, I lose it and have to hunt for it again among the others." Analogous difficulties were experienced by these subjects in the other problems in the experiment.

The students in this group typically strived to use any possible auxiliary technique to help them mentally reconstruct the initial graphic representation. They rotated it in various directions, trying to write down the particular element on paper to keep it from moving out of their field of vision once it assumed a new position, and only then attempted to determine a second position.

These difficulties appeared most clearly when the students were confronted with diagnostic problem 9, in which they had to mentally follow changes occurring in a metal blank as it moves through production, and record them in the form of sketches of manufacturing steps and a diagram of the finished part. These difficulties also occurred with problem 7.

The third group of subjects (244 students) consisted primarily of seventh-, eighth-, and ninth-graders, although it also included a few students in the younger grades (28%) placed in this group because of their work. These students use clearly expressed criteria for analyzing representations, for the most part specifically geometric representations. They typically displayed a different approach to the tests than the subjects in the other two groups. They did not rush to start on a problem immediately, but instead tried to first draw out a mental plan of the course of its solution. As a rule, these students started by creating a general plan for the analysis of the diagram, and also followed various "trajectories" for their analysis, moving from right to left and, conversely, from left to right, based on any reference point (vertex, midline, central point, etc.). For example, Irina B. (grade 7) looked at the diagram for a long time without sketching anything; indeed, she essentially did not even start the problem. When the experimenter asked why she was not sketching anything, she responded, "I am looking and thinking. There are so many figures that I first have to decide how they may be best grouped if I am not to become confused and repeat them." The subjects of this group first selected criteria, and only then analyzed the diagram. This method was applied to virtually any diagram, regardless of its specific set of elements. The subjects first tried to analyze the geometric features of the diagram and its method of construction, and then set about identifying its constituent elements.

These students did not repeatedly identify the same element, nor did they leave any undivided elements. The precision of analysis increased, and the number of correctly identified figures approached the model. They identified practically all the polygons in the diagram, and did this sequentially; a change in analytic criteria (reference point) was clearly evident. Figures with common or overlapping elements were identified on the basis of their distinctive attributes. They made extensive use of principles of symmetry, similitude, and complementarity, i.e., specifically geometric criteria.

Our observations of these students enabled us to establish the ease and speed with which they completed the problems, the absence of any effort to rely on visual and practical aids, and their flexibility and independence in selecting analytic criteria, shifting from one set of reference points to another, and subordinating their actions to selected criteria. Moreover, these subjects constantly exhibited this style of mental activity. It appeared whenever they had to solve problems of varying levels of complexity based on different types of subject matter.

The three groups of subjects we have identified can be correlated with age. The first group consists primarily of fourth- and fifth-graders, the second group of sixth-graders, and the third group of seventh-, eighth-, and ninth-graders. Gradual shifts could be observed in the distribution of subjects into groups. Thus, the fourth- and fifth-graders form the majority of the first group, more than half (57%) of all the subjects in grade 6 were in the second group. The subjects from grades 8 and 9 were placed primarily in the third group, although some fraction (9%) of them were placed in the second or even the first group.

Our analysis of the data on quantitative and qualitative indices led us to conclude that students' ability to use conceptual analytic criteria for problem-solving improves with age. The older the student, the richer the store of geometric experience, graphic knowledge, and skills. Older students also show improved forms of representational analysis, and this analysis becomes rational, sequential, and controlled. All mental processes become more natural and self-regulated with age. The ability to act according to representations without relying on physical activity also increases. Age-group differences appear in the subject's ability to vary his reference point. Subjects in the younger group tended to establish spatial relations based on the position of their own body. They seemed to mentally place themselves in a definite position relative to which the given objects are "distributed," thereby establishing their spatial relations.

As they grow, children begin to freely assume other systems of reference, and the position of their own body ceases to be the principal point of reference. This is particularly clear in the process of solving problems which require the following abilities: 1) to establish spatial relations in which the subject is part of the general system formed by these relations; and 2) to establish spatial relations between moving objects which change their position in space independent of the subject. Let us give a few examples of such problems.

Problem 1. A bicyclist travels along a highway. He rides forward 100 m, turns to the right and goes 500 m, and then again turns to the right and rides another 300 m. Finally he turns left and goes another 100 m. Draw and compute the bicyclist's path.

In order to solve this problem, it is necessary to place oneself mentally in the bicyclist's position, and vary the reference point relative to the direction (left-right-forward), taking into account not only one's own position, but also the change of this position in the course of travel. Our experiment demonstrated that many third- and fourth-graders are unable to solve this problem. After completing the control lesson, they physically "traced" this path, turning to the left, to the right, and moving forward, in order to see if they had correctly solved the problem.

Problem 2. Two cars simultaneously set out from two points A and B, 50 km apart. After traveling 800 km toward each other, they arrive simultaneously at the destination, point C. Determine whether the cars could have moved at the same speed all the time.

The position of the observer is not important in solving this problem, since he remains fixed. What is important is to consider the spatial relations between the cars moving toward each other at different speeds.

These problems demonstrate that the transition from a fixed reference point based on the body to another reference point based on other objects may be considered an important index that changes with age. The arbitrary change in reference point typical of younger schoolchildren is manifested in other ways as well. In certain graphic problems, particularly those which involve three-dimensional representations, it is important to arbitrarily alter the observation point. Our experiments have shown that when analyzing a representation, younger schoolchildren view all the different surfaces of the representations (front, rear, side) in their minds. This change in observation point is nurtured in students under the influence of objective activity. When working on reaming in shop class, they routinely alter their observation point, working with the object or a graphic representation of the object. Therefore, younger schoolchildren are quite ready to learn the projective method, which is introduced in the school only in grade 7.

In the older age group (grades 5-8), this dynamism of observation points is less marked, due, we believe, to the position students assume

when perceiving a representation, i.e., exclusively from the front relative
to the observer. Therefore, comprehension of the method of projective
relations on a scientific basis at this age encounters considerable difficulties. In this regard, the younger age group has certain advantages.

The features noted earlier that reflect the dynamics of age-group
differences are not only a function of age. This can be seen from the
following facts. First, through special instruction, we have been able to
cause students' age-group abilities to diverge markedly. For example, by
teaching students special techniques for the analysis of diagrams, many
students who were in the first level at the start of our experiment were
able to make it into the second group, and some even to the third. Second,
a comparative analysis of the creativity of the solutions of the same
problem by students of the same age carried out by the present author
using the cross-sectional method in 1965 and 1975 demonstrated that the
distribution of students by groups also varied. Students in grades 4-7
surveyed in 1975 belonged to the second and third groups based on their
solution of the experimental problems, whereas their peers surveyed in
1965 belonged primarily to the first group. This resulted from major
changes in instruction, particularly in mathematics. The potential of the
younger students, however, is still not being fully utilized.

In analyzing age-group differences, one more interesting fact may be
noted. The spatial images created by younger schoolchildren are highly
animated and dynamic. The students have no trouble solving problems
which require the transformation of elements of a representation, readily
isolate geometric shapes, are interested in creating evolutes of solid
objects from visual representations, and learn to represent them graphically. However, when they start the basic geometry course (grades 5-6),
their experience seems to become impoverished. Their experience reduces to the mastery of the operations of displacing geometric figures in
the plane. The students try to apply their previous experience at recoding
three-dimensional representation into two-dimensional ones and vice
versa, and manipulate the image not only in the plane, but also in space.
But this experience is neither reinforced nor expanded. In geometry class

in grades 6 through 8, the students deal primarily with the transformation of two-dimensional figures in the plane.

Let us illustrate this with an example. In their study of axial symmetry in grade 6, many students complete this type of transformation by mentally plucking a given figure out of the plane and into space, rotating it about its axis, and superimposing it on another figure until the figures coincide. This method is carried over from their prior experience of working with books, finishing physical objects, etc., but as an empirical and limited method it is not utilized in mathematics. In mathematics a different method is recommended, one which requires that they determine the shortest distance of given elements from an axis of symmetry and plot these distances on either side of an axis. This is how the method of constructing a point symmetric to a given point is described: "Through point A, draw a line perpendicular to the axis. Designate the point where it intersects the axis by the letter O. Draw segment OA_1 of length $[OA]$ along line AO on the other side of the axis. Point A_1 has been constructed." [*Mathematics: A Textbook for Grade 6*, 1976, p. 43]. If a set of points is specified, the method may be applied to each point, and the points then combined to yield the desired figure.

The textbook recommends another method (using a compass) which differs from the first one only in the method of graphic design. The textbook presents many other analogous types of displacement defined in mathematics as distance-preserving mappings of a figure onto itself. But if students learn only mathematically correct methods for mathematical transformations, their activity is restricted to a single plane, since they must handle two-dimensional representations and transform them within the plane. Their accumulated experience of translating three-dimensional representations into two-dimensional ones and manipulating them not only in the plane, but also in space, is supplanted by more uniform experience in grades 5-8. Then, in grades 9-10, they begin to actively manipulate not only two-dimensional, but also three-dimensional representations, orienting these representations both within the plane and in space. Thus, the student's experience of spatial orientation is at first lost, and then resurrected at a more complex level.

This, we believe, may explain the many psychological difficulties observed in mathematics students in secondary school. Some of our data demonstrate that if different geometric objects (plane and solid) are used right away—of course, taking into account their complexity—in teaching methods of transformation beginning with the early grades, the transition from two-dimensional to three-dimensional representations and vice versa, as well as learning to apply transformations not only within a single plane, but also outside it in space, proceed smoothly and creatively. Here the age-group differences are smoothed out, which is of great importance not only for mathematics, but also for mechanical drawing. This becomes particularly clear when moving from plane to solid geometry.

These facts indicate that various teaching methodologies require a scientific foundation for a unified line of development in spatial thinking in children, starting with knowledge of the psychological laws underlying this development at various stages of the child's growth. Unfortunately, psychology has devoted far too little attention to this question.

The outline of the development of spatial representations in ontogenesis suggested by Jean Piaget is of extraordinary interest here. According to Piaget, the development of the child's understanding of space proceeds from topological representations to projective representations, and subsequently to metric representations. The child first reflects the topology of objects. In orienting himself to spatial relations, he isolates the outline of objects readily, and has no difficulty distinguishing open and closed figures. As a result, he can differentiate objects (physical articles and geometric figures), relate them, identify them, etc. Then he acquires an understanding of projective representations, orienting himself to the world of objects in light of different spatial positions, and only then acquires a conscious understanding of metric relations.

The current mathematics curriculum actually realizes a reverse pattern. Through specially organized activity (measuring, computing, constructing), the student starts by learning the metric relations of space, then projective relations, and finally topological relations. The logic underlying the development of spatial understanding is a fundamental issue; it defines not only the theoretical issues in learning, but also the practical organization of instruction designed to nurture spatial thinking in light of developmental considerations. The correct approach to this question may be found only through the combined efforts of educators, methodologists, and psychologists.

Analyzing the dynamics of the age-group differences in manipulating spatial images in different graphic representations requires that indices of a dual nature be taken into account. Some of these indices depend on the content and nature of the teaching process; any improvement in the latter leads at once to a change in the overall picture of age-group differences. Other indices depend to a lesser extent on teaching conditions, and are defined, apparently, by deeper systems of spatial orientation fostered by preceding phylogenic experience as a result of the enduring body image orientation. Critical points of development are more clearly manifested here.

Evaluation of the reliability of our indices and the study of their psychological nature require further in-depth and careful investigation. This investigation will define the future direction of any curriculum for the development of spatial thinking in students throughout their years in school.

Several Prerequisites for the Study of Individual Differences in Spatial Thinking

The psychological literature contains considerable data dealing with individual differences in spatial thinking. What is the nature of these differences? What do they depend upon? These are controversial questions. Some writers suppose that, like any form of thinking, spatial thinking is formed in the course of learning. Its special organization levels out individual differences. Other researchers, proceeding from empirical data, support the view that although it is possible to develop spatial thinking in the course of instruction, this development proceeds along highly varied paths; furthermore, schoolchildren, and even college students, retain individual difficulties that hinder the acquisition and manipulation of spatial images. This fact reflects the complex nature of spatial thinking.

Spatial thinking, like all of man's mental processes, is social and is formed on the basis of certain anatomical and physiological attributes. Its structure comprises elements that differ genetically. Spatial thinking is formed within the context of knowledge at a certain level of verbal and graphic fluency. Furthermore, it is determined by functional features of the perceptual analyzers (their level of development and degree of coherence) and by topological features in the perception of spatial properties and relations, particularly the relation between signal systems that engender individual differences in the retention and reproduction of spatial images (predominantly artistic or mental images). There are data which show the influence of the functional features of brain structures on the way in which spatial images are created and manipulated, and demonstrate the presence of certain inherited factors that define the individual's success in spatial orientation.

We are interested in all literature on the identification and analysis of the parameters which define individual development of spatial thinking. Individual differences in spatial thinking can be seen in the procedural characteristics underlying the perception of spatial properties and relations. Here may be found both an analytic (gradual identification of individual parts) and synthetic (integral, nondifferentiated) perception of the object or its representation, as expressed in both quantitative (sequential-simultaneous) and qualitative (fragmented-integral) indices.

Individual differences are manifested especially sharply in the creation and manipulation of spatial images based on graphic material. This primarily affects the individual's ability to vary his frame of reference, in learning methods for the mental transformation of visual (graphic) material, in techniques for conceptual processing of this material, in the selective manipulation of elements in the structure of the image (its shape and size), in the ease with which images at varying degrees of visualization are manipulated, and so forth.

All these factors indicate that spatial thinking does not consist of a sequential collection of mental functions. Rather, it is a complicated dynamic system which ensures the coordinated work of functional and operational mechanisms, based not only on social factors, but also biological (anatomical and physiological) factors. The distinctive combination and elaboration of these mechanisms, along with their level of development, also define the nature of individual differences in spatial thinking.

The complexity and lack of uniformity in the elements that make up the structure of spatial thinking are manifested in the high level of compensability of its various aspects, and also in the diversity of types of compensation. In ontogenesis we constantly see, on the one hand, that instruction has a decisive effect on the development of spatial thinking, and on the other hand, that students under identical teaching conditions persistently exhibit modes of activity aimed to creating and manipulating spatial images. This becomes quite clear whenever it is necessary to shift to different systems of reference, abstract from the body image, and use spatial relations.

In the course of ontogenesis, because of the effect of instruction (in the broad sense of the term), the influence of the anatomical and physiological features of the personality weakens, although this process is highly idiosyncratic (A.R. Luriya, B.M. Teplov, I.V. Ravich-Shcherbo, and others). For this reason, the relation between biological and social factors in spatial thinking is highly complicated and varied. Far too little attention has been devoted to this subject.

Studies carried out by E.N. Kabanova-Meller [1934, 1956, 1960], B.G. Ananev et al. [1960, 1968, 1970, 1972], B.F. Lomov [1959], F.N. Shemyakin [1940, 1958], and others have demonstrated that persistent individual differences are manifested in the student's creation and manipulation of spatial images. This is expressed in the way students perceive and manipulate graphic representations. When given a representation that they must use to create an image, some students establish all its concrete features in detail, and gradually reconstruct the image from the individual parts by combining them into a unified whole. Others first "capture" in their representation a general outline of the object, and subsequently "fill in" the outline with the appropriate details. In this way students confer on the image a definite and complete structure and a clear configuration. These features are seen in every student, whether he is handling various types of graphic aids (diagrams, figures, geographic maps), or solving classroom problems, which attests to the stability of these features. They are characteristic not only of students, but also engineers, planners, and artists.

All other conditions being equal (identical background and work experience, level of education, nature and complexity of production tasks), we find that the activity of design engineers may be distinguished in terms of design style and methods of reading and creating diagrams. According to S.I. Avgustevich [1970], some designers isolate the most difficult unit in a construction to start their work, while others draw all the elements of the construction in turn from start to finish. Individual differences are apparent in the compositional features of the resulting solution. Typically, some engineers try to attain maximal detail in their designs, while in others complicated, multi-functional chassis-type details predominate. For example, some engineers carefully think out all the elements of the construction when developing a plan at the draft stage, while others first solve the basic design problem, and only then begin creating drawings of the assemblies, followed by the elaboration of design solutions for the individual elements. Their ultimate solution is often generated in the form of diagrams and so-called skeleton designs.

Interesting data have been obtained by V.A. Molyako [1972], B.M. Rebus [1965], and others. These investigators discovered that designers can be distinguished by their method of creating spatial images (more "analytic" or "synthetic") and their choice of reference elements. Some engineers may employ the geometric shape of perceived or created objects as reference elements, while others prefer to establish functional relations between specific shapes. It is therefore no accident that the former group prefers problems that require creating novel design forms through diverse combinations of preexisting forms, whereas the latter group has greater success in solving problems that require novel operating principles within the scope of preexisting structural forms. According to these investigators, these are enduring characteristics that appear at various stages, e.g., when studying raw data, at the point of searching for and finding the design solution, and in the course of elaborating mechanical drawing documentation. For example, mechanical drawing documentation produced by designers who rely mainly on transformations of shapes are rich in modifications of these shapes (combinations, cuts, and sections). In others, by contrast, we observe a tendency towards the use of a narrow range of simple shapes. Design decisions are judged predominantly from the standpoint of adaptability to production conditions, and in certain cases, even at the expense of functional potential (according to Avgustevich). Furthermore, individual differences may be found quite clearly in the process of creating spatial images even at the stage of direct perception of the initial visual material.

In our own studies [1958, 1960], we found that students who have no trouble establishing spatial relations in various types of graphic material have their own method of elaborating this material mentally. Even at the moment when visual information (e.g., a diagram) is present, these students subject the sensory data to active mental reworking. They identify the most important elements of the diagram for problem-solving and seemingly all at once incorporate these elements into the full set of elements depicted in the diagram, interpret them, and establish at a glance the most significant "spots" (points, lines, planes of intersection). Other students do this slowly and gradually, without explicit criteria for analyzing the representations.

Thus, individual differences in the manipulation of spatial relations occur even at the level of perceiving graphic representations. These differences affect the style of perception (more detailed or integrated), the features underlying the solution based on perception (establishing certain elements at the expense of others), the choice of reference elements (shape, size, etc.), and the distinctive methods for mental elaboration of perceptual data (more visual-sensory or more conceptual).

These features of perception display a persistent, individual affinity. They can be observed in the same subjects with different problems, and also with different types of graphic representations. For example, when confronted with problems requiring the application of different types of graphic aids, some students start by establishing spatial relations in the given objects "on the spot", independent of the methods underlying their expression. Others establish this gradually by comparing the visual attributes of the different objects element by element. Moreover, the first group isolates spatial relations by direct consideration ("I see it that way"). The second group resorts to a complex conceptual apparatus for this purpose, as well as a highly developed system of inference and proof (M.E. Botsmanova [1962], V.I. Zykova [1961], N.P. Linkova [1964], and I.S. Yakimanskaya [1961]).

Differences can also be observed in the methods used for sensory generalization. In some students, generalizations from visual material proceed sequentially through a detailed, partitioned analysis of isolated data, while in others it occurs rapidly and concisely, i.e., all at once; furthermore, the most significant relations between the visual attributes are generalized. This feature of generalization has been regarded as an important prerequisite for the successful comprehension of geometry (V.A. Krutetskii, 1968; P.A. Sorokun, 1966; and others). In the apt words of the well-known mathematician D.D. Mordukhai-Boltovskii, "The geometrician does not recall the visual image of a diagram. He recalls only the relative position of lines and surfaces or parts of lines and surfaces" [1908: 3]. These individual features in the perception of visual material are found in students from various age groups.

We have found vivid individual differences under specially organized instruction. Under identical conditions, having all the necessary knowledge and habits for solving the experimental problems, 19 students of the same age display varying receptivities to teaching, even when placed under the same conditions.[19] Some students require minimal explanations and a rather small number of exercises in order to learn effective methods of analyzing representations. For these students, the quantity, predictability, accuracy, and speed with which the elements of a representation are identified all improve. In contrast, other students, given the same teaching conditions, retain their customary imperfect methods of analysis for some time. In order the teach them effective methods for reading representations, we are forced to use visual aids in the form of cardboard models, illustrate methods of transforming the elements physically, draw circles around the elements to be transformed, and apply other secondary techniques. These facts indicate that the individual characteristics of spatial perception are persistent. Some writers attribute these characteristics to the predominance of one or another signal system (M.N. Borisova, 1954; B.B. Kossov, 1956; and others); others attribute them to the discrete individual mechanisms underlying spatial recognition and discrimination (M.S. Shekhter, 1969); finally, a third group attribute them to features in the structure and functioning of the visual system which make it possible to create images (V.P. Zinchenko, 1968).

L.L. Gurova [1976] has shown that three-dimensional vision is based on unique mental events that make it possible to select spatial relations and connections, either sequentially or simultaneously. Three-dimensional vision is related to the continuous and integral transformation of a visual problem-oriented situation, the simultaneous imposition of constraints on the search domain, the use of isolated spatial relations, and their arrangement into a system in a definite "representational" logic (in Gurova's words), and is also sharply individual in nature.

Spatial transformations are based on actions aimed to "inserting" the same perceived or imagined element into various sets of relations (S.L. Rubinshtein, 1956). Some students learn these transformations readily and freely, which helps them discover new attributes in the perceived or represented objects which did not previously catch their eye. Others acquire an imperfect understanding of this act, which limits their ability to transform and reinterpret visual material, and also makes it hard for them to solve problems (K.A. Slavskaya, 1961; I.S. Yakimanskaya, 1955; and others).

The creative element in working with graphic material is determined largely by the student's ability to regard the same figure from different standpoints (V.G. Vladimirskii, B.D. Zhuravlev, E.N. Kabanova-Meller, and others). This is the basis for the ability to read diagrams correctly (A.D. Botvinnikov), since the shape of an object depicted in a diagram can be determined only through repeated analysis from the standpoint of different projections. As has been demonstrated in a number of studies

(V.A. Krutetskii, G. Mikshite, and others), the ability to regard a representation dynamically (multi-dimensionally) correlates with high grades in mathematics and mechanical drawing, and with inclination and interest toward these subjects.

Individual differences, according to the data of our studies, are manifested not only in the nature of the perception of graphic representations, but also in the flexibility and freedom with which spatial images are created and manipulated. There are students who do not find it difficult to create and manipulate spatial images. As a rule, these students "see" the image created from a representation quite clearly, and are able to manipulate it freely without resorting to the original visual aid. The static and dynamic elements of the image merge for these students. They display equal facility at focusing on and transforming the existing image.

Other students experience significant difficulties when trying to create and manipulate images. We can identify two groups in this regard. The first group consists of those students who are unable to retain images in their memory for very long. They tend to become blurry and lose their clear outline and structure. These students typically resort to the visual aid, which helps them establish the conceived image, revive it in their memory, and retain it. In the second group we include students who have no trouble creating images from an illustration (figure, drawing, diagram), but are unable to modify it mentally. Unlike the students in the first group, these students possess vivid, static images, but are unable to mentally transform these images. Recourse to the initial visual aid only aggravates their difficulty. The visual aid helps them retain the image and establish its basic characteristics. But when they have to transform a preexisting image (by shape, size, or position), it is not retention that is desirable, but rather abstraction of the initial characteristics. The static and dynamic elements of the image are in contradiction for these students. In such cases, the visual aid makes it difficult to manipulate the image freely, and plays a negative role. The visual aid seems to attach itself to the content, whereas it is the content that the student must abstract. This is especially clear in solving design-engineering and manufacturing problems. These features also occur in the same students when they have to solve geometry problems, mechanical drawing, and technology, which attests to the stability of these features.

The conflict between the results of activity aimed at creating images and manipulating them for solving graphic problems is clear from the fact that a student may prefer problems involving reading representations and finding specified objects based on them. He may painstakingly compare these representations, regard them with interest, talk about their characteristics, but avoid trying to solve problems where it is necessary to transform the resulting images. A second student, by contrast, may regard this work as boring and uninteresting, paying little attraction, and may become animated only when it is necessary to mentally conceive and transform an existing image; he may do this rapidly, easily, and without any need for visual aids.

Our data lead us to conclude that there are several degrees of freedom in the manipulation of spatial images, corresponding to the three types of manipulation considered above. Some subjects find it easier to transform images in a situation where they must vary the spatial position of an object, while others have less trouble when they have to vary the structure of an object, and finally a third group has the least trouble when they must transform the position and structure of an initial image. These differences have been discovered with material in geometry, mechanical drawing, and technology, as well as in the study of descriptive geometry, in working with nonverbal tests.[20]

Another area of individual differences is the index of manipulability. Using this index, it has been found that some students find it easier to manipulate spatial images within homogeneous representations (e.g., figures, drawings, or diagrams), while others manipulate various types of representations freely and easily, so that they can shift back and forth from visual to projective or conventional representations, and vice versa.

Interesting individual differences have also been found in the index reflecting the comprehensiveness of the spatial image. In an experiment involving younger students [M.G. Bodnar, 1974], it was shown that the most persistent individual differences in students' creation and manipulation of spatial images occur when they wish to establish spatial relations; but these differences are not as explicit in the manipulation of shape and size. Bodnar also developed special problems in which he was able to identify the following elements in the structure of the spatial image: 1) reproduction of the shape of a figure (corresponding to a given model); 2) the relation between the size of the figures and their individual elements; and 3) correct arrangement of a figure and its elements in the plane.

Individual differences have also been found in an index that may be referred to provisionally as verbal or visual. In a number of studies (V.I. Zykova, 1955; V.A. Krutetskii, 1965; I.S. Yakimanskaya, 1959; and others), it has been shown that some students experience difficulties when trying to analyze a drawing, while others have trouble in trying to analyze the conditions of a problem expressed in verbal form. Two groups of problems (five problems in each group) were designed in one experimental study (Yakimanskaya, 1959). The first group consisted of oral versions of essentially the same geometry problems. The problems were distinguished by the concrete data, and they were expressed either in words and letters, or in words alone. Let us give an example of these problems.

1. In $\triangle ABC$, lines AD and CE are drawn from angles A and C. Where they intersect the sides of the triangle, they cut off equal segments BE and BD, which form equal angles with lines AD and CE. Prove that the lines are equal.

2. Perpendiculars are drawn through the midpoints of each leg of an isosceles triangle to meet the opposite sides. Prove that these perpendiculars are equal.

In the second group of problems, the verbal formulation of the conditions of each problem remains unchanged, although different types of diagrams are given in which the position of the figures required for the solution are varied (the labels of the figures remain unchanged). Here is one of these problems:

In triangle ABC, the bisector of angle A is drawn to intersect side BC at point D. Line DE is drawn from point D such that $[DE] \parallel [AC]$, and line EF is drawn from point E such that $[EF] \parallel [BC]$. Prove that $[AE] = [FC]$.

Five versions of the diagram were given for the problem. In these diagrams, the unknown relations (even their alphabetic symbols) remained unchanged, but their spatial position was varied (see Figure 38a, b, c, d, and e). This technique made it possible to identify persistent differences in flexibility, speed, and precision of realization, primarily with regard to verbal or visual analysis of the material. The results demonstrated that the subjects continue to prefer a verbal or visual form of problem analysis and problem-solving methods in solving other problems with different material and content.

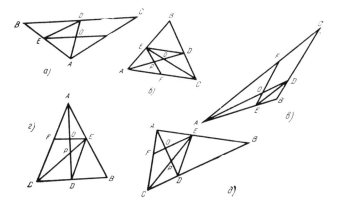

Figure 38.

We have obtained analogous data based on mechanical drawing material. In reading the illustrations given in Figure 39, the majority of subjects (10 ninth-graders) had no trouble differentiating the geometric features of the screws from the diagrams and finding the corresponding isometrics. Three of the ten students had trouble only in determining which diagrams matched isometrics *e* and *l*. In fact, they are quite similar, which forces the student to make a precise differentiation (in one case the screw has a spherical head, and in the other case it has a flat head).

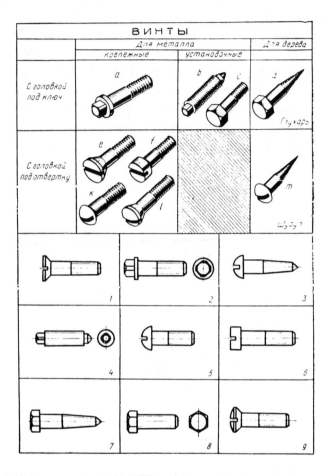

Figure 39.

However, the students were able to complete the test successfully by specifically concentrating on these isometrics.

Only one subject was unable to "see" the difference between isometrics *e* and *l*, and thus could not find the drawing corresponding to each of these isometrics on his own. This student's method of attacking the problem is of interest. He tried to establish the difference verbally (deductively), instead of through the perception of the given illustrations. He reasoned as follows: "We are given technical isometrics and diagrams. According to the condition, each isometric has a corresponding diagram. I will proceed by eliminating the diagrams which can be easily related to the isometrics. Then I keep e, f, and l, which are similar, but e and f may be distinguished by the shape of their head, this is clear. Then diagrams 1 and 9 remain unallocated. But since one of them correlates exactly with figure e, only one diagram is left, number 9, and it corresponds to figure l."

In order to establish the correspondence between a diagram and an isometric, this subject undertook a chain of logical reasoning and verbal inferences, whereas other students remarked that "everything is so obvious," and selected the isometric corresponding to each drawing by visual means.

Summarizing our discussion of these indices, individual differences are clearly manifested in the following areas: the ability to create static and dynamic images, the flexibility with which images are created or manipulated, and image manipulability. This is clear from the way in which visual aids are utilized, the comprehensiveness of the resulting image, the methods used to transform it (type of manipulation), and the predominant use of verbal or visual attributes.

In studying the appearance of individual differences in these indices, we adhered to specific principles, which guided us to develop a special program for identifying individual differences. Let us briefly survey these principles.

1. The individual differences were identified against a backdrop of equal instruction. For this purpose, the subjects were placed under identical teaching conditions. The subjects in each group were the same age, had achieved the same grade levels, and had shown the same positive attitude towards the experimental problems.

2. Only enduring individual differences were studied; this was achieved applying various methodologies and using a longitudinal test.

3. The stability of individual differences was determined from specially designed qualitative and quantitative indices of the structure of spatial thinking.

4. The susceptibility of certain indices to adaptation or reorganization under environmental influence, primarily in the course of teaching the corresponding subjects, was analyzed, since it is only under the influence of organized actions is it possible to judge the stability of individual differences and their psychological nature.

5. These differences should influence the formation of personality, define its inclinations and interests, and motivate the student to select an occupation in which the creation and the manipulation of spatial images are of major importance, i.e., they should influence the motivational area.

Precisely how the last index "shows" itself within the context of other indices has been studied by G. Mikshite [1974]. It was demonstrated that there is a close relation between how spatial relations are established and the individual's propensity for a particular occupation. The subjects were ninth- and tenth-graders in ordinary and specialized (mathematical, language) schools. To determine their propensity for a chosen occupation, Mikshite utilized special questionnaires and student profiles, individual interviews with students, and an analysis of school grades in each of the corresponding subjects.

Based on this experiment, several groups of students were identified. Depending upon their occupational propensities, the groups were divided into "geometricians," "physicists," "algebraicists," "geographers," "literature specialists," and "linguists." A total of 72 students with explicit propensities were selected (12 in each of the six groups) from the total number of 326 students surveyed. These students formed the body of the basic experiment, which consisted in identifying the student's individual aptitudes for manipulating spatial relations.

The experiment demonstrated major differences in the way students completed various groups of experimental problems,[21] which was expressed not only in certain quantitative indices, but also in qualitative indices (precision in evaluating the length of lines, selecting and determining shortest distances, arbitrary shift in reference points, etc.).

Mikshite declared that there is a close relation between individual characteristics in the establishment of spatial relations and the level of development of spatial thinking (the correlation coefficient between these attributes was 0.439 at p = 0.01). Features underlying the establishment of spatial relations are closely related to the degree of creativity with which images of two- and three-dimensional figures are created (a corresponding correlation coefficient of 0.372 at p = 0.05). There is also a close relation between features underlying the establishment of spatial and quantitative relations (correlation coefficient 0.421 at $p = 0.01$). However, no statistically significant relation could be established between the characteristics underlying the establishment of spatial relations and the ability to solve verbal problems.

Based on a dispersion analysis, Mikshite concluded that the "geometricians" had the highest level of development of spatial thinking (with the application of the entire group of techniques), the "physicists" and "geographers" had an average level, and the "algebraicists" and students with a propensity for the humanities ("literary specialists" and "linguists") had the lowest level. The greatest differences were found between the development of spatial thinking in the "geometricians" and "algebraicists," between the "geographers" and "linguists," between the "physicists" and "algebraicists," and between the "algebraicists" and the "literary specialists" (the differences were reliable to the level of p 0.01 for t = 3.78, 3.67, 3.59, and 2.98, respectively). The differences between the "geometricians" and the "literary specialists" (and also the "linguists") were the most significant for p 0.001, t_1 = 8.27, t_2 = 5.64.[22]

The data obtained in Mikshite's study provide an experimental confirmation that the level of development of spatial thinking is inseparable from individual characteristics of relations in two- and three-dimensional space. Some are related directly to perceptual features, others to the way in which spatial images are created, and a third set to the manipulation of spatial images as part of the problem-solving process. The qualitative nature of expressive activity at different levels of development is not leveled out in the course of learning, but, quite to the contrary, is manifested rather vividly. This is expressed in the individual nature of representational methods, in students' propensities, and in students' real achievements in the study of school subjects.

Spatial thinking as a mental development is both structurally and functionally complex. Its level of development depends upon harmonious interrelations between the various elements in its structure. If these elements do not develop uniformly, there will be individual differences in the structure of spatial thinking. The less developed elements may be compensated for by other elements, which must be taken into account not only in analyzing the nature of individual differences, but also in deciding upon steps to take in order to ensure favorable conditions for the development of spatial thinking.

As we have already noted, the structure of spatial thinking comprises elements of various origins, both social and biological. This fact underlies the activity of the anatomical and physiological systems and the mental events which occur during learning, and which are social in nature. There is now considerable data in the educational literature attesting to the relations between the level of development of spatial thinking and the activities of corresponding sites in the cerebral cortex (A.R. Luriya, 1969; D. Kimura, 1964, 1973; A.N. Sokolov and E.N. Shcheblanova, 1974; V.V. Suvorova, 1976; and others).

For example, Luriya et al. [1966, 1973] have demonstrated convincingly that the tertiary zones of the cortex play a major role in making spatial distinctions. Here the projective regions of the perceptual analyzers are superimposed; we should add that the combined activity of the analyzers underlies the perception of spatial properties and relations. In his study of patients suffering from impaired functioning of various regions of the cerebral cortex, Luriya identified two basic types of disturbances of design activity involving the manipulation of spatial relations. In the first type, there is damage to the parieto-occipital sections, while the second type involves damage to the frontal lobes. In the first case, the patient retains the ability to create a general design plan (construct Koss cubes), guided by definite plans, but he finds it difficult to put his plan into reality. In the second case, the patient manipulates the cubes, has no trouble orienting himself to their spatial relations, but is unable to subordinate this activity to a definite purpose and work toward a particular goal in practice.

Interesting data may be found in a study by V.I. Korchazhinskaya and L.T. Popova [1977]. It was shown that the right hemisphere is dominant for nonverbal visual and spatial thinking. "Our observations," write the authors, "like numerous examples in the literature, attest to the routine predominance of left hand ignorance in the case of focal damage to the brain. This leads us to conclude that the right hemisphere plays a special role in visual and spatial perception" [1977: 80].

This conclusion is supported by facts obtained in other studies (L. Franco and R.W. Sperry, 1976). According to this study, the individual's success in manipulating geometric properties in various types of spaces (Euclidean, projective, topological) depends upon features underlying the functioning of different sections of the right hemisphere. Franco and Sperry suggested that high intra-hemispheric integration promotes the development of geometric thinking. The determination of preverbal, intuitive ideas of geometric relations is essentially the function of the right hemisphere.

Interesting data regarding the influence of intrahemispheric asymmetry on the nature of binocular vision are also found in studies by V.V. Suvorova [1975]. Suvorova found that methods used to establish spatial relations in three-dimensional space (perception of perspective representations) by people who stammer differ markedly from methods employed by people with normal speech development.

There are several studies dealing with the basic EEG characteristics in ninth- and tenth-graders' solution of nonverbal and verbal test problems (conducted by E.I. Shcheblanova). Three ninth-graders were tested in this study, after they were subjected to systematic work aimed at identifying stable indices of the level of development of spatial thinking.[23] The study involved subjects who stood out as representatives of the verbal, visual, and mixed types of intelligence in experimental and classroom problems, and the actual features identified were stable. EEG study of these subjects discovered that when given suitable tests (verbal and nonverbal), they displayed a selective alteration in the level of activization of projective zones. Moreover, the degree of expressiveness of the EEG parameters varied in each subject according to his current, stable work methods.

There are also interesting data regarding the relation between the establishment of spatial relations based on the perception of graphic representations, and the distinctive combination of two semiotic systems (M.N. Borisova, 1956).

The complex structure of spatial thinking is also defined by the fact that it comprises elements which are genotypically dependent. The use of twins (A.R. Luriya and A.I. Mirenova, 1936; N.I. Annenkov, 1969; I.V. Ravich-Shcherbo, 1972; S.G. Vandenberg, 1969; and others) has shown that various aspects of intelligence are related in different ways to the genotype. The more ancient and earlier the mental function in terms of phylogenetics, the more strictly determined it is in genetic terms. In the structure of spatial thinking, the role of this mental function is played by body image orientation. Our results have shown that body image orientation is a highly stable index which affects all other indices. The redistribution and reconstruction of this mode of orientation and the transition to other systems of reference cause well-known difficulties in all people, since the mode develops at a very early point in ontogenesis.

The child's acquisition of a vertical position relative to the earth's gravitation helps develop spatial orientation grounded in the body image. Body image orientation is a genetically early development, and therefore is of major importance for the formation and development of spatial thinking. It is used in orientation in both physical and geometric space. Essentially, body image orientation asserts that one takes the position of his own body in space as the initial reference point. Moreover, various activities require a shift from this natural system of reference to other systems in which the initial reference point is not oneself, but any arbitrarily selected entity (point, line, plane, surface), real object, etc. A shift from the natural reference point grounded in the body image to an arbitrarily selected or specified point is one of the most important aspects of the development of spatial thinking. The psychological conditions motivating this transition, along with persistent individual differences, have yet to receive sufficient attention. A number of productive lines of inquiry on these questions have recently been opened.

N.I. Annenkov's study [1969], based on twins, showed that pairs of monozygotic twin subjects did not differ at all in their solution of problems requiring an orientation relative to parts of their own body, whereas with dizygotic twins there was a sharp divergence in the problems solved. S.G. Vandenberg [1967] suggested that different spatial abilities that are all part of the structure of intelligence are controlled in different ways by the genotype. According to Vandenberg, the ability to perform mental rotations of figures is dependent upon heredity. These data require careful and repeated evaluation, however, and the experimental methodology must be improved.

Although it is the earliest function in terms of phylogenetics, body image orientation changes substantially in the course of social ontogenesis. It has been demonstrated in a number of studies (A.V. Zaporozhets, 1965; N.N. Poddyakov, 1977; S.L. Novoselova, 1978; L.A. Venger, 1976; and others) that even in the early years of childhood, body image orientation develops under the influence of the child's activity, in the course of interaction, with the acquisition of speech, and as part of acquiring knowledge and mental techniques for use in transforming initial graphic material.

Moreover, body image orientation is a highly persistent mental development that defines individual features in the establishment of spatial relations and their manipulation. I.V. Tikhomirova [1976] has shown that instruction can rapidly overcome difficulties in solving problems involving the manipulation of the shape and size of depicted objects, although difficulties in the manipulation of spatial relations are rather stubborn. These difficulties are seen to an equal degree in superior as well as average students. This indicates that not all elements of the structure of the spatial image share the same psychological nature. Some change under the influence of instruction, while others endure.

Tikhomirova selected problems from various school subjects (geography, mechanical drawing, geometry, design, shop) and also utilized textbooks by UNESCO, Raven, Amthauer, and others. The subjects for the study were carefully selected, the nature of their work observed for three years, their grades in school analyzed, and so forth. An experimental group of eleven-, twelve-, and thirteen-year-old students (boys and girls) was formed. The selection of subjects of this age was dictated by the following considerations.

According to physiological studies, by this age the formation of analyzer systems has been completed, the activity of the higher portions of the cerebral cortex stabilized (as is clear from the stability of EEG indices), a dynamic unity between the sensory and verbal components of spatial orientation has arisen, and the use of different coordinate systems has become conscious and controlled. Based on observations and a survey of students of the same age under identical teaching conditions, it was possible to identify enduring individual differences in the manipulation of spatial relations. This stability was apparent in the invariant application of methods of orientation in space and in the difficulty of rearranging preexisting methods of orientation. In other words, a dual type of stability was observed: 1) it was difficult to modify through the influence of teaching; and 2) it was creative.[24] Tikhomirova emphasized that in the former type of stability, subjects routinely select a system of reference focused "on themselves" (grounded in their body image). The second type of stability is manifested in the ability to utilize any of a series of suggested systems of relations to oneself, a specified reference point. The teaching experiment demonstrated that these types of stability may be distinguished by the flexibility with which they are used, their "susceptibility" to change under the influence of instruction, and the rigidity or dynamism at the basis of the representational methods.

The experimental data given above and obtained both in our studies and in studies by other authors demonstrate that individual differences in spatial thinking are determined by a set of indices of differing nature. The identification and analysis of these indices requires "decomposition" of the structure of spatial thinking into its constituent components, taking into account their lack of uniformity, their genesis, and the analysis of the psychological and physiological nature of the underlying mechanisms.

Conclusion

The analysis of spatial thinking in our work corresponds to the basic assumptions of Soviet psychology on the relation between teaching and mental development and the nature of psychological development. Spatial thinking has been treated as a complex structural development in which both the general and specific laws underlying mental activity are manifested. Because of its vivid and unique qualitative nature, spatial thinking is not a limited mental quality. It is a fundamental feature of the mind which makes it possible to orient oneself in space in practical and theoretical contexts.

The gradual development of spatial thinking takes place within the context of the individual's general mental development, through his mastery of the objective world, in the course of interaction and special instruction, which makes him fully aware of spatial properties and relations in their universal and regular connections. As special objects of cognition (learning), these relations and connections become the content of spatial thinking, defining its distinctive features. The basic content of spatial thinking also includes the manipulation of these relations and connections in representational form.

The development of spatial thinking has been treated here as a social process. It proceeds under the direct and decisive influence of teaching. But this process is complex and internally contradictory, i.e., truly dialectical. The structure of spatial thinking incorporates elements of various origin. The complexity and abundance of the factors underlying their formation explain why the functional structure of spatial thinking and features in its ontogenetic development, the critical points fundamental to any transition from one level of mastery of spatial relations to another, qualitatively improved level, are not uniform.

Studying the features of spatial thinking brings into vivid relief the general psychological law that the development of thought proceeds as the individual masters techniques of mental activity. From our standpoint, the mental activity takes the form of representational activity, and constitutes the central element in the acquisition of spatial thinking.

As has been shown in numerous psychological studies, including ours, this activity is often left to develop spontaneously under current teaching practice. The basic techniques of this activity—representational tools and methods—do not become a special subject for development, which in our opinion accounts for the rather low level of development of spatial thinking in children. Comparatively few psychological studies have attempted to analyze representational activity.

The development of representational activity, which makes it possible to create and manipulate spatial images, depends upon a host of heterogeneous factors. Among these factors, we may cite specific techniques of orientation based on body image and teaching conditions that depend upon the specific knowledge to be learned.

The transition from the mapping of physical space to a system of conventional graphical substitutes for this space, as used in various school subjects, requires the acquisition of specialized representational tools, the use of different systems of reference and methods of reorientation, and the acquisition of a complex system of knowledge, abilities, and skills. The relation between general and specialized techniques of orientation in imaginary space has attracted inadequate study in psychology. We feel that this is among the most promising lines of research.

Our works have been devoted to a differentiated approach to the study of representational activity, based on an analysis of the structure of spatial thinking. In particular, we have tried to show that the manipulation of such attributes as shape, size, and spatial relation does not proceed uniformly. This is determined by learning conditions and differences between problems which can be solved by means of spatial images.

The relation between the structure of the spatial image and its function in the problem-solving process is highly dynamic. In accordance with the conditions of a problem, a spatial image suited to its content is formed.

The features of spatial thinking that we have investigated may be applied to the design of a broad curriculum for nurturing this type of thinking through teaching. The demand for such a curriculum has been felt not only in the general educational school, but also in post-secondary educational institutions. This work must be carried out through the combined creative forces of educators, methodologists, teachers, and psychologists.

There is no doubt that the study of spatial thinking must be continued with an eye towards more in-depth theoretical and experimental analysis, as well as further development of practical recommendations for nurturing it in the teaching process.

Notes

Notes to Chapter 1

1. It would be more precise to speak of thinking in terms of spatial images. But for the sake of brevity, and on purely conventional grounds, we will use the term "spatial thinking."

2. The term, "image-expressive activity" [*predstavlivanie* hereafter "expressive activity"], in contrast to "presentation" [*predstavlenie*], was introduced into Soviet psychology by B.M. Teplovto to describe complex intellectual activity aimed at creating and using images. It subsequently became widely employed to denote the process of intentional and arbitrary reproduction of the image and its mental manipulation for solving graphic problems. The psychological content of this term has been discussed by B.G. Ananev, F.N. Shemyakin, E.N. Kabanova-Meller, B.F. Lomov, and others.

3. An analogous classification of visual aids may be found in V.A. Shtoff [1966] and A.D. Botvinnikov [1916].

4. See A.D. Botvinnikov [1973: 9-10, 13, 15].

5. See V.S. Stoletnev [1977].

6. O.V. Khotimskaya and G.A. Naumova [1963: 15].

Notes to Chapter 2

1. We will not consider here cases where the image is used simply, without any modification.

2. From our standpoint, we find specific manifestation of the general principles underlying the relation between thought and knowledge manifest themselves, experimentally demonstrated by K.A. Slavskaya [1968], A.V. Brushlinskii [1968], A.M. Matyushkin [1972],and others.

3. With respect to the use of the visual base, we singled out the individuals in each group of subjects who were most successful in the use of either graphic or conventional symbolic representations.

4. Such a classification of spatial images can be found in our presentation of a technique for teaching mechanical drawing [1966, pp. 146-147].

5. The students were introduced to signs that replace projective representations by means of a table containing all the notations.

6. This generalization is based on 1,000 students in various Soviet schools. Many mechanical drawing teachers participated in these tests, which were conducted by A.D. Botvinnikov together with the present author under the auspices of the Institute for the Study of Educational Content and Methods, USSR Academy of Pedagogical Sciences.

7. *Teaching the Fundamentals of Design. Teacher's Manual [Obuchenie osnovam proektirovaniya. Posobie dlya uchitelei].* Moscow: 1975, p. 21.

8. In F.N. Shemyakin [1940], this feature is referred to as "travel—map" and "survey—map."

9. Cf. *Mathematics Exercises for Grades 4 and 5 Teacher's Manual [Sbornik up-razhnenii po matematike dlya IV-V klassov. Posobie dlya uchitelei].* Moscow: 1971; *Teaching Material for The Grade 6 Geometry Course. Teachers Manual [Didakticheskie materialy po geometrii dlya VI klassa. Posobie dlya uchitelei].* Moscow: 1975, 2nd ed; N.A. Ermolaev and G.G. Maslova. *Mathematics in the Eight-Year School [Matematika v vosmiletnei shkole].* Moscow: 1976.

10. A technique for the formation of these representations may be found in Z.I. Lebedeva, "Methods for the Development of Notions of Size" ["K voprosu o metodakh razvitiya predstavlenii o velichine"]. *Preschool Education [Doshkolnoe Vospitanie],* 1971, No. 12).

Notes to Chapter 3

1. The basic principles underlying the development of these techniques have been set forth in an article by A.N. Leontev, A.P. Luriya, and A.A. Smirnov [1968].

2. $V = 1$ denotes that the number of figures identified by the subject is equal to the standard; $V > 1$ denotes that they have repeated certain figures.

3. For brevity's sake, these other versions will not be given here. The material in the problems consisted of various geometric figures (line segments, angles, polygons, along with perspective representations of cubes, prisms and tetrahedrons).

4. When the rules for compiling three projections are specially taught, this problem was fully accessible to second- and third-graders, particularly with the use of a physical model. It was only necessary to create it by combining simple geometric bodies.

5. A "practical" version of this problem was also used. In this version, the subject was given four cardboard triangles, which, when manipulated, can be combined to form all the above figures. This version of the problem was given whenever the subject could not mentally make the given figures.

6. Versions of these tests have been described in earlier studies (Yakimanskaya 1965, 1969).

7. These problems may be varied in terms of graphical content, though it is important to retain the psychological model.

8. A total of 38 versions of the problem were developed. The first problem went through 10 versions, the second 3, the third 2, the fourth 5, the fifth 3, the sixth 1, the seventh 2, the eighth 1, the ninth 6, and the tenth 5.

9. Experimental problems were presented to students of different ages (grades 3-10, technical institute, university) from various cities (Moscow, Chelyabinsk, Tobolsk, Ivano-Frankovsk, Ussuriisk, and others). A total of 2,566 students were tested.

10. The increase in time for problem 1 may be attributed not so much to the complexity of the test as to the number of steps required to solve it.

11. A more detailed description of each level is given in I.Ya. Kaplunovich [1977, 1978].

12. The age-group characteristics of students' learning depend largely on the content of teaching, as demonstrated by studies carried out under the direction of V.V. Davydov and D.B. Elkonin.

13. Collections of in geometry and mechanical drawing problems and exercises compiled by A.B. Botvinnikov, G.G. Maslova, L.M. Eidel's, O.N. Khotimskaya, and others served as the material for selecting the experimental problems.

14. The diagnostic problems were developed from material accessible to the students at their stage, although the type of problem was held constant. Within each problem category, we developed versions of varying complexity.

15. Results of our combined research have been presented in several articles (cf. Botvinnikov and Yakimanskaya 1968, 1970).

16. These experiments were carried out at School No. 611 in Moscow, which was the main center of our study.

17. A detailed description of the diagnostic problems is given in section 3.

18. The problems used in the tests were taken from the following methodological collections: S.A. Ponomarev et al. [1971: 136 (exercise 1115), 275 (ex. 2344), and 276 (ex. 2369)]; V.A. Gusev, G.G. Maslova, et al. [1975: 32 (C-20) and 67 (DC-14)]; V.A. Gusev, G.G. Maslova, Z.A. Skopets, and R.S. Cherkasov [1975: 12 (ex. 16), 15 (ex. 6B), 16 (ex. 7A), 15 (ex. 5), 9(ex. 34), 38 (ex. 73), 41 (ex. 15), 21 (ex. 27B), and 38(ex. 70)]; and *Teaching Mathematics In Grades 4-7: (Methodological Letter)* [*O prepodavanii matematiki v 4-7 klassakh: (Metodicheskoe pismo)*]. Minsk: 1976.

19. Before presenting the experimental problems, we "equalized" the subjects in terms of this index, checking to see whether they had the appropriate knowledge and abilities. If these abilities and knowledge were lacking, we closed this gap.

20. These differences are described in more detail in other studies by I.S. Yakimanskaya, I.Ya. Kaplunovich, V.S. Stoletnev, and I.V. Tikhomiroa.

21. Diagnostic problems designed by I.S. Yakimanskaya, a battery of verbal intelligence problems (Koss and Amthauer tests), and a problem named after the Swiss mathematician Steiner were used.

22. Mikshite utilizes other indices to identify a relation between the qualitative character of the way spatial relations are manipulated and an affinity for an occupation, which are not considered here for the sake of brevity.

23. The level of their spatial thinking was determined by a diagnostic technique developed by the present author.

24. Lengthy and careful individualized work was carried out with each subject in the study. In the course of this work, the subject was asked to solve about 50 problems requiring body image orientation, mental rotations, and displacements, and symmetric and reflectional transformations.

Bibliography

Aidarova, L.I. *Psychological Issues in Teaching Russian to Younger Pupils* [*Psikhologicheskie Problemy Obuchenii Mladshikh Shkol'nikov Russkomu Yazyku*]. Moscow: 1978.

.Ananev, B.G. *The Psychology of Sensory Cognition* [*Psikhologiya Chuvstvennogo Poznaniya*]. Moscow: 1960.

_____. "New discoveries in spatial perception" ["Novoe v uchenii o vospriyatii prostranstva". *Issues in Psychology* [*Voprosy Psikhologii*], no. 1, 1960.

_____ and B.F. Lomov, [*eds.*]. *Problems in Spatial Perception and Spatial Representations* [*Problemy Vospriyatiya Prostranstva i Prostranstvennykh Predstavlenni*]. Moscow: 1961.

_____ and E.F. Rybalko. *Spatial Perception in Children* [*Osobennosti Vospriyatiya Prostranstva u Detei*]. Moscow: 1964.

Annenkov, N.I. "A Study of the System of Spatial Orientation and Its Hereditary Conditioning" ["Izuchenie sistemy prostranstvennoi orientirovki i ee nasledstvennoi obuslovlennosti"]. *Neuropathology and Psychiatry* [*Nevropatologiya i Psikhiatriya*], no. 69(10), 1969.

Arnheim, R. *Visual Thinking*. London: 1970.

_____. *Art and Visual Perception* [*Iskusstvo i vizualnoe vospriyatie*]. Translation into Russian. Moscow: 1974.

Arsenev, A.S., V.S. Bibler, and B.M. Kedrov. *An Analysis of the Developmental Concept* [*Analiz Razvivayushchegosya Ponyatiya*]. Moscow: 1967.

Atutov, P.R. "Several Issues in the Use of Visual Aids in Teaching" ["Nekotorye voprosy ispolzovaniya naglyadnosti v obuchenii"]. *Soviet Pedagogy* [*Sovetskaya Pedagogika*, no. 5, 1967.

Bakst, Aaron. "Mathematical Recreations." *The Mathematics Teacher*, no. 4, 1951.

Beritov, I.S. "Man's Spatial Orientation in the Animal Kingdom and in Nature" ["O prostranstvennoi orientatsii cheloveka i zhivotnykh v okruzhayushchei srede"]. *Issues in Psychology] Voprosy Psikhologiya*, no. 4, 1956.

Berlyne, D. "Structure and Direction in Thinking". 1965, no. 4.

Blauberg, I.V. and E.G. Yudin. *Development and Essence of the Systems Approach* [*Stanovlenie i sushchnost sistemnogo podkhoda*]. Moscow: 1973.

Blyumenfeld, B.M. "A Description of Effective Visual Thinking" ["K kharakteristike naglyadno-deistvennogo myshleniya"]. *Proceedings of the RSFSR Academy of Pedagogical Sciences Izvestiya APN RSFSR*], no. 13, 1948.

Bodnar, M.G. "Structure of Spatial Representations in Young Schoolchildren" ["O strukture prostranstvennykh predstavlenii mladshikh shkolnikov"]. *New Studies in Psychology* [*Novye Issledovaniya v Psikhologii*], no. 3, 1974.

Bogoyavlenskii, D.N. and N.A. Menchinskaya. *The Psychology of Learning in the School* [*Psikhologiya Usvoeniya Znanii v Shkole*]. Moscow: 1959.

Boltyanskii, V.G. "The Formula of Visualization—Isomorphism Plus Simplicity" ["Formula naglyadnosti—izomorfizm plyus prostota"]. *Soviet Pedagogy* [*Sovetskaya Pedagogika*], no. 5, 1970.

Borisova, M.N. "Technique for determining the relation between the right and left signal systems in visual recall" ["Metodika opredeleniya sootnosheniya pervoi i vtoroi signalnykh sistem v usloviyakh zritelnogo zapominaniya"], in the collection Psychological Features in Man's Higher Neural Activity [*Psikhologicheskie Osobennosti Vysshei Nervnoi Deyatelnosti Cheloveka*]. Moscow: 1956.

Borodai, Yu.M. *Imagination and Cognitive Theory* [*Voobrazhenie i Teoriya Poznaniye*]. Moscow: 1966.

Botvinnikov, A.D. *Basic Trends in the Classification and Study of Methods of Solving Graphic Problems in the School* [*Osnovnye napravleniye klassifikatsii i issledovaniya sposobov uchebnykh graficheskikh zadach*]. Moscow: 1966.

_____. *Collection of Drafting Problems* [*Sbornik zadach po chercheniyu*]. Moscow: 1973.

_____, ed. *Fundamental Techniques for Teaching Drafting* [*Osnovy metodiki obucheniya chercheniyu*]. Moscow: 1966.

_____. "Perception of the Original [*Full-Scale Model*] When Creating a Diagram" ["Vospriyatie originala (antury) pri vypolnenii chertezha"]. *Issues in Psychology* [*Voprosv Psikhologii*], no. 3, 1965.

_____, V.N. Vinogradov, I.S. Vyshnepolskii, and S.I. Dembinskii. *Drafting in the Secondary School* [*Cherchenie v srednei shkole*]. Moscow: 1977.

_____ and I.S. Yakimanskaya. "Student Manipulation of Various Types of Graphic Representations" ["Osobennosti operirovaniya uchashchimisya raznymi vidami graficheskikh izobrazhenii"]. *Proceedings of the USSR Academy of Pedagogical Sciences* [*Izvestiya APN SSSR*], no.143, 1968.

_____ and I.S. Yakimanskaya. "Teaching Certain Forms of Spatial Transformations Using Various Types of Graphic Base" ["Obuchenie nekotorym formam prostranstvennykh preobrazovanii na raznom graficheskom materiale"]. *New Research in the Pedagogical Sciences* [*Novye issledovaniya v pedagogicheskikh naukakh*], no.1, 1970.

Botsmanova, M. E. "Psychological Issues in Elementary Schoolchildren's Use of Graphical Diagrams" ["Psikhologicheskie voprosy primeneniya graficheskikh skhem uchashchimisya nachalnykh klassov"], in the collection *The Application of Knowledge in the Children's Classroom Activity* [*Primenenie znanii v uchebnoi praktike shkolnikov*]. Moscow: 1961.

Brushlinskii, A.A. *Cybernetics and the Psychology of Thought* [*Psikhologiya myshleniya i kibernetika*]. Moscow: 1970.

Chebysheva, V.V. *Psychology of Vocational Training for Schoolchildren* [*Psikhologiya trudovogo obucheniya shkolnikov*]. Moscow: 1969.

Chetverukhin, N.F. *Methods of Geometric Constructions* [*Metody geometricheskikh postroenii*]. Moscow: 1952.

Chetverukhin, N.F., ed. *Formation and Development of Spatial Representations in Schoolchildren* [*Formirovanie i razvitie prostranstvennykh predstavlenii uchashchiksya*]. Moscow: 1964.

Cooper, Z.A. "Mental Rotation of Random Two-Dimensional Shapes." *Cognitive Psychology*, v. 7, no. 1, 1975.

Davydov, V.V. *Forms of Generalization in Teaching* [*Vidy obobshcheniya v obuchenii*]. Moscow: 1972.

Djang, S. *The Roles of Past Experience in the Visual Apprehension of Masked Form.* 1937.

Eysenck, G. *Test Your Abilities* [*Proverte svoi sposobnosti*]. Translation into Russian. Moscow: 1976.

Fetisov, A.I. *Geometry in Problems* [*Geometriya v zadachakh*]. Moscow: 1977.

Fishbein, H.D., G. Decker, and P. Wilcox. "Cross-Modality Transfer of Spatial Information." *British Journal of Psychology*, no. 68, 1977.

"Formation and Development of Spatial Representations and Imagination" ["Voprosy formirovaniya i razvitiya prostranstvennykh predstavlenii i voobrazheniya"]. *Proceedings of the RSFSR Academy of Pedagogical Sciences* [*Izvestiya APN RSFSR*], no. 21, 1949.

Galkina, O.I. *Development of Spatial Representations in Elementary Schoolchildren* [*Razvitie prostranstvennykh prestavlenii u detei v nachalnom shkole*]. Moscow: 1961.

Galperin, P.Ya. "The Study of the Child's Intellectual Development" ["K issledovaniyu intellektualnogo razvitiya rebenka"]. *Issues in Psychology* [*Voprosy psikhologii*], no. 1, 1969.

Gamezo, M.V. *Signs and Semiotic Modeling in Cognitive Activity* [*Znaki i znakovoe modelirovanie v poznavatelnoi deyatelnosti*]. Candidate's dissertation. Moscow: 1977.

Gregori, R.L. *The Eye and the Brain: the Psychology of Visual Perception* [*Glaz i mozg: Psikhologiya zritelnogo Vospriyatiya*]. Moscow: 1970.

Grunebaum, A. *Philosophical Problems of Space and Time* [*Filosovskie problemy prostranstva i vremeni*]. Translation into Russian. Moscow: 1969.

Gurevich, K.M. *Individualized Approach to Students in Vocational Training* [*Individualnyi podkhod k uchashchimsya v proizvodstvennom obuchenii*]. Moscow: 1963.

Gurova, L.L. *Psychological Analysis of the Problem-Solving Process* [*Psikhologicheskii analiz reshenii zadach*]. Voronezh: 1976.

Gusev, V.A., G.G. Maslova, et al. *Instructional Material In Geometry for the Sixth Grade: Independent and Test Material. Teacher's Handbook* [*Didakticheskie materialy po geometrii dlya 6 klassa: Samostoyatelnye i kontrolnye raboty. Posobie dlya uchitelei*]. Moscow: 1975, 2nd ed.

Ignatev, E.I. *The Psychology of Pictorial Activity in Children* [*Psikhologiya izobrazitelnoi deyatelnosti detei*]. Moscow: 1961.

Janmer, M. *Concepts of Space*. Cambridge, 1954.

Kabanova-Meller, E.N. "Analysis of the Development of Spatial Thought" ["Analiz razvitiya prostranstvennogo myshleniya"]. *Soviet Psychotechnology* [*Sovetskaya psikhotekhnike*], no. 3, 1934.

_____. *The Formation of Techniques of Mental Activity and Mental Development in Schoolchildren* [*Formirovanie priemov umstvennoi deyatelnosti i umstvennoe razvitie uchashchikhsya*]. Moscow: 1968.

_____. "The Role of Diagrams in the Application of Geometry Theorems" ["Rol chertezha v primenenii geometricheskikh teorem"]. *Proceedings of the RSFSR Academy of Pedagogical Sciences*] [*Izvestiya APN RSFSR*], no. 28, 1950.

_____. "The Role of the Image in the Problem-Solving Process" ["Rol obraza v reshenii zadach"] *Issues in Psychology*] *Voprosy psikhologii*], no. 5, 1970.

Kagan, M.S. *Human Activity* [*Chelovecheskaya Deyatelnost*]. Moscow: 1974.

Kalmykova, Z.I. *Problems in Diagnosing the Mental Development of Schoolchildren* [*Problemy diagnostiki umstvennogo razvitiya uchashchikhsya*]. Moscow: 1975.

Kaplunovich, I.Ya. "The Structure of Spatial Thinking in Solving Mathematics Prob lems" ["O strukture prostranstvennogo myshleniya pri reshenii matematicheskikh zadach"]. *Issues in Psychology* [*Voprosy psikhologii*], no. 3, 1978.

Kapnin, L.V. *Lenin's Philosophical Ideas and Logic* [*Filosofskie idei V.I. Lenina i logika*]. Moscow: 1969.

Karandashev, Yu.N. *Projective Representations in Children—The First Stage in the Development of the Cognitive Reflex* [*Proektivnye predstavleniya u detei— nachalnyi etap stanovleniya poznavatelnoi refleksii*]. Candidate's dissertation. Len ingrad, 1975.

Kimura, D. "Cerebral Dominance and Perception and Verbal Stimuli." *Canadian Journal of Psychology*, v. 15, no. 3, 1961.

Kireenko, V.I. *The Psychology of Aptitude for Pictorial Activity* [*Psikhologiya sposobnostei dlya izobrazitelnoi deyatelnosti*]. Moscow: 1959.

_____. "The Psychology of Aptitude for Spatial Activity" ["Psikhologiya sposobnostei k prostranstvennoi deyatelnosti"] *Proceedings of the RSFSR Academy of Pedagog ical Sciences Izvestiya APN RSFSR*, no. 76, 1956.

Korchazhinskaya, V.I. and L.T. Popova. *The Brain and Spatial Perception* [*Mozg i prostranstvennoe vospriyatie*]. Leningrad, 1977.

Kossov, B.B. *Problems in the Psychology of Perception* [*Problemy psikhologii vospriyatiye*]. Moscow: 1971.

Krutetskii, V.A. *The Psychology of Mathematical Aptitude in Schoolchildren* [*Psikhologiya matematicheskikh sposobnostei shkolnikov*]. Moscow: 1968.

Kudryavtsev, T.V. *The Psychology of Technical Thought* [*Psikhologiya tekhnicheskogo myshleniya*]. Moscow: 1975.

_____. ed.. *Student Thought Processes in Vocational Training* [*Osobennosti myshleniya uchashchikhsya v protsesse trudovogo obucheniya*]. Moscow: 1970.

_____ and I.S. Yakimanskaya. *The Development of Technical Thought in Students* [*Razvitie tekhnicheskogo myshleniya uchashchikhsya*]. Moscow: 1964.

Lekhtman-Abramovich, R.Ya. *Stages in the Development of the Child's Ability to Handle Objects in the First Year of Life* [*Etapy razvitiye deistvii s predmetanii u detei pervogo goda zhizni*]. Moscow: 1949.

Lektorskii, V.A. "Principles for the Reproduction of the Object in Knowledge" ["Printsipy vosproizvedeniya obekta v znanii"]. *Issues in Philosophy* [*Voprosy filosofii*], no. 4, 1967.

Lenin, V.I. *Complete Collected Works* [*Polnoe Sobranie Sochinenii*], V. 14, 29.

Leonov, A.A. and V.I. Lebedeva. *Psychological Aspects of the Activity of Cosmonauts* [*Psikhologicheskie osobennosti deyatelnosti kosmonaytov*]. Moscow: 1971.

Leontev, A.N. *Activity, Consciousness, Personality* [*Deyatelnost, soznanie, lichnost*]. Moscow: 1975.

_____, ed. *Psychological Studies* [*Psikhologicheskie Issledovanii*]. Moscow: 1976, no. 6.

_____. "Sensory Images and Models in the Light of the Leninist Theory of Reflection" ["Chuvstvennyi obraz i model v svete leninskoi teorii otrazheniya"]. *Issues in Psychology* [*Voprosy psikhologii*], no. 2, 1970.

_____, A.R. Luriya, and A.A. Smirnov. "Diagnostic Methods for the Psychological Study of Schoolchildren" ["O diagnosticheskikh metodakh psikhologicheskogo issledovaniya shkolnikov"] *Soviet Pedagogy* [*Sovetskaya pedagogika*], no. 7, 1968.

Linkova, N.L. "On Spatial Thought" ["K voprosu o prostranstvennom myshlenii"], in the collection *Psychological Issues in Student Aptitudes* [*Voprosy psikhologii sposobnostei shkolnikov*]. Moscow: 1964.

Lomov, B.F. *The Development of Graphic Knowledge, Abilities, and Skills in Schoolchildren* [*Formirovanie graficheskikh znanii, umenii i navykov u shkolnikov*]. Moscow: 1959.

_____. *Man and Machine* [*Chelovek i tekhnika*], Moscow, 1966, 2nd ed.

_____. "The Systems Approach in Psychology" ["O sistemnom podkhode v psikhologii"]. *Issues in Psychology* [*Voprosy psikhologii*], no. 2, 1975.

Luriya, A.R. "The Variability of Mental Functions in the Child's Developmental Processes" ["Ob izmenchivosti psikhicheskikh funktsii v protsesse razvitiya rebenka"]. *Issues in Psychology* [*Voprosy psikhologii*], no. 3, 1962.

Marx, K. and F. Engels. *Works* [*Sochinenii*], v. 20, 42.

Maslova, G.G. "The Development of Spatial Conceptions in Students in the Eight-Year School through Solving Geometry Problems" ["Razvitie prostranstvennykh predstavlenii uchashchikhsya vosmiletnei shkoly pri reshenii zadach po geometrii"]. *Mathematics in the School* [*Matematiki v shkole*], no. 3, 1964.

Mathematics: A Textbook for Grade 6 [*Matematika: uchebnik dlya VI klassa*]. Moscow: 1976.

Menchinskaya, N.A., ed. *The Application of Knowledqe in Schoolchildren's Classroom Activity* [*Primenenie znanii v uchebnoi praktike shkolnikov*]. Moscow: 1961.

236   Bibliography

_____, ed. *The Psychology of Student Solution of Industrial-Engineering Problems* [*Psikhologiya reshenii uchashchimisya proizvodstvenno-tekhnicheskikh zadach*]. Moscow: 1965.

_____. "Thought in the Learning Process" ["Myshlenie v protsesse obucheniya"], in the collection *The Study of Thought in Soviet Psychology* [*Issledovanie myshleniya v sovetskoi psikhologii*]. Moscow: 1966.

Merzon, E.A. *Methodological Instructions for the Determination and Development of Spatial Notions* [*Metodicheskie ukazaniya po resheniyu zadach na opredelenie i razvitie prostranstvennykh predstavlenii*]. Leningrad, 1969.

Mikshite, G.I. *The Relation between Determination of Spatial Attitudes and Propensities for Particular Professions* [*Svyaz mezhdu ustanovleniem prostranstvennykh sootnoshenii i sklonnostyu k spetsialnosti*]. Candidate's dissertation. Vilnius, 1974.

Molyako, V.A. "Psychological Approaches to the Study of Technical System Design" ["Psikhologicheskie podkhody k izucheniyu proektirovaniya tekhnicheskikh sistem"]. *Issues in Psychology* [*Voprosy psikhologii*], no. 1, 1976.

Mordukhai-Boltovskii, D.D. "The Psychology of Mathematical Thought" ["Psikhologiya matematicheskogo myshleniya"]. *Issues in Philosophy and Psychology* [*Voprosy filosofii i psikhologii*], v. 4(94). Moscow: 1908.

Novoselova, S.V. *Mental Development during the Early Years of Life* [*Razvitie myshleniya v rannem vozraste*]. Moscow: 1978.

Piaget, J. and B. Inhelder. *The Genesis of Elementary Logical Structures* [*Genezis elementarnykh logicheskikh struktur*]. Moscow: 1963.

Poddyakov, N.N. *The Thought of the Preschooler* [*Myshlenie doshkolnika*]. Moscow: 1977.

Ponomarev, S.A. *Knowledge, Thought, and Mental Development* [*Znaniya, myshlenie, i umstvennoe razvitie*]. Moscow: 1967.

Posner, M.I. "Characteristics of Visual and Kinaesthetic Memory Codes." *Journal of Experimental Psychology*, v. 75, 1967.

"The Psychology of Vocational Training in the School" ["Voprosy psikhologii obucheniya trudu v shkole"]. *Proceedings of the RSFSR Academy of Pedagogical Sciences* [*Izvestiya APN RSFSR*], no. 144, 1968.

Pushkin, V.N. *Operative Thinking in Large Systems* [*Operativnoe myshlenie v bolshikh sistemakh*]. Moscow: 1965.

Ravich-Shcherbo, I. V. "Studies in Human Psychogenetics" ["Issledovaniya po psikhogenetike cheloveka"]. *Issues in Psychology* [*Voprosy psikhologii*], no. 2, 1972.

Rebus, B.M. "Spatial Imagination as a Key Aptitude for Engineering Creativity" ["Prostranstvennoe voobrazhenie kak odna iz vazhnykh sposobnostei k tekhnicheskomu tvorchestvu"]. *Issues in Psychology* [*Voprosy psikhologii*], no. 5, 1965.

Representational Thought and Its Role in the Development of the Child's Personality: Abstracts of Scientific Papers of Soviet Psychologists at the XXI International Congress of Psychology [*Obraznoe myshlenie i ego rol v stanovlenii lichnosti rebenka: Tezisy nauchnykh soobshchenii sovetskikh psikhologov k XXI Mezhdunarodnomu psikhologicheskomu kongressu*]. Moscow: 1976.

Rubakhin, V.F. *Psychological Foundations of Primary Information Processing* [*Psikhologicheskie osnovy obrabotki pervichnoi informatsii*]. Moscow: 1974.

Rubinshtein, S.L. *Being and Consciousness* [*Bytie i soznanie*]. Moscow: 1957.

_____. *Fundamentals of General Psychology* [*Osnovy obshchei psikhologii*]. Moscow: 1946, 2nd ed.

_____. *Thought and Methods for the Study of Thought* [*O myshlenii i putyakh ego issledovaniya*]. Moscow: 1958.

Sakulina, N.P. *Drawing in the Preschool Years* [*Risovanie v doshkolnom vozraste*]. Moscow: 1965.

Serov, A.M. ed. *Drawing: A Handbook for Students in Art and Graphic Departments of Teachers Colleges* [*Risunok: Uchebnoe posoboe dlya studentov khudozhestvenno-graficheskikh fakultatov pedinstitutov*]. Moscow: 1975.

Shekhter, M.S. *Psychological Problems in Pattern Recognition* [*Psikhologicheskie problemy uznavaniya*]. Moscow: 1967.

Shemyakin, F.N. "On the Psychology of Spatial Conceptions" ["K psikhologii prostranstvennykh predstavlenii"]. *Proceedings of the Institute of Psychology* [*Uchenye Zapiski Instituta Psikhologii*], v. 1, 1940.

_____. "Orientation in Space" ["Orientatsiya v prostranstve"], in the collection *Psychological Research in the USSR* [*Psikhologicheskie nauka v SSSR*], v. 1. Moscow: 1959.

_____. "Several Theoretical Issues in the Study of Spatial Perception and Conceptions" ["Nekotorye teoreticheskie problemy issledovaniya prostranstvennykh vospriyatii i predstavlenii"]. *Issues in Psychology* [*Voprosy psikhologii*], no. 4, 1968.

Shepard, R.N. and G. Metzler. "Transformational Studies of the Internal Representation of Three-Dimensional Objects," in Losso, R. ed., *Theories in Cognitive Psychology*. Academic Press, 1974.

_____. "Mental Rotation of Three-Dimensional Objects." *Science*, no. 17, 1977.

Shteinman, R.Ya. *Space and Time* [*Prostranstvo i vrema*]. Moscow: 1962.

Shtoff, V.A. *Modeling and Philosophy* [*Modelirovanie i filosofiya*]. Moscow-Leningrad: 1966.

Slavin, A.V. *The Visual Image in the Structure of Cognition* [*Naglyadnii obraz v strukture poznaniya*]. Moscow: 1971.

Slavskaya, K.Ya. *Thought in Action* [*Mysl v deistvii*]. Moscow: 1968.

Smirnov, A.A. et al., eds. *Psychology: A Textbook for Teachers Colleges* [*Psikhologiya: Uchebnik dlya peda gogicheskikh institutov*]. Moscow: 1962, 2nd ed.

Sokolov, A.N. and E.I. Shcheblanova. "Changes in Total EEG Rhythmic Energy in Certain Types of Mental Activity" ["Izmeneniya v summarnoi energii ritmov EEG pri nekotorykh vidakh umstvennoi deyatelnosti"] *New Research in Psychology* [*Novye issledovaniya v Psikhologii*, no. 3, 1974.

Sperry, R.W. and L. Franco. "Hemispheric Differences in Intuitive Processing of Geometry." *21st International Congress of Psychology*. Paris, 1976.

Stoletnev, V.S. "Manipulation of Spatial Images in the Problem-Solving Process" ["Operirovanie prostranstvennymi obrazami pri reshenii zadach"]. *New Research in Psychology* [*Novye issledovaniya v psikhologii*], no. 1, 1979.

_____. Collection of Problems and Exercises in Descriptive Geometry [Sbornik zadach i uprazhnenii po nachertatelnoi geometrii]. Ussuriisk, 1977.

Suvorova, V.V. "The Functional Asymmetry of the Hemispheres as a Subject for Differential Psychophysiology" ["Funktsionalnaya asimmetriya polusharii kak problema differentsialnoi psikhofiziologii"]. Issues in Psychology [Voprosy psikhologii], no. 5, 1975.

Teplov, B.M. "The Mind of the General" ["Um polkovodtsa"], in the collection Problems of Individual Differences [Problemy individualnykh razlichii]. Moscow: 1961.

Tikh, N.A. "On the Genesis of Spatial Perception" ["K voprosu o genezise vospriyatiya prostranstva"]. Proceedings of the RSFSR Academy of Pedagogical Sciences [Izvestiya APN RSFSR], no. 86, 1956.

Tyukhtin, V.S. The Nature of the Image [O prirode obraza]. Moscow: 1963.

Vaitkunene, L.V. The Development of Spatial Thought in Schoolchildren [Razvitie prostranstvennogo myshleniya u shkolnikov]. Candidate's dissertation. Vilnius, 1969.

Vandenberg, S.Y. "The Hereditary Abilities Study: Hereditary Components in a Psychological Test Battery." American Journal of Human Genetics, v. 14, no. 2, 1962.

Venger, L.A. "The Structure of Perception and Its Characteristics in the Younger Schoolchild" ["K voprosu o strukture vospriyatiya i ee osobennostyakh u detei mladshego shkolnogo vozrasta"]. Issues in Psychology [Voprosy Psikhologiya], no. 2, 1959.

Volkov, N.N. "Perception of Pictures in Lessons" [O vospriyatii risunka na uroke"]. Soviet Pedagogy] Sovetskaya pedagogika], no. 7, 1947.

_____. The Perception of the Object and the Picture [Vospriyatie predmeta i risunka]. Moscow: 1950.

Vygotskii, L.S. The Development of Higher Mental Functions [Razvitie vysshikh psikhicheskikh funktsii]. Moscow: 1960.

Yakimanskaya, I.S. Creation of Specialized Psychological Diagnostic Techniques: Papers from a Conference on the Problem of Aptitude [O sozdanii spetsialnykh psikhodiagnosticheskikh metodik: Materialy konferentsii po probleme sposobnostei]. Moscow: 1970.

_____. "Development of Spatial Conceptions and Their Role in the Apprehension of Elementary Geometric Knowledge" ["Razvitie prostranstvennykh predstavlenii i ix rol v usvoenii nachalnykh geometricheskikh znanii"], in D.N. Bogoyavlenskii and N.A. Menchinskaya, eds. Methods of Increasing the Level of Apprehension of Knowledge in the Early Grades [Puti povysheniya kachestva usvoeniya znanii v nachalnykh klassakh]. Moscow: 1962.

_____. "Development of Spatial Thought in the Learning Process" ["Razvitie prostranstvennogo myshleniya v protsesse obucheniya"], in the collection Mental Development and Its Diagnosis [Umstvennoe razvitie i ego diagnostiki]. Gorkii, 1971.

_____. "Development of Technical Thought in Training Mechanized Equipment Operators" ["O razvitii tekhnicheskogo myshleniya pri podgotovke operatorov avtomaticheskogo oborudovaniya"], in A.A. Smirnov, ed. Issues in the Psychology of Vocational Training [Voprosy psikhologii obucheniya trudu]. Moscow: 1962.

_____. *Enhancing the Sensory Depth of Work* [*Vospitanie sensornoi kultury truda*]. Moscow: 1969.

_____. "Individual Psychological Differences in Schoolchildren's Spatial Orientation" ["Individualno-psikhologicheskie razlichiya v prostranstvennoi orientatsii shkolnikov"]. *Issues in Psychology* [*Voprosy psikhologii*], no. 3, 1976.

_____. "The Mechanisms of Creating the Sensory Image" ["O mekhanizmakh sozdaniya chuvstvennogo obraza"]. *New Research in Psychology* [*Novye issledovaniya v psikhologicheskikh naukakh*], no. 3, 1971.

_____. "On the Nature of the Spatial Image" ["O prirode prostranstvennogo obraza"], in the collection *The Problem of Activity in Soviet Psychology* [*Problema deyatelnosti v sovetskoi psikhologii*]. Moscow: 1977, ch. 1.

_____. "Representational Activity and Its Place in Teaching" ["Obraznoe myshlenie i ego mesto v obuchenii"]. *Soviet Pedagogy* [*Sovetskaya pedagogika*], no. 12, 1968.

_____."Several Features in Mental Activity Which Appear When Reading a Diagram" ["O nekotorykh osobennostyakh myslitelnoi deyatelnosti, proyavlyayushchikhsya pri chtenii chertezha"]. *Reports of the RSFSR Academy of Pedagogical Sciences* [*Doklady APN RSFSR*], no. 3, 1958.

_____. "Several Methods of Diagnosing Spatial Thought in Schoolchildren" ["O nekotorykh putyakh diagnostiki prostranstvennogo myshleniya shkolnikov"] *Issues in Psychology* [*Voprosy psikhologii*], no. 3, 1971.

_____. "The Use of Visual Aids in Teaching" ["Ob ispolzovanii naglyadnosti v protsesse obucheniya"]. *Secondary Special Education* [*Srednee Spetsialnoe Obrazovanie*], no. 10, 1971.

Yakobson, P.M. "Engineering Thought in Schoolchildren" ["Tekhnicheskoe myshlenie uchashchikhsya"] *Vocational and Technical Education* [*Professionalno-tekhnicheskoe obrazovanie*], no. 11, 1958.

Zavalishina, D.N. "Several Techniques of Solving Spatial and Combinatory Operational Problems" ["O nekotorykh priemakh resheniya prostranstvenno-combinatornykh operativnykh zadach"]. *Proceedings of the RSFSR Academy of Pedagogical Sciences* [*Izvestiya APN RSFSR*], no. 138, 1964.

Zhuravlev, B.B. "On Mathematical Insight" ["O matematicheskom videnii"]. *Mathematics in the School* [*Matematika v shkole*], no. 5, 1940.

Zinchenko, V.P. and N.Yu. Vergiles. *Formation of the Visual Image* [*Formirovanie zritelnogo obraza*]. Moscow: 1969.

Zuckerman, C.B. and I. Rock. "Reappraisal of the Roles of Past Experience and Innate Organizing Processes in Visual Perception" [*Psychological Bulletin*, 54, no. 4, 1957.

Zykova, V.I. *Development of Practical Abilities in Geometry Classes* [*Formirovanie prakticheskikh umenii na urokakh geometrii*]. Moscow: 1963.

5984